EMPIRE'S MISTRESS

starring Isabel Rosario Cooper

DUKE UNIVERSITY PRESS *Durham and London* 2021

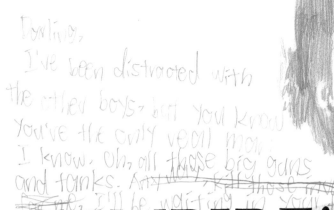

EMPIRE'S MISTRESS

starring Isabel Rosario Cooper

✳ VERNADETTE VICUÑA GONZALEZ ✳

Designed by Aimee C. Harrison
Typeset in Arno Pro by Westchester Publishing Services

LIBRARY OF CONGRESS CATALOGING-IN-PUBLICATION DATA
Names: Gonzalez, VernadeTTe Vicuña, [date] author.
Title: Empire's mistress, starring Isabel Rosario Cooper / VernadeTTe Vicuña Gonzalez.
Description: Durham : Duke University Press, 2021. | Includes bibliographical references and index.
Identifiers: LCCN 2020035287 (print)
LCCN 2020035288 (ebook)
ISBN 9781478011866 (hardcover)
ISBN 9781478014003 (paperback)
ISBN 9781478021315 (ebook)
Subjects: LCSH: Cooper, Isabel Rosario, 1914–1960. | MacArthur, Douglas, 1880–1964—Relations with women. | Motion picture actors and actresses—Philippines—Manila—Biography. | Filipino American women—Biography.
Classification: LCC PN2918.C66 G669 2021 (print) | LCC PN2918.C66 (ebook) |
DDC 791.4302/8092 [b]—dc23
LC record available at hTTps://lccn.loc.gov/2020035287
LC ebook record available at hTTps://lccn.loc.gov/2020035288

Cover and title page art: Studio portraits of Isabel Rosario Cooper by Jose Reyes, Hollywood, CA, circa 1942.

Duke University Press gratefully acknowledges the Center for Philippine Studies at the University of Hawai'i at Mānoa, which provided funds toward the publication of this book.

For my parents,
ERNESTO & VIVIAN GONZALEZ

CONTENTS

ARCHIVAL DETRITUS,
FABRICATIONS, SECOND TAKES,
AND OTHER PROVOCATIONS

one * This Is Not a Love Story * 1

two * *Death Certificate, Partial* * 13

three * A General and Unruly Wards * 15

four * *The Flower of Cathay, Excerpts* * 28

five * *Misapprehensions* * 30

six * The Farm Boy and the Unbiddable Wife * 32

seven * *The Delicate Moonbeam* * 48

eight * "Dimples": Innocence (Colonial Kink) * 49

nine * *Stage Presence* * 67

ten * *Letters Lost at Sea, Imagined, Excerpts* * 69

eleven * The New Filipina, Kissing * 72

twelve * *Gossip: Fiction and Nonfiction* * 86

thirteen * *"It Girl" Meets General* * 89

fourteen * *Recipe for the Douglas* * 93

fifteen ✳ The Washington Housewife,
the Hollywood Hula Girl, and
the Two Husbands: Reinventions ✳ 94

sixteen ✳ *Out of Place* ✳ 111

seventeen ✳ 1st Filipina Nurse, Geisha,
~~Little Sergeant,~~ Javanese Nurse, Uncredited ✳ 112

eighteen ✳ *Lolita's Lines* ✳ 127

nineteen ✳ Bit Parts: Racial Types, Ensemble ✳ 128

twenty ✳ Caged Birds ✳ 149

twenty-one ✳ *For Future Archives,
Apocrypha, and Fictions* ✳ 160

twenty-two ✳ *Death Certificate, Entire* ✳ 165

twenty-three ✳ The Suicide ✳ 167

twenty-four ✳ *Last Review* ✳ 170

Acknowledgments ✳ 173
Notes ✳ 177
Filmography (with Roles) ✳ 199
Bibliography ✳ 203
Index ✳ 215

This story begins with a dead woman whose death was caused by heart-break. At least, we are told this repeatedly, so that it becomes truth. Women dying for love are tragically beautiful, inspiring wistful longing. The pathos of thwarted romance obscures what might otherwise be ugly, or bitter, or something yet unimagined.[1]

She is caught in a familiar and worn plot, a clichéd convention of empire. Surrounded by the chaos and uncertainty of war and colonial occupation, the lovely, exotic young woman falls in love with the powerful white soldier. Their affair is illicit but inexorable, defying the obstacles of race, culture, and nationality that ultimately derail their devotion. The last act always ends with her impossible yearning for his fidelity and return. Her death is inevitable. *She can only die in this plot.* He goes on to live the rest of his life happily ever after, his future secured by her sacrifice.[2] Nonetheless, it is a delicious and compelling fiction, told again and again until it acquires a force of its own.

This book is an attempt to unravel the story of one particular dead, beautiful woman named Isabel Rosario Cooper, whose life has always been reduced to this story or something like it.

Isabel Cooper, when she is talked about at all, is cast as General Douglas MacArthur's notorious one-time mistress. Most often, she is invoked only to lend flavor to otherwise predictable accounts of his military and political career, which pivots around the dramatic "rescue" of the Philippines from Japanese occupation near the end of World War II. As the story goes, the mixed-race vaudeville and film actress is plucked from the Philippine Islands by the much older MacArthur and brought to Washington, DC, to continue their affair. After some time, they part ways acrimoniously. He then redeems a lackluster military career in Washington by becoming a hero in the noblest war, returning to the Philippines dramatically (and in well-documented fashion) as its liberator.[3] She labors in obscurity in Hollywood and dies of a drug overdose. Her death is labeled a suicide, the cause, unrequited love.

In the decades that follow, as biographies both lionizing and denigrating MacArthur are published, her death (when noted at all) is ascribed to her despair at her lover's rejection. No matter that she died three decades and two husbands after MacArthur, Isabel Cooper cannot extricate herself from the arms of the general or from the gravitational pull of this cherished story line.

I have tripped over variations of this plot over the last two decades, trying to piece together Isabel Cooper's side of the story.

❊ ❊ ❊

My first encounter with Isabel Cooper—or her thinly veiled counterpart—was through Ninotchka Rosca's novel *State of War*, which depicts the surreal colonial world of the United States' occupation of the Philippines in the twentieth century. In it, Isabel Cooper's double is the unnamed mistress of the American military governor, a "Eurasian chanteuse who came to the club now and then—'only as a diversion.'" Rosca describes a well-kept, exquisite woman with a "sultry, passionate contralto, which suited her slim, high-breasted, lithe body, her blue-black hair piled high on her head, crowning an oval face of incredibly delicate beauty."[4]

In the novel, as the object of desire, she haunts the edges of the action, a pleasurable distraction from (and a softened metonym of) the main plot of torture, war, and revolution. Rosca's songbird finds herself pulled along in the wake of her lover and is lost in the ebbs and flows of modernity and tradition. She languishes in an opiate hallucination after the war. Her fate reflects the treacherous consequences of the American empire's so-called deliverance, those unfortunate side effects of "white love."[5] Neither romance—with the general or with colonialism—are plots in which the heroine survives, no matter the promises whispered in the fevers of desire.

Rosca's fictional chanteuse, it turned out, was a real-life woman, and not just an archetype of the tragic mixed-race concubine. Biographers of the general note her intriguing presence in the margins, but for the most part, treat her like a shallow side dish, the classic Oriental seductress. In William Manchester's sprawling 1978 biography of MacArthur, *American Caesar*, she is a juicy morsel of gossip. Manchester describes a powerful older man wheedling love from a petulant and spoiled young woman with gifts of a lavish apartment and an "enormous wardrobe of tea gowns, kimonos, and black-lace lingerie."[6] Predictably, Isabel Cooper is depicted as a lovely doll that could be kept in boudoir costume, at the ready for his sexual whims. Manchester quotes a Washington lobbyist who met her: "I thought I had never seen anything as exquisite. She was wearing a lovely, obviously expensive chiffon tea gown, and she looked as if she were carved from the most delicate opaline. She had her hair in braids down her back."[7] That the lobbyist uses opaline—an opaque, colored glass—to describe Isabel Cooper is illuminating. Encounters with Isabel Cooper, even those seemingly intimate ones, cannot or do not choose to delve beneath the smooth surface of her exoticized beauty and sexuality. Her typecasting demands no further explanation.

Other biographies of MacArthur portray Isabel Cooper as a Delilah to his Samson, as the linchpin to a potential scandal that could destroy his career, or as the adoring and submissive lover who appeases the wounded masculinity eroded by his recalcitrant first wife and his domineering mother.[8] In the decades since the first flurry of MacArthur biographies, the occasional tabloid, magazine article, newspaper column, website, or blog resurrects Isabel Cooper as an entertaining bit of trivia, solidifying the patterns and plots that define her.[9] There is little variation from the familiar archetype, because it is easier to repeat, with some embellishment, a titillating but almost comforting story of a beautiful woman who yearns, to a tragic end, for her man. With repetition, all these narratives congeal into a truth that is hard to shake.[10]

A beautiful woman dying of heartbreak is a seductive fiction.

Sixty years after her suicide, this fiction has proven its durability. Yet there is something there, too, in the way that the dead refuse to rest. Her apparition lingers, I suspect, because this flimsy plot—the tragic romance, and her casting as the doomed Eurasian—cannot contain her. The mix of romance, sexual scandal, and tragedy that narrates Isabel Cooper has an undeniably magnetic pull: it has the stuff of epics and the tantalizing elements of gossip and rumor. It also has blind spots and refusals.

Perhaps it is time to tell her story in a different way.

❋ ❋ ❋

In 2016, I found myself on a dry, grassy hillside in Culver City, in Los Angeles County, looking for Isabel Cooper's grave. It had been almost two decades since I had first encountered what I thought was a stock fictional character of the Eurasian seductress. Over that time, I pursued her story in piecemeal fashion. The trip to Holy Cross Cemetery was a kind of pilgrimage, nearing the end of the different leads I had followed over time. At the cemetery, the graves of luminaries like Bela Lugosi, Bing Crosby, and Rita Hayworth are marked and identified for zealous fans of Hollywood history. The object of my search did not burn so brightly. I imagined the simplest headstone mark-ing her plot, and some kind of resolution to my search. I had called earlier for her plot number and enlisted the help of my mother's childhood friend who was a longtime Hollywood resident.

Isabel Cooper's final resting place is not easy to find: the cemetery's well-kept grounds are expansive, and even with the small concrete markers denot-ing the rows of gravestones, there is no sign of her burial ground. I consult the map given out at the entrance. I walk up and down the hill that is marked in the map as her section, the hazy sun beating down on my head. My mother's friend and I get excited when a number closely matches the one in the crumpled sheet in my hand, only to be foiled by the seeming lack of logic in the ordering of the graves. The numbers and letters on the circular concrete markers make no sense in their arrangement. It is getting hotter, and the hill feels steeper.

Finally, a wandering groundskeeper helps us find the plot's location. He takes a look at the grave number and motions for us to follow him. As we walk along a gradually sloping knoll, he explains how the plots are arranged.

It was the lack of a gravestone that had thrown us off. The groundskeeper identifies the unremarkable parcel of scrubby, thirsty grass near the top of the hill as Isabel Rosario Cooper's final resting place.

"So, if this is the number," he says, "then her feet would have been over here and her head would be here." He gestures over the plot. I can't help but imagine Isabel Cooper's body laid out under the grass.

We thank him, and he ambles off. I take photographs of her burial site, but the stretch of grass captured in the images is lackluster. A shade tree stands sentinel, with the vague outline of the city peeking over the hillside. It pro-vides the only cool spot in this place. We linger for a few minutes, but there really is nothing to see.

❋ ❋ ❋

I discovered that her first husband, Frank Kennamer, paid for the plot upon her death. I had not realized that he did not pay for a gravestone. By the time Isabel Cooper died, he had remarried and started a family. He had no obliga-tions to her. Somehow, even though Isabel Cooper married again, he was named as her nearest kin on her death certificate.

Around her plot, other graves are marked with simple headstones, with epitaphs like "Beloved Wife and Mother" or names with birth and death dates. I had hoped for the same for Isabel Cooper, some last trace of who she was, even if again only in relation to someone else. But her unmarked grave resists this. And to my surprise, this feels right.

It is fitting, somehow, that her grave has no headstone. Isabel Cooper is a cipher, in the sense of being both an anonymous minor figure and a text needing decryption for which the code is lost. Like many other women in history, her characterization as a sexualized object reflects a failure to come to terms with a complex personhood from whom little is demanded other than to play to type. The infamous liaison with MacArthur, which prompts the search that finds me on a hillside in Culver City, is also the very thing that obscures her as a historical subject in her own right. She is always the kept woman in the story, the accessory, MacArthur's mistress. Yet I'm also here because this story, the way it is determined to contain her, never quite succeeds.

Faced with the small rectangle of dry grass where she is buried, I realize that this moment captures how historical figures like her evade or even refuse scrutiny. I can't help but compare her grave to that of her erstwhile lover, whose mausoleum in Norfolk, Virginia, is a museum to his life, complete with an archive (albeit sanitized) dedicated to his heroism. His is a burial site primed for pilgrimage and posterity, shored up by tourists and historians. It reflects his 1964 memoir, one in which Isabel Cooper is disappeared.[11] While she was apparently an open secret in both American and Philippine circles during her life, here in a small burial plot in Los Angeles County, she is anonymous among other dead. At her gravesite, there are no flowers or visitors. The historical traces of Isabel Cooper's life are scattered far and wide, ephemeral, and lost. Here on the stark hillside, with the sun weakly beating down on her grave through the LA smog, Isabel Cooper refuses easy narration.

※　※　※

What does it mean to take Isabel Cooper seriously? Grappling with her life is not a radical act. If anything, hers is a story filled with uninspiring elements: the seamy details of illicit relations, a protagonist who does not look past her own self-interest, a life lived without particularly noble ambitions. This is no bottom-up historiographical project that reveals heroic resistance to oppression. Instead, it is more about the supporting players of empire, the ones who render colonialism palatable, or mask its unsavory workings. It is about those who take and make opportunities in order to survive. It is perhaps about how agency sometimes looks like blackmail, or lying, or death.

This is not a love story. War, imperialism, and occupation are its defining conditions—the violent historical forces that move the action along. Going beyond the salacious details of a scandalous affair, this account illuminates the shifting intimate relations that underpinned the project of American empire in the Philippines just before and well after the brutal sweep of the

Philippine-American War. It is as much about the personal registers of American empire—the ways in which empire's effects play out on the bodies, relationships, and lives of colonized people—as it is about Isabel Cooper. While she takes center stage in this version of the story, her choices embody how the dimensions of the geopolitical are carried out through the close encounters between colonizer and colonized. Isabel Cooper's life is intimately stitched into the larger canvas of American empire in the Philippines. Likewise, the threads of American empire are woven into her story. Bookending the six decades of her life, from the early 1900s to 1960 when she died in Los Angeles, this account is sutured into the progressive and modern project of American civilization and its obsessive policing of intimacy that followed its genocidal pacification campaign in the Philippines.

As with stories narrated just off the axes of power, the interrelated workings of gender, sexuality, and race are essential to the telling. Isabel Cooper grew up as a first-generation mixed-race Filipina/American in a colonial society where race mixing was commonplace yet somehow still scandalous.[12] Her body was a constant reminder of how the unruly desires of empire ran aground on the shoals of the colony. While her notoriety is tied to MacArthur, Isabel Cooper's story is much more than the *querida*, or the *kabet* (literally, hook, snag, a term used to signify the position that mistresses held in the Philippines).[13] She personified the most illegitimate and disavowed consequence of American imperialism, and was at the heart of the constantly shifting legal and social boundaries of race during the unsettled aftermath of war. In other words, Isabel Cooper's liaison with MacArthur is only exceptional because of his political stature and the colossal shadow he casts over the landscape of Philippine and American history.

At the same time, she was herself a dangerously desiring subject, wielding her ambiguous status for her own ends. She flouted social proprieties. In colonial Manila, she witnessed how imperial rule manifested itself in everyday life, especially in the ways that people from vastly different worlds encountered each other. There were spoken and unspoken rules about who could socialize with each other. She saw when and how those rules could be broken, and by whom. She grew up absorbing the tensions of a colony pushing to become independent—and within her own family witnessed some of the divisions and complicities of this struggle playing out. Debates about women's political and social independence were intertwined with the question of an emerging Philippine nation.[14] She took in the push and pull of these ideas. She even came to embody some of them, coming of age during an especially vibrant time of invention and creativity. The infusion of Hollywood dreams

Isabel Cooper in her vaudeville days in Manila. Photograph unattributed, original source unknown.

and glamour rubbed up against Filipino theater and song, producing new forms and orientations. Filipino cinema was born during her childhood. All of these forces propelled her into the currents of fame and infamy.

In many ways, Isabel Rosario Cooper was a woman who refused to know her place or stay in place. She traversed oceans, chasing her own desires and dreams as a professional actress. She contended with the demands of the industry and the audience, cunningly strategizing around her own desirability as a young, mixed-race, modern woman. She was a successful professional actress in a colony with Hollywood dreams and a wandering colonial ward of indeterminate belonging who wanted companionship and adventure. She transplanted her life across two oceans at a young age at the lovelorn beseeching of the much older MacArthur. She provoked a powerful lover. In the messy aftermath of that defining relationship, she remade her life. Her choices illuminate how people adapted and survived in conditions not of their own making, and in circumstances that were designed to wear away their dignity and humanity.

This is a story of a woman caught in the currents of history, who was at times adept and at times ill-equipped to navigate them. Even as she played with the strictures of colonial race and gender, she was also subject to them. Her American mestiza identity, her embrace of cosmopolitan Hollywood cultures, the position she occupied as a colonizer's mistress, the reality of her expendability as a mixed-race actress in Hollywood, and her death by suicide narrate key moments and instances of American intimacy and its continuing afterlives.

Isabel Cooper personified the double-edged and interrelated meanings of what it meant to be empire's mistress. The apostrophe linking empire to mistress gestures to the possessive—the mistress of empire—Isabel Cooper as the kept woman of a powerful imperial player. But the terms joined by the apostrophe also capture another meaning from the old French feminine of master—*maistresse*—a figure of authority and power in the household. In this second sense, the mistress of empire points to someone conversant in the intimate workings of the colonial world. Isabel Cooper's mastery of and familiarity with the languages, cultures, and social relationships of empire both reinforced and unsettled the hierarchies upon which empire relied. As someone who pieced together a life that was profoundly fragmented by its violence, the bit parts she played on its larger stages yield an account of empire's reach and its limits, and of its own contingent and improvised nature.

Object of and subject to empire's dubious love, Isabel Rosario Cooper was also at the heart of its deepest anxieties.

❊ ❊ ❊

As I drive away from Holy Cross Cemetery, I realize that it is not so much Isabel Cooper's story that has called to me from beyond the grave. It is the reality that her story—one both profoundly exceptional and commonplace—is only one of many that are told and repeated, forced into genres that do not quite fit. The story that follows is an attempt to imagine and narrate otherwise—beyond the plots and materials that we inherit.[15] It is a reminder to generate new forms when the ones we are mired in fail us.

UNPLOTTING EMPIRE

This book was born out of my dissatisfaction with how Isabel Cooper has been repeatedly reduced to a scandalous footnote—that she comes into focus only as the Eurasian mistress—flattening out a full and complex life, much of it lived outside the shadow of the general. In all the versions in which she appears, MacArthur is inevitably the sun, and she, the satellite. Finding a way to tell her story with her at the center troubles our inherited histories, which in content and form dictate how we make sense of our present.

When I went looking for Isabel Rosario Cooper, I had to come to terms with her flickering presence and absence in the archival record. That the colonial archive excludes and obscures is not new: its function as an apparatus of power is as much to conceal or distort as it is to record, categorize, and make banal the workings of empire.[16] Over the course of my research, I shuttled between the promise and pleasures of the archive as source of documentary evidence (the more difficult to find, esoteric, and singular, the more triumphant the sense of discovery) and an understanding that this "seduction of access" was a dead-end affair.[17] The colonial archive, for all the secrets it promises to keep and divulge, is ultimately a ruse of power. And yet it beckons—a repository of empire that elicits a desire to put together what it has fragmented and disappeared.

Unsurprisingly, like many other women before her, Isabel Cooper barely registered in the government records of the United States' time in its Philippine colony. Compounded by the ways in which imperial administrators decided which lives were worth documenting, the prejudices of people doing the recording, and the types of material selected for archiving, someone like Isabel Cooper slips in and out of archival focus. Her archive is thin and scattered, what remains of it barely enough to hold together a story. Some moments of her life blaze through with startling clarity, and others are discernable only through what Evelyn Hammonds, in encountering the absence of material about African women in slave history, calls the effect of the "black (w)hole"—the ways in which the sheer gravitational force of an unseeable object warps the light around it.[18]

Given the violent occlusions and, at best, ambiguous encounters the colonial archive entails, I learned to plumb for meaning in silences and distortions. Others have walked this path before, seeking out the ghostly contours of slave history, wrestling with absence in the records of queer life in the colonial age, or delving headlong into the dusty repositories of imperial governance.[19] They have found ways to "mine and undermine the evidence of the archive," to make meaning out of the fragmentary and the ephemeral by "following traces, glimmers, residues and specks of things" or by scavenging derided sources, generating alternative archives of grief and survival for lives considered less-than.[20] Understanding that archives are not merely inert records but rather "charged sites" where knowledge is produced and contained, they urge us to take the "pulse of the archive," by reading alongside and against it.[21]

An early photograph of a vaudeville performer, who might be a very young Isabel Cooper. Collection of Juan Martin Magsanoc.

I found myself patching together Cooper's movements through the unreliable reports of entertainment magazines and the slightly more reliable filings of legal documents. I chased down her traces in ship manifests and movie payrolls, and lingered over letters written to and by her. I dug into gossip and rumor, scoured the tiny print of Manila entertainment and Hollywood industry publications, and combed through film production records to get a sense of how she inhabited her world and how others saw her. I watched her extant films, where she appears for a total of minutes of screen time, to learn how she moved, what her voice sounded like, and if she was any good as an actor. I scavenged the census, birth records, marriage licenses, divorce rulings, and death certificates for dates and details. Pulling these bits of archival detritus together, I became acquainted with someone who was much more than a beautiful accessory for a powerful man's flaccid ego.

Yet Isabel Cooper also deflected and misdirected attempts at getting to know her. What there is of her records makes up a sometimes-apocryphal archive that eludes authoritative, documentary claims to truth. She is discernable only through the warped lens of conjecture and rumor, her story refracted through what remains of ephemeral performances or tangential anecdotes in other people's stories. She herself embraced the distortions of gossip and submitted lies on official documents, sometimes as part of a survival strategy. These moments of creation and absence point to how alternative possibilities and imaginations emerge when we are willing to reexamine what has acquired the patina of truth.

A beautiful woman dying of heartbreak is a seductive fiction.

The gaps and silences of the archive can house myriad speculations, other versions of the story where she is not predictably cast over and over again as empire's beloved archetype. This story, then, is shaped by the tensions between the archive and the desires it stirs up and confounds. Perhaps the story that emerges from these tensions—incomplete, unsatisfying, and riddled with silences, absences, and refusals—might be enough.

Just as Isabel Cooper's life defies easy categorization, so too must the forms that attempt to narrate it—those "blurred genres" generated by imperial life.[22] Isabel Cooper's life story reveals a portrait of someone grappling with how imperial love is by turns seductive, perverse, violent, and impossible. While rendering her story in the interrupted and even erratic fashion in which her archive appears, this approach better captures the effects of the imperial relations that produced her, that she traversed, and that continue to diminish her in the present. This fragmentation is borne out in the form of the book, which reflects how the stories we inherit are always already distorted by gossip, further confused by conflicting archival evidence, altered by the woman at its center, and warped by the narrative forms of imperial desire. The assemblage offered here is meant as a provocation for thinking through how empire operates from the perspective of those not in power; of how intangible elements like emotions, rumor, and fantasy are embedded in and crucial to imperial success; and what surviving or rejecting the embrace of imperial love looks like.

What follows is a response to and critique of the imperial fictions that have fixed Isabel Cooper's story in their rigid plots. These messy entanglements are captured by a shadow narrative of archival detritus, fabrications, second takes, and other provocations, distinguished by italicized text or nonstandard type, and marked by a right-justified title. Some take the shape of genres that Isabel Cooper used and encountered—such as letters and recipes—gesturing to the alternative and devalued forms of writing and expression through which women's stories are often told. Others present speculative scenes or moments that draw from archival records and the spaces in between them, adding to and diffusing the fictions of empire, and the sometimes-fantastic plots, characterizations, and twists that themselves are outstripped by reality. Others address the archive's limits by reimagining events as they might have happened through what Lisa Lowe has described as alternative past conditional temporalities.[23] These are not meant to make coherent a life story that might be best left fragmented, but rather to illuminate how fiction and imagination—and the genres we choose—are always already complicit in how history is narrated.[24] Just as the fictional pieces are steeped in a shadow story of archival research, these archival documents are not just unassailable sources but also a place for parallel, connected, or conflicting stories. On occasion, they are the sites through which Isabel Cooper is able to write herself into history. Sometimes, these records contradict each other, troubling our trust in the archive and the interpretations it generates and forecloses.[25]

This confusion of genres, of authorities and authorship, deflects those desires for resolution, even as I also rely on them to stitch together yet another way to tell her story, one, I hope, that gives it more room to breathe.

Isabel R. Cooper #56740

STATE FILE NUMBER

CERTIFICATE OF DEATH

STATE OF CALIFORNIA—DEPARTMENT OF PUBLIC HEALTH

LOCAL REGISTRATION DISTRICT AND CERTIFICATE NUMBER 7053 14250

DECEDENT PERSONAL DATA

1A. NAME OF DECEASED—FIRST NAME: ISABEL
1B. MIDDLE NAME: ROSARIO
1C. LAST NAME: COOPER
2A. DATE OF DEATH—MONTH, DAY, YEAR: 6-29-60
2B. HOUR: 430 P M
3. SEX: Female
4. COLOR OR RACE: White
5. BIRTHPLACE (STATE OR FOREIGN COUNTRY): Philippines
6. DATE OF BIRTH: January 15, 1914
7. AGE (LAST BIRTHDAY): 46 YEARS
8. NAME AND BIRTHPLACE OF FATHER: Isaac Cooper, Unknown
9. MAIDEN NAME AND BIRTHPLACE OF MOTHER: Josephine Unknown, Phil.
10. CITIZEN OF WHAT COUNTRY: USA
11. SOCIAL SECURITY NUMBER: Unknown
12. LAST OCCUPATION: Actress
13. NUMBER OF YEARS IN THIS OCCUPATION: 20
14. NAME OF LAST EMPLOYING COMPANY OR FIRM: Free-Lance
15. KIND OF INDUSTRY OR BUSINESS: Motion Pictures
16. IF DECEASED WAS EVER IN U.S. ARMED FORCES, GIVE WAR OR DATES OF SERVICE: No
17. SPECIFY MARRIED, NEVER MARRIED, WIDOWED, DIVORCED: Divorced
18A. NAME OF PRESENT SPOUSE:
18B. PRESENT OR LAST OCCUPATION OF SPOUSE:

PLACE OF DEATH

19A. PLACE OF DEATH—NAME OF HOSPITAL:
19B. STREET ADDRESS: 6244 Delongpre Avenue [X] INSIDE CITY CORPORATE LIMITS
19C. CITY OR TOWN: Los Angeles
19D. COUNTY: Los Angeles
19E. LENGTH OF STAY IN COUNTY OF DEATH: 20 YEARS
19F. LENGTH OF STAY IN CALIFORNIA: 20 YEARS

LAST USUAL RESIDENCE

20A. LAST USUAL RESIDENCE—STREET ADDRESS: 6244 Delongpre Avenue
20B. IF INSIDE CITY CORPORATE LIMITS: [X]
20C. CITY OR TOWN: Los Angeles 083 ✓
20D. COUNTY: Los Angeles
20E. STATE: California
21A. NAME OF INFORMANT (IF OTHER THAN SPOUSE): Frank E. Kennamer
21B. ADDRESS OF INFORMANT: 821 Market St., San Francisco

PHYSICIAN'S OR CORONER'S CERTIFICATION

22A. PHYSICIAN: I HEREBY CERTIFY THAT DEATH OCCURRED AT THE HOUR, DATE AND PLACE STATED ABOVE, FROM THE CAUSES STATED BELOW AND THAT I ATTENDED THE DECEASED FROM ... AND THAT I LAST SAW THE DECEASED ALIVE ON ...
22A. CORONER: I HEREBY CERTIFY THAT DEATH OCCURRED AT THE HOUR, DATE AND PLACE STATED ABOVE FROM THE CAUSES STATED BELOW AND THAT I HAVE HELD AN Investigation ON THE REMAINS OF DECEASED AS REQUIRED BY LAW
22C. PHYSICIAN OR CORONER—SIGNATURE: Theo. J. Curphey, M.D., Coroner
22D. ADDRESS: HALL OF JUSTICE LOS ANGELES
22E. DATE SIGNED: 7-14-60

FUNERAL DIRECTOR AND LOCAL REGISTRAR

23. SPECIFY BURIAL, ENTOMBMENT OR CREMATION: Burial
24. DATE: 7-5-60
25. NAME OF CEMETERY OR CREMATORY: Holy Cross Cemetery
26. EMBALMER—SIGNATURE, LICENSE NUMBER: Robert E. Snyder 3787
27. NAME OF FUNERAL DIRECTOR: CALLANAN MORTUARY
28. DATE ACCEPTED FOR REGISTRATION BY LOCAL REGISTRAR: 7-18-60
29. LOCAL REGISTRAR—SIGNATURE: George W. Uhl, M.D.

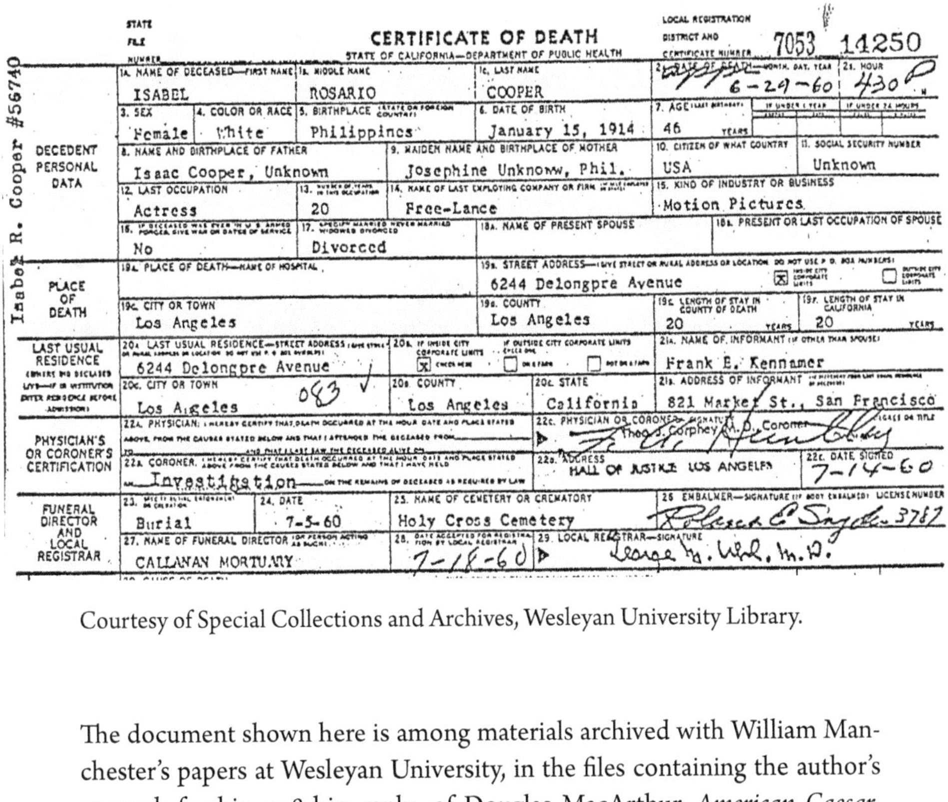

Courtesy of Special Collections and Archives, Wesleyan University Library.

The document shown here is among materials archived with William Manchester's papers at Wesleyan University, in the files containing the author's research for his 1978 biography of Douglas MacArthur, *American Caesar*. This death certificate has been used as definitive proof of Isabel Cooper's tragic fate, as evidence of the inevitable endpoint of her relationship with MacArthur.

In the Manchester papers, the death certificate is accompanied by a letter to Manchester (dated May 2, 1978) from his editor, detailing how she acquired it from Dan Schwartz at the *National Enquirer*: "He is the person who really did all the work. He tracked Isabel Rosario Cooper to Los Angeles and got the death certificate. It took him four months!"[1] Schwartz was another man who embellished the archetype of the mistress languishing in unrequited love. He was happy to titillate his readers with the scandal of the general and his very much younger Filipina amour, doing so two years before Manchester's book was published.[2] He enclosed two newspaper articles (one of them his) about the letters along with the death certificate, and sent them to Manchester, who then further embellished the story.

I am struck by the way that these two men bound Isabel Cooper into plots of their own making, pressing the raw material of her life and death into a suffocating archetype. Yet another man is caught in the stark form of this document: Frank E. Kennamer, Isabel Cooper's first husband—the "Informant." That he is there at the end of her life confirming the deceased's race and date of birth is yet another instance of a woman's story being authored by men.

It was my first encounter with the documentation of her death. But documents, read askance, push back against a stubborn adherence to dearly held ideas about women and love. A death certificate, holding details given by a distant and distanced survivor, might also gesture to the success that the dead one has had in shaping lies into truth, or keeping some secrets to herself. That this reticence is taken up as an invitation says more about the living than the dead.

1   Letter to Manchester, box 5, folder 2, William Manchester Papers, Wesleyan University.
2   Dan Schwartz, "Passionate Letters Reveal . . . the Sensational Love Affair of 50-Year-Old Gen. Douglas MacArthur—& a 16-Year-Old Filipino Girl," *National Enquirer*, September 21, 1976, from box 262.4, Morris Leopold Ernst Papers, Harry Ransom Center, University of Texas at Austin.

Because this story is not about the general, it begins with him in order to move him out of the way. This version of the story takes issue with the re- peated, settled truths positioning the general and other men at the center of the action. It tracks the disorderly power of people deemed disposable and makes room for Isabel Cooper's desires to drive the plot.

❀ ❀ ❀

On the ninth of December, 1930, a young woman disembarks from the *President Filmore*, which has just docked in New York City after a long ocean voyage.[1] Isabel Cooper has finally arrived from Manila, having come to the United States at the behest of her lover, General Douglas MacArthur. She is eighteen, or twenty-one, or somewhere in between.[2]

She follows a trail of love letters strewn across the Pacific, written by Mac- Arthur and posted from Hong Kong, Shanghai, Kobe, Yokohama, Tokyo, Honolulu, and San Francisco. They mark his route home after being recalled from his two-year assignment as the commanding general of the Philippines Department. They also mark the intensity of his ardor for the charming, worldly Filipina performer he had met the year before.[3]

Just weeks before Isabel Cooper's arrival, the fifty-one-year-old MacArthur is promoted to the rank of general, ordered to Washington, DC, and appointed by President Herbert Hoover as the chief of staff of the United States Army.

MacArthur installs Isabel Cooper in a suite at the Chastleton Hotel, con- veniently near his State, War and Navy Building office. His redoubtable mother, Pinky, lives with him in the official chief-of-staff residence in Fort Meyer, Virginia.[4] He lavishes Isabel Cooper with gifts, mostly clothes. Their

The Chastleton Hotel at Sixteenth and R Streets NW, Washington, DC, circa 1921. National Photo Company. National Archives and Records Administration.

liaison is not a secret to Washington insiders—it is his mother that he wants to keep in the dark.[5]

Their relationship in both capital cities, Washington and Manila, lasts approximately five years, but its power to define her story endures well after her death.

Those biographers of MacArthur who discuss this brief affair predictably portray Isabel Cooper as an exotic yet submissive plaything whose sole duty was to prop up MacArthur's insecure masculinity. Replicating a fantasy of the colonial harem, they confine her to the Chastleton with a wardrobe best suited for the bedchamber rather than life outside.[6] They concur that as MacArthur's duties intensified, this arrangement came apart. One of his most prominent biographers attributes this collapse to Isabel Cooper's ingratitude and disloyalty—that she seduced other men despite MacArthur's gifts of a chauffeured limo, access to the city's night spots, paid trips, and cash.[7] Another chalks it up to her rapacious sexuality—that she began to seek her pleasures elsewhere.[8] No pieces of evidence are offered to back up these claims, other than rumor, and the existence of a beautiful young woman in proximity to power. The ease with which her characterization slides from passive Oriental doll to promiscuous seductress is hackneyed—they are, after all, opposite sides of the same gendered coin.

Beleaguered on political and personal fronts, he ends their arrangement in 1934 on an injudiciously sour note (and, fortunately for us, in writing).

Months later, the letters MacArthur so devotedly composed are used as leverage by Drew Pearson, a Washington journalist he sues for libel. MacArthur drops the suit. Freedom of the press wins in underhanded fashion. In this accounting, Isabel Cooper is a lurid side note to the intrigues of men in power.

This retelling turns on the love letters in question, and the comings and goings of unruly colonial wards. It supposes that while relatively young, Isabel Cooper was a sophisticated and shrewd person capable of weighing her choices and aware of the stretch of her power, that she too was capable of taking action.

It also starts with an understanding that no matter how Isabel Cooper and MacArthur felt about each other, or the lingering archival evidence of his sentimental words, *there is no romance to be found here.*[9] Rather, we have desire, brokered by states and statesmen in fraternal collaboration with each other, and tendered through the currency of women caught in the webs of sex, intimacy, and empire.[10] These entanglements of patriarchy and imperialism profoundly shaped the opportunities of women like Isabel Cooper who took part in the work of empire and whose labors of "love" were crucial to the maintenance of U.S. colonial power in the Philippines.[11]

The men who waded through the tedious bureaucracy of colonial administration, the military presence that MacArthur oversaw, and the fleet of teachers civilizing the "savages"—all relied on the unrecognized labor of women.[12] And where white women were unavailable or unwilling, Filipinas took up the slack. For Isabel Cooper and women like her, keeping house, entertaining, even expressions of love and attraction—from flirting to seduction and sex—were elements of the labor of caretaking that upheld the personal and social needs of imperial men.

The misrecognition of this labor as romance or love forgets the profound racism and sexual violence at the heart of empire. It exposes the colonizer's wish for innocence, to be loved despite the violence he exercises.

The pivotal nature of this illicit labor gave many women a means of survival in a rapidly shifting world. Isabel Cooper's story is both ordinary and exceptional. She was one among innumerable Filipinas who engaged in sexualized relationships with white American colonial men. Her swain happened to be among the highest-ranking soldiers in the U.S. military. Like many Filipinos during this period, she traveled to the metropole. Unlike them, she was sponsored by a powerful man, demonstrating that the borders between metropole and colony could be more porous for those wards of the nation fulfilling obligations of a more intimate nature than for those toiling in canneries and fields.

This intimate labor also represents a site where the order and authority of empire might be unsettled or even overrun.[13] If indeed MacArthur met Isabel Cooper on Pier 9 on the Hudson, as he promised her in his letters, he was demonstrating a perilously intemperate commitment to a colonial subject by the brand-new chief of staff of the United States Army.[14]

❀ ❀ ❀

Reading the general's love letters with Isabel Cooper at the center is an act of agitation. It solidifies her as the authority, if not the author, in this particular plot twist.

Photostatic copies of the letters in question are held in the archived papers of Morris Ernst, the attorney who represented Drew Pearson in the libel suit.[15] They cannot be reproduced or quoted at length due to MacArthur's rights as the letter writer. The originals were returned to him in exchange for a $15,000 settlement with Isabel Cooper following the showdown between the general and the muckraker.[16] I imagine he promptly destroyed them. The excerpts included here are those already published elsewhere in exposés of the general's proclivities.

There are twenty-two of them, and most are written in MacArthur's slanted, efficient hand. There are occasional telegrams. The entire collection spans from the beginning of their arrangement to its end.

The items filed in Ernst's papers also include the correspondence between Pearson and his lawyer regarding their strategy, and letters from them to MacArthur and his legal representative regarding the libel suit. There are no love letters from Isabel Cooper to fill in the gaps, only a typewritten and signed letter authorizing Ernst to act on her behalf regarding the terms of a possible settlement.

❀ ❀ ❀

The first insight: Isabel Cooper, three decades younger than MacArthur, with no real social or political status, wields considerable emotional power in their relationship.

MacArthur is besotted. In late September to mid-October 1930, he sends a constant stream of dispatches to her as his ship makes its way from Manila to San Francisco, attempting to bridge the ever-widening distance between them with extravagant expressions of adoration. Bracketing anecdotes about Chinese flappers hovering over gambling "chinks" in Hong Kong, a story of having a stranger try on a fur coat that he buys for his Baby Doll in Shanghai, and an account of a lackluster meeting with an ambassador in Tokyo, the general's lovesick tributes doggedly remind their recipient of his devotion.[17]

Reading the letters again and again manifests the phantom outlines of their recipient. I imagine Isabel Cooper inundated by bursts of mail delivered to her home on Calle Herrán, in Manila's modest Paco district. I wonder whether she feels assured by their sender's unrelenting ardor, or glad to have some respite from him, or a little of both.

MacArthur's maudlin paeans to his Baby Girl describe his heartbreak as her lithe figure, clad in green, is silhouetted against the receding Manila landscape. He lovingly recalls the beginning of their affair five months prior in the tropical heat of the city. His feelings saturate the pages, pressing themselves against her.

> Every hour of every day I but love you deeper and more truly . . . with all the passion of my starving, panting body.

> My love encompasses you and enshrines you deep in my heart. . . . I kiss your dear lips and press your soft body to my own. . . . I long for you so that the memory makes me feel ill and faint.

> I am so happy in the thought that you are coming. . . . I kiss your lips and eyes and feet. . . . Come back to me my precious one, or I perish.[18]

My Own Sweetheart. The Darling of My Life. Babe, My Beloved. My Baby Girl. Bella.[19] The general's missives address and build a fictional figure, drowning out the ways she might not fit into his fantasy, leaving little room to imagine Isabel Cooper otherwise. MacArthur's prose casts her over and over again as the object of his obsession, the paramour around whom his destiny manifests. Yet his ardent turns of phrase, his determination to confine her to the small spaces of his desire, reveal the acute anxieties undercutting intimate arrangements such as theirs.

MacArthur imagines—wants—his Bella to be an innocent, childlike object of his devotion while also knowing her to be a woman who made her living onstage, and who earned her notoriety through the steady dismantling of her reputation. He gravitates toward her because of her beauty but also out of a deep-seated belief that Asian women, unlike his first wife, are demure and docile, biddable—even if all evidence before him is to the contrary.

To some extent, Isabel Cooper plays the part, no matter that it is a part riddled with the contradictions and corruptions of imperial desire. She has long become familiar with the demands and turns of this type of role in her years on stage and screen. This is merely stagecraft on a more intimate level. She indulges a powerful man whose fantasies about Asian women are at odds with her occupation and social position, yet also very much served by them. The mental acrobatics required by both of them to maintain their affair are considerable.

MacArthur's desires to play Daddy to his Baby Girl are stymied by the independence and worldliness of the young vaudeville star. Despite their three-decade age difference, and his position as one of the highest-ranking colonial men in the Philippines and hers squarely in the Manila demimonde, Isabel Cooper is not at the general's beck and call.

His letters constantly imagine her refusal.

His fantasy, succored by the gentle promises of Isabel Cooper's acquiescence, is haunted by the possibility of failure. He reminds her to "pack early and put your luggage on the boat as soon as she arrives," to secure her cabin the night the ship docks, to write him the day she sails, and under no circumstances to stay ashore overnight at other stops.

He entreats her, over and over, not to miss her boat.

Baby Girl's arrival in New York is by no means assured.

      ❀ ❀ ❀

The archive's one-sided documentation of transoceanic love obscures Isabel Cooper's deliberations about uprooting her life to Washington, DC, and becoming entirely dependent financially on MacArthur. She would be abandoning vaudeville and cinema at the height of her hard-earned success.

In his letters, he asks her to write back to him. It is unclear if Isabel Cooper writes back, how often, and with what tone. She is a diligent correspondent, as later letters to Pearson show. If her replies to MacArthur once existed, I imagine what kind of rage fueled their eventual destruction.

The last word from him in this sequence is a telegram asking her to disregard a dismaying rumor, keep to her plans, and to cable him at once.[20] It is unclear what rumor gives MacArthur such great anxiety.

In the end, Isabel Cooper sails.

      ❀ ❀ ❀

The letters are the only documentation of their relationship, which becomes increasingly turbulent. The pure happiness MacArthur promises Isabel Cooper at the end of 1930 collides with the realities of the Great Depression in full swing, the weighty responsibilities of his new office, and, most of all, the inevitable erosion of the fantasy MacArthur had built.

Her position is both clandestine and an open secret. I wonder about the young woman that Washington lobbyist Dorothy Detzer describes as having "a face that could have been sculpted out of alabaster," and how she might feel to be the unacknowledged ornament on the arm of a powerful mover and shaker.[21] I think about how the luxurious suite at the Chastleton could begin to feel like a gilded cage to a woman who had the run of the Washington of the Orient.

Perhaps a thirty-year age gap begins to chafe, or she eventually tires of the role he has cast her in.

❊ ❊ ❊

The next set of letters holds the silences and spaces of a slow-motion disintegration.

MacArthur's career is ascendant. Absorbing some of Isabel Cooper's lessons about the importance of public relations, he has hired his own staff to promote an image of a strong military leader to the public.[22] He travels to Europe on official duties in late 1931. He leaves an increasingly restless Isabel Cooper behind. She ventures beyond the Chastleton to Washington and Baltimore nightclubs. She is a young, vibrant woman hungry for the world outside. But she has always been. It is as if he just begins to notice.

His infatuation with someone who is his social inferior continues, but instead of incessant four-page letters, he sends infrequent postcards from Paris and Hungary. The sentiments of his love are shorter, less effusive.

His writing describes his royal treatment by dignitaries and the accolades he receives, as if to remind her that he is quite the catch: the Hungarian regent has decorated him with yet another medal. He notes that it is nothing without her. He remembers the second anniversary of their parting in Manila, holding on to his memory of the "lovely girl in green."

A year later, he is back in Europe.[23] While he is away, she takes an excursion of her own to Havana, to take in the pleasures in the city known as the Paris of the Caribbean.[24] She arrives back in New York on September 10, 1932.[25] The silence between these comings and goings is ripe with possibility.

She returns, coincidentally, on the same day that the *Philippines Free Press* runs an article about former vaudeville stars. It includes gossip about her running off with the second mate of the boat she took to Marseilles, marrying him, and settling down in New York.[26] It is amusing and provoking. Isabel Cooper's continuing Washington arrangement with the general has clearly not made the rounds in Manila.

Two postcards, sent en route from the ss *Leviathan*, wistfully hope she is enjoying herself in Havana (but not too much) without him. Another one reminds her of his love and deep longing and promises that it is the last time he will ever leave her until he dies.

I wonder if his eruption of sentiment is conciliatory—perhaps they quarreled before parting. Or if it is deluded—that he remains committed to a fantasy of Isabel Cooper that she is increasingly stripping bare.

The trip he takes to Europe in 1932 is deeply political: MacArthur has become a liability to President Herbert Hoover. Just a month prior to his departure, the Bonus Army veterans had descended on Washington, DC, to petition for government assistance in the midst of the Depression. He had driven out the marchers and dismantled their protest using tear gas and tanks, personally leading the rout. It was a public relations disaster, generating an intense backlash that, among other things, contributed to Hoover's failed bid for reelection.[27] MacArthur's brutality is censured and vilified by the press.

He is in Europe to lick his wounds.

He sends more postcards from Warsaw, from Bucharest. He describes how he has to play king on these visits, as if his ambitions were not flattered by the attention, as if he were not reeling from a blunder that has eroded his political capital.

In October, on his way home, he sends a telegram, daringly signed "Doug." It is the only letter he signs with his name.

※ ※ ※

There is a gap of two years until MacArthur's last written communication, which is decidedly not a love letter. In the interim, their relationship runs its course. His biographers blame her: she is greedy, restless, mercenary. The break between the letters allows other stories to incubate: she has affairs with other men; she takes a stab at art school, or law school; she becomes uncontrollable in her desire to have a life outside of the general.[28] He, apparently, is an innocent party.

Their arrangement ends, discordantly, by May 1934.[29] Isabel Cooper moves out of the Chastleton into a rooming house just a few blocks from MacArthur's office. It is to this new address that the terse, typewritten letter to Bella Cooper is sent on September 11, 1934.

She has asked him for assistance of some sort, possibly for her father, a military veteran a few years older than MacArthur, who is working as a hospital steward in Los Angeles, or for her brother Bruce, who has served a sentence for robbery and fled back to Manila after parole.[30] He is offended by her presumption.

He responds by telling her to apply to the Humane Society for any assistance for her brother and father, and encloses a job ad for women clipped out of a newspaper's classified section.[31] His unending love for his Baby Girl has run its course, helped along by her expectations of aid to her family.

❋ ❋ ❋

Their separation would have been historically inconsequential were it not for the letters MacArthur wrote to Isabel Cooper, the fact that she kept them, and her willingness to use them for her own ends.

The letters' fate has been understood primarily through narratives that exhibit the political swaggering of powerful men. They are fuel for a game of legal one-upmanship that ends with the triumph of a wily, street-smart journalist over an egotistical and thin-skinned bully. Framing this moment as a masculine showdown denies Isabel Cooper its ownership.[32] Yet without her, the action stalls.

Drew Pearson, a muckraking journalist, dares to criticize MacArthur's handling of the Bonus Army march. In retaliation, MacArthur sues him and a collaborator for libel to the tune of nearly $2 million. Pearson, a longtime fixture in the capital, has allies—or at least, people who have a common interest in MacArthur's downfall. Ross Cooper, a Mississippi Congressman who was one of MacArthur's nemeses, leaks the existence of a lovely young former neighbor of his at the Chastleton, who had frequently received the general.[33] By May 1934, Pearson has hired someone to actively search for Isabel Cooper: "So far I have been unable to locate the lady in the telephone book but am making every effort to find her."[34]

Evicted from her suite at the Chastleton and smarting from MacArthur's hostility and dismissiveness, Isabel Cooper spikes his guns. When she is found by the beleaguered Pearson—possibly in New York City—she consents to the journalist's use of the letters in her possession to pressure MacArthur to drop his lawsuit. Her caveat: that she would return the letters to the general only in exchange for a monetary settlement. She gives Pearson's attorney the authority to represent her.

Drew Pearson is exultant. Morris Ernst sends a confidential letter to the general, indicating that he now represents Isabel Cooper, and that "a strong ethical and moral claim" could be laid against him based on what she has shared with him, which includes the letters.[35] The issue of the libel suit is almost incidental. At first, L. S. Tillotson, MacArthur's lawyer, denies any such possibility, but later requests a conference with Ernst, who plays coy.

In the meantime, "the flower of Cathay" or "Ling" (aliases assigned to Isabel Cooper by Pearson) was living at the Park Central Hotel, and later at the Algonquin, possibly moved around by Pearson to stymie MacArthur.[36] Tillotson (and by extension, MacArthur) begins to capitulate: "Please understand that I do not want this matter to get out of your hands."[37]

The men in question meet, lawyers in tow, in December 1934. Pearson shows his hand, a full complement of saccharine love letters. In a communiqué before the meeting, Pearson also tells his lawyer that should it be needed, "a few discreet hints" might be dropped about how unfortunate it might be if Isabel Cooper were called to witness at a public trial and had to divulge MacArthur's imprudent confidences about other powerful men.[38]

The general waves the white flag immediately and drops the libel suit.[39]

The originals are returned to MacArthur, in exchange for Pearson's legal costs and a significant sum—$15,000—paid to Isabel Cooper. She is to relinquish "forever" any kind of suit, damages, or claims against the general. She agrees never to approach MacArthur again.[40]

⁕ ⁕ ⁕

The original letters, unsurprisingly, are not archived in MacArthur's papers in Norfolk.

There is no known contact between MacArthur and Isabel Cooper after this exchange, though the ghostly echoes of their relationship play out for decades after.

Pearson claims that Isabel Cooper takes the settlement and moves to the Midwest to open a beauty parlor, but there is no evidence of this.[41] She does live in Oklahoma briefly, with the law student she had met in Washington, DC, whom she would eventually marry.[42]

⁕ ⁕ ⁕

Not included in the love letters that Isabel Cooper returns to MacArthur is the one-way ticket to Manila that he enclosed in his last correspondence.

His indecision about how to solve his particular Filipino problem mirrors the confused American policy toward its Filipino wards in the 1930s. In the 1920s and 1930s, the United States was struggling to define its political relationship vis-à-vis the Philippines and Filipinos. It sought to exert a more definitive political rule in the islands while attempting to appease the rising calls for Filipino independence. On its own shores, the United States also contended with thorny issues of racial exclusion and racist violence when its newest imperial subjects traveled to North America for work.[43]

Isabel Cooper did not have to claim her father's citizenship or rely on her relationship with a powerful man to evade the anti-Asian immigration laws on the books when she crossed the Pacific to join the general. As colonial wards, Filipinos were exempt from racialized immigration laws that limited the entry of Asians—"aliens ineligible for naturalization."[44] But rising anti-Filipino violence, incited by images of "sexually deviant" Filipino laborers laughing and dancing with white women—touching them—ended the porosity of the borders between imperial metropole and colonial outpost.

By 1934, the year that MacArthur and Isabel Cooper's arrangement ends, the Tydings-McDuffie Act passes. In essence a breakup on a larger scale, it allows for a ten-year transition period for Philippine independence, but instantly reclassifies all Filipinos living in the United States as aliens (and hence subject to Asian exclusion).

Filipino laborers working in the United States are offered a return fare, much like the one MacArthur offers Isabel Cooper.

❊ ❊ ❊

At some point after the Pearson showdown in Washington, DC, Isabel Cooper does sail back to Manila. (I find myself hoping she used the ticket that MacArthur sent her.) Her stay is temporary.

In 1936, just days before the birthday she declares (this time) to be her twenty-sixth, she arrives back in Seattle from Manila on the *President Jackson*.[45] She travels in the opposite direction of the approximately two thousand Filipino migrant workers who took up the United States' offer of a one-way ticket back to the islands.[46]

She claims citizenship through her father at her port of entry, but someone like her, a mestiza Filipina, is not the target of the dragnet aimed at Filipino men. Her labor, while explicitly sexual in nature, is not a threat to white male virility. It is expected, even essential, to colonialism.

❊ ❊ ❊

It is telling that MacArthur's last communication with Isabel Cooper includes both a ticket and a job ad. The classified ad column—"For Women"—lists a variety of occupations deemed appropriate for women in 1934, ranging from commission sales and demonstrations of various products (food, Christmas cards, cosmetics), caretaking (for a young attorney and son), food services, nursing, and office work. It reflects his thinking that Isabel Cooper was a kept woman no more, that there would be no more generosity to support her life of leisure. Isabel Cooper could get a job.

But it also gestures to the fact that she had had one. While her work was unwaged, she exchanged sexual and emotional intimacy for room, board, and lavish gifts. He understood it as love—that was his fantasy. I suspect she was much more pragmatic about it, having become familiar with many such arrangements in the Philippines.

The domestic arrangements are tacit, but clear: MacArthur relies on his mother to provide him with the comforts of home while he ensures her well-being. He turns to Isabel Cooper for sex and emotional fulfillment, but also to buttress his fragile ego. Her role is not just to be adored but also to admire him.[47] Her presence is an indicator of his virility. Even though she is not officially his hostess, enough people in Washington know of her presence to conclude that MacArthur's sexual prowess must reflect his military rank.

As an object of desire and a desiring subject, Isabel Cooper burnishes MacArthur's image. The illicitness of the arrangement roughs up his good-boy aura, makes him more of a man's man. Her beauty, her mixed-race heritage, her youth—all of these embellish MacArthur.

Read through the warped prism of colonial desire and power, their relationship is an entirely different thing—an intimacy pressed into service for survival. It is an imperial occupation, a business born out of subjugation that she cunningly turns into a means for mobility.

Once she refuses to stay in her place, she, like her compatriots, is deemed expendable. Her desires are reframed as excessive and unseemly—she wants too much. MacArthur's gift of a return ticket positions Isabel Cooper alongside Filipino migrant laborers—as the help who oversteps the bounds of interracial intimacy. In this moment, he inadvertently recognizes the labor she has done to uphold his illusions of romance.

✵ ✵ ✵

The love letters that haunt this five-year arrangement remain in their photostatic form, in the archived papers of a man whose relationship to Isabel Cooper was fleeting at best. Morris Ernst's act to safeguard copies was likely driven by a need to check MacArthur's autocratic tendencies, particularly when aimed at his client, Drew Pearson. But read differently, the letters' stubborn existence is less about the legal maneuverings of men and more about the ways that a woman like Isabel Cooper exploited empire, generating moments when her own circulations through the imperial landscape flicker through the archive and beckon for historical consideration.

Isabel Cooper's unruliness filters through these letters—in the lines of their emotional prose, in the empty spaces between them. She materializes through them as a resourceful and recalcitrant mistress of her own desires. The letters evidence how empire operated on a more personal scale, what Ann Laura Stoler so aptly describes as the micropolitics of the intimate.[48] That the letters—preserved by the vanity of imperial men—capture the contrary mobilities of a woman determined to wrest her own narrative from them illuminates how intimacies are an essential element of empire, and perhaps, on occasion, of its undoing.

December 6,1934.

(Personal - Strictly confidential)

Gen. Douglas MacArthur,
Chief of Staff,
War Department Building,
Washington, D. C.

Dear General MacArthur:

      I have been retained and represent Isabel Cooper.
My client has discussed with me at length her relations with
you and has shown me various letters, etc. Before advising
my client as to any definite legal steps, I am writing to you
because I am thoroughly convinced that a strong ethical and
moral claim lies irrespective of any other rights.

      I deem it quite important that I see you, with or
without your attorney, no later than Wednesday of next week.
I will not be in New York on Monday but would thank you to let
me know just when you can see me on Tuesday or Wednesday.

      Very truly yours,

MLE-PG

Form 18

Postal Telegraph-Cable Company

PRESS TELEGRAM

Dear Morris,

[illegible]

[illegible]

[illegible]

We had dinner with Pecora tonight [illegible] and read him some of the letters written by the Flower of Cathay to the General. He expressed the opinion that she was very reasonable in asking for only $15,000 and that he should be glad to pay this much. He said that [illegible] any Broadway flapper would have [illegible] gone at him for about $500,000.

[illegible]

Will telephone you tomorrow, Drew

(*above*) Letter from Drew Pearson to Morris Ernst, no date. Courtesy Morris Leopold Ernst Papers, Harry Ransom Center. (*left*) Letter from Morris Ernst to Douglas MacArthur, December 6, 1934. Courtesy Morris Leopold Ernst Papers, Harry Ransom Center.

Curated from author's collection of statements about and by Filipina women, published and unpublished sources.

In some parts of the Philippine island the women, it is true, are neither interesting or amusing, for they are less than half-civilized. . . . It is the Tagal women and girls principally that Americans have come to know. . . . A right adherence to the truth forbids saying that as a general thing a fair Tagal is pretty at any age. She isn't. She may have charms, but beauty isn't one of them.[1]

The Igorot keep their women away from Americans but when an American gets an Igorot woman for a wife—she gets well fed & rounds out into a plump, healthy rosey cheekt woman that is a beauty that would more than hold her own with the average American girl. The Amer-Igorot mestizos that I saw lookt as tho there was something to them.[2]

1 John Fitzgibbon, "The Filipino Woman: She's Not Handsome but She's Strangely Interesting," Frank H. Burton Papers, Bentley Historical Library, University of Michigan at Ann Arbor. No date or source information in news clip, or notes on why this article in particular merited preserving in Mr. Burton's album of his time in the Philippines.
2 David Murray Gates, "Frank Caleb Gates, Botanist and Ecologist, and His Companion, Margaret Thompson Gates," 2000, 141, from Frank C. Gates Collection, Bentley Historical Library.

As a moral force one may make the assertion and be far within the bounds of truth, that woman outranks man in Las Islas Filipinas.[3]

Today, the Filipino woman ranks equal with man. She is the mistress, wife, or both of them jointly, managing the business. This confidence of the man in the woman with regard to the interest and economic welfare of the family made an English writer assert "that the Filipino woman occupies a position in law as well as in custom at least equal to the position of woman in the most advanced countries in the world."[4]

The girl of today is very different from that of an earlier period. She enjoys all kinds of active outdoor exercises and competes with the other sex in scientific or artistic endeavor, considers men not as superiors or masters, but her equals. This type of girl is new in our country, and like anything which is new, is looked upon with suspicion and condemned as rude and unfeminine.[5]

What some of these girls consider freedom, might rightly be termed libertinage. Anyone who has a roadster these days, or even a flivver, for that matter, can pick up one of these modern coeds of the eccentric type. . . . In fact, in some instances, they need not pick them up. Some of the ultra modern "babies" take the initiative to pick up the "sugar daddies."[6]

3 Emma Sarepta Yule, "The Woman Question in the Philippines," *Filipino People* 3, no. 10 (February 1916): 9.
4 Carmen R. Aguinaldo, "The Filipino Woman in Society and before the Law," box 7, 1922, Walter W. Marquadt Papers, 1896–1952, Bentley Historical Library. No other publication information or date in bound collection of papers. Carmen R. Aguinaldo is the daughter of Emilio Aguinaldo.
5 Maria Paz Mendoza-Guzaon, *My Ideal Filipino Girl*, 1931 (no publisher), volume of informational articles and informal talks in American Historical Collection, Rizal Library, Ateneo de Manila University. This quote is from Mendoza-Guzaon's notes from a "Heart to Heart Talk with Filipino Girls," read before the Women's Club of the University of the Philippines, September 1922, 4.
6 Perfecto E. Laguio, *Our Modern Woman: A National Problem* (Manila: Philaw Book Supply, 1931), 7. In American Historical Collection, Rizal Library.

Intimacies of desire, sexuality, marriage, and family are inseparable from the imperial projects of conquest, slavery, labor, and government.—Lisa Lowe, *The Intimacies of Four Continents*

The archives reveal scandals.

The big scandal, of course, was empire itself. The purchase of the Philippines from Spain was the concluding transaction of the Spanish-American War in 1898. Seven thousand islands reduced to a real estate deal. Bypassing the irksome demands of Filipinos for independence, the United States took it upon itself to "uplift" its "little brown brothers."[1] Contrary to its stated political ideals but in keeping with its blood-soaked historical practice, it instigated a "pacification campaign" resulting in a massive Filipino death toll, a razed countryside, and political sovereignty wrested from a people who had long been struggling against Spanish colonizers. In tandem with this brutal war, the United States brought "civilization"—the built infrastructures and cultivation of cultural and social norms that were the colonizer's gifts to the colonized.[2]

The more titillating scandal was colonial love writ small—the birth of the first generation of mixed-race Filipino Americans in the islands.[3] Their existence was incontrovertible evidence that the racial line the civilizing project of empire was so keen on upholding was being crossed all the time.[4] Mobilizing mostly young (mostly) white men for the military and bureaucratic work of colonizing the islands, the United States created the conditions that enabled people from very different walks of life to encounter each other. In the colonial outpost, people fucked each other, with or without consent, sometimes indiscriminately and imprudently—but mostly with a sense of their place—across the color line.

Tracking Isabel Cooper's roots, I am fixated by these paired scandals. There is a story worth lingering over here.

As the offspring of these scandals, Isabel Rosario Cooper is proof of the personal indiscretions that are the unintended outcome—and dirty secret—of bringing civilization to the savages. Her very existence provokes anxieties about racial truths held dear by colonial authorities, her body a reminder of the fragility and porousness of racial categories. Though they regularly remark on the appeal of her mixed-race beauty, those who have written about her have not pursued the question about how someone like Isabel Cooper—a woman of Filipina and white American ancestry—came to exist in the first place.[5]

The records of her parentage and birth are murky. There is no birth certificate that definitively names her as the progeny of her parents, nor an indisputable birthdate. In 1912, an unnamed daughter is born to Isaac Cooper, an American fireman from Wisconsin, and Protacia Rubin, a Filipina housewife from Nagcarlan, Laguna, who cohabit at 347 Madrid Street in the barrio of San Nicholas in Manila, and who are already parents to two other children.[6] These are the two names that Isabel Cooper lists as her parents in travel documents as an adult. In those and other records, however, she moves her birthdate back and forth from 1909 to as late as 1921.[7]

Isaac Cooper and Protacia Rubin are strange bedfellows, brought together in the vibrant maelstrom of a colonial city in the aftermath of the Philippine-American War.[8] In fleshing out their stories, I stumble across other, more intimate, scandals. If their daughter's life can be read as a text of the lessons she absorbs during childhood, then one could say their disregard of social and cultural mores is one she took to heart. Between the two of them, they commit at least two noteworthy, exceptional acts that upend the tacit rules of colonial society.

Isaac Cooper, a white veteran of the U.S. war against the Philippines, marries a Filipina and legally recognizes her and the children he has with her. In doing so, he flouts the prejudices of colonial society by legitimizing a type of relationship that had become commonplace but was still frowned upon. He then—whether consciously or not—flies in the face of antimiscegenation laws in the continental United States by returning there with his mixed-race family in tow, with the intention of permanent re-settlement.

For her part, Protacia Rubin ultimately rejects the promises of the metropole and the protections of her husband. Reversing the trajectory of most Filipinos of the period, she sails back to Manila, where she almost immediately takes up with another American soldier, possibly committing bigamy.

These were the limited expressions and practices of rebellion and survival that were available to the minor actors of empire—both colonizer

Birth certificate, unnamed daughter, 1912, Philippine Islands. FamilySearch.

and colonized. In the frontier spaces of the Philippine archipelago, where interracial relationships were discouraged but also ordinary, and where legal and social categories were inchoate and mutable, it was perhaps inevitable that the personal desires of individuals would override the usual order of things. These creative, somewhat disreputable transgressions invert the established understandings of colonial relations that placed white men in positions of power over the Filipinas that they took up with. While empire's broader power structures proved largely unassailable, in the space of intimate encounters there was room for small subversions and other expressions of desire.

❋ ❋ ❋

Isaac Cooper and Protacia Rubin would not have met were it not for the United States' ambition to join the imperial land grab that was already well underway in the late 1800s. Isaac Cooper's path to the Philippines was not unusual. Many of his new fellow soldiers hailed from the rural heartland, where the prospect of a lifetime toiling on the land was a near certainty. He was born in the sparsely populated town of Boaz, Wisconsin, around 1875, the middle child of seven. Like many of their neighbors, fellow midcentury settlers from Europe and states like Ohio, Kentucky, and Virginia, the Coopers eked out a living as small farmers.[9] At the age of twenty-five, Isaac Cooper had enough of farming.[10] The wider world called, and it beckoned with adventures that would have been familiar to someone who had grown up with accounts of the United States' sustained and lethal military campaign against Indians. He was surrounded, after all, with stories about a fellow Wisconsin native, Arthur MacArthur. This was the infamous "Boy Colonel" of the Civil War, whose later genocidal exploits against Native Americans in the West—culminating with his capture of Geronimo in 1889—fired the imagination of many white settlers.

After the violent extermination campaigns against Indians had ebbed, the declaration of war against Spain provided a new generation with prospects for manly adventure. Yellow journalism stirred up the emotions of the public against Spanish military atrocities in Cuba and its other colonies, and war broke out in April 1898.[11] The routine of Isaac Cooper's life as a farm laborer in Wisconsin and, later, Kansas paled in comparison to the heroic accounts of men on exotic frontiers. They made war "splendid"—Commodore George Dewey and his quick dispatch of the Spanish navy in the Battle of Manila Bay and Theodore Roosevelt storming up San Juan Hill in Puerto Rico with his Rough Riders.[12] Surrounded by farmland, with few prospects other than the promise of unrelenting physical labor, Isaac Cooper, like thousands of young men from Ohio, Nebraska, Minnesota, and Kansas, chose adventure.

On Christmas Day in 1898, Isaac Cooper enlisted. American volunteer expeditions had already taken part in the assault and capture of Manila in 1898, wresting it from Spain with a show of force in August of that year. Just days before Isaac Cooper signed up for his three-year tour, President McKinley issued the Benevolent Assimilation Proclamation, which announced the United States' "altruistic" intentions of keeping the Philippines as a colony under the "mild sway of justice and right," much to the dismay of Filipino independence fighters.[13] The Spanish-American War in the Philippines had ended with a whimper, but another war was brewing.

Over the weeks it took Isaac Cooper to cross the Pacific, the tensions generated by the U.S. military occupation of the Philippines sparked a new conflict. Skirmishes between American soldiers and Filipino troops and

DESCRIPTIVE AND ASSIGNMENT CARD OF RECRUIT.

Isaac L Cooper

forwarded to the *20'* Regt. of *Inf*

pursuant to *Gen 853 A.R.* , dated

_____, 189 .

DESCRIPTION.

WHERE BORN.		AGE.	OCCUPATION.
Town or County.	State or Kingdom.		
Fork Andrew	*Wis*	*24*	*Laborer*

EYES.	HAIR.	COMPLEXION.	HEIGHT.	
			Feet.	Inches.
Blue 10	*Bro*	*Swarth*	*5*	*7 1/2*

ENLISTED.

DATE.	PLACE.	BY WHOM.	PERIOD.
Dec 98	*Fort Dsworth Wis*	*Lt. Cavenaugh*	*3*

LAST PAID.		Year of Continuous Service.	PRIOR SERVICE.		
By Paymaster.	To What Time.		Co.	Regt.	Date of Discharge.
Due from recruit		*1*			

LAUNDRY WORK	DUE UNITED STATES.

Isaac Cooper's enlistment papers. National Archives and Records Administration.

civilians, exacerbated by drunken revelry that laid bare the prejudices of un-supervised young men far from home, were reported in American papers—framed as "Filipinos Killing Our Troops."[14] Military violence between the United States and Filipino "insurrectos" finally broke out in February 1899, cementing American intentions to hold on to Spain's former colonies. By the time Isaac Cooper's transport docked in Manila that year, he was just in time to serve in what the United States was euphemistically calling a "pacification" campaign.[15]

As far as I have found, Isaac Cooper did not record his time in the islands. Diaries and letters home written by his fellow soldiers during this early pe-riod juxtapose hearsay about "losing ground" and predictions of "some hard fighting" with yearnings for baths, notes about wildlife, complaints about food, and descriptions of Manila.[16] Young white Midwestern men tried to make sense of the tropical landscape that they were moving through. They complained about the wool uniforms in the tropical heat and the tedium of garrison life, and were felled by indigestion and other illnesses. The short, blue-eyed, brown-haired Isaac Cooper found himself headed to the province of Batangas, in the southern region of Luzon, a stark difference from the flat farmland of Boaz. In its rugged countryside, American soldiers with barely six weeks' worth of training waged a protracted and disorienting fight against a guerrilla force familiar with the lay of the land.[17]

One might call it coincidence, but given that the Philippines was imagined to be an extension of the Western frontier, it was no surprise that one of the cowboys who leaped the ocean to find new Indians was Isaac Cooper's fel-low Wisconsinite Arthur C. MacArthur, now a brigadier general. The former Boy Colonel, now a family man and father to a teenager named Douglas who was heading to an officer's career at West Point in 1899, would become an instrumental player in American military rule in the islands.[18] Son would fol-low father, and along with Isaac Cooper (who was just five years older than the MacArthur scion) and other young American men, they would find the Philippines ripe for career advancement and personal pleasures.

Occupation was a strangely surreal experience for many soldiers, as the war soon turned into a guerrilla conflict across the islands. They went out into the "boondocks" to engage in military maneuvers against Filipino rebels, not knowing sometimes how to tell the enemy from civilians. Meanwhile, in the capital, business went on as usual even after the outbreak of hostilities. Soldiers on their few days of rest and recuperation had freedoms they had not imagined back in the United States. Even as they fought against guerrillas in the country-side, American soldiers also socialized with Filipinos in organized activities such as concerts, dances, and meals, mixing with their Filipino hosts and appreciating the welcome they extended.[19] The contrast was dizzying for the average American soldier: holding a Filipino in his gun sights during the day, and a warm Filipina in his arms in the red-light district in Manila at night.[20] They caroused, got drunk, and took part in the prostitution trade already in place from Spanish times. Venereal disease among American troops shot up, demonstrating what historian Tessa Winkelmann names the "dangerous intercourse" of colonial relations.[21] Unsurprisingly, the Philippine-American War saw the U.S. military in the business of regulating prostitution to control sexually transmitted diseases among its troops.[22]

Exacerbated by the shortage of white women, Manila's urban proximity bred interracial familiarity, exchanges, and illicit relationships between natives and colonizers. Filipinas and Filipinos kept house for their colonizers, providing comfort as servants, cooks, and launderers, or providing succor, entertainment, and pleasure through companionship and sex.[23] To the dismay of some American colonialists, the race thinking that had underpinned the colonial venture did not translate into segregation in the bedroom. While the new governor-general encouraged "closer social relations between the Americans and Filipinos," hosting fêtes at Malacañang Palace, this was not quite what he had in mind.[24] Those in the diplomatic ranks were not so open in their commingling, but soldiers and civilians of Isaac Cooper's status were less discreet about consorting with the natives, and set up an array of arrangements with Filipinas and, occasionally, Filipinos.[25]

Even as American newspapers attacked the lingering immorality of the "*querida* system," a Spanish colonial practice of keeping mistresses outside of marriage, they also noted American crossings of the color line.[26] The Americanos were no exception, no matter the supposedly progressive and modern brand of imperialism they practiced. A. V. N. Hartendorp, a colonial educator and journalist, noted that "indeed many American and civil officials of the highest rank, scientists, professors, and others who were bachelors, entered into discreet alliances with Japanese and also Filipino women without marrying them for the reason that most of these men did not expect to remain in the Philippines for any great length of time and therefore did not wish to enter into any permanent relationships."[27] Hartendorp matter-of-factly narrates his own sexual exploits (including diseases caught and given) alongside his eclectic Philippine career.

The July 4, 1903, *Sunday Sun* shared gossip designed to titillate and police Manileños: "They say that the Cavite Captain who nightly drives with two demure brown sisters through Paco, should reflect that open air exhibitions of affection, particularly where the principals are of such diverse nativity, are not calculated to exalt the uniform he wears." Another aside on an "Escolta storekeeper of prominence" who "pays visits to a chocolate-hued sister on Calle Echague" captures the petty public censuring that followed these commonplace relationships.[28] Read a different way, they also document how American men and Filipinas persisted in negotiating arrangements with each other regardless of what was deemed acceptable.

Colonial anxiety about the purity of racial lines was further tested by relationships that veered dangerously into the respectable. Social observers often wrote in disapproval of how Manila social life fostered intimate relations between white men and Filipinas, so that "'the white men are friendly with many of the Mestizos, and dance with their pretty daughters,' and were 'occasionally foolish enough to marry the latter.'"[29] Charles W. Hack, an American medical officer during the war, observed with distaste how some of his fellow officers had gone so far as to marry Filipinas: "We hear of marriages every few days. . . . We heard an army officer we knew is to marry a philippina who lives near us in an adjoining pueblo. These things are hard to understand."[30] Those who chose to marry were able to do so because antimiscegenation laws were not enforced in the islands and "no Jim Crow laws ever made it across the Pacific," but also because, in practice, these marriages were often ephemeral: they were not legally binding and could be dissolved with little effort, even if they produced children.[31] Many Filipina "wives" were eventually abandoned by their American "husbands" and had little or no legal standing or knowhow to demand any kind of support from them.

As the United States settled into a longer-term occupation, both casual and illicit interracial intimacies became the rule, rather than the exception. Isaac Cooper tried his hand at both.

By 1903, twenty-eight-year-old Isaac Cooper was living in Manila, having served out his three-year enlistment in the Twentieth Infantry.[32] The city played host to a spectacular medley of Filipino and mestizo elites, natives of more modest backgrounds, and foreigners, including over half of the more than 8,135 American soldiers, colonial administrators, teachers, entrepreneurs, and tourists in the islands.[33] They lived in a city that was rapidly being modernized for "the American lifestyle."[34] As a child attending the one-room schoolhouse in rural Boaz, Isaac Cooper could not have imagined the diverse and cosmopolitan community he would live in as an adult, halfway across the world.

Amid the growing number of public spaces in the city, American men found ways to meet Filipinas. Where church and school might have introduced him to a potential mate in Wisconsin, in Manila, Isaac Cooper and other American

Escolta, Manila, circa 1910–20. Photo Supply Co., Library of Congress Prints and Photographs Division.

men dined together with Filipinos in restaurants, attended public entertainments like the theater, horse racing, and sporting events, strolled the paths of Luneta Park, rode streetcars, and shopped in the same stores on the busy streets of the Escolta district. Trading the uniform of the soldier for pale linen suits, they went about their business in the bustling heart of the city. Others partook in the more illicit pleasures of Manila, from the cabaret to prostitution. A streetcar connected the Santa Ana Cabaret, owned by former soldier John Canson, who married a Filipina, to the city. The club strategically catered to a wide clientele: sit-down dinners with linen tablecloths for higher-ranking officers and government administrators took up one side of a white picket fence. On the other side, peso-a-dance Filipina dancers swayed with military bachelors seeking the comfort and companionship of women.

In many ways, the "American lifestyle" that Manila accommodated was that of the white American bachelor. As the military campaign against Filipino revolutionaries moved further afield from the capital, Isaac Cooper and many of his fellow veterans took up the kind of civil service positions that came with bringing civilization and progress to the islands, and which were primarily reserved for white men. He became a fireman in Manila's municipal service.[35]

As a wage-earning single man, Isaac Cooper saw Manila as his oyster. While of vastly different backgrounds, he and other American men—like the twenty-three-year-old Douglas MacArthur, a freshly minted second lieutenant from West Point taking a tour of Asia in October 1903—were the agents of the civilizing mission. They felt entitled to the urban entertainments Manila had on offer, from the American social clubs to the array of vaudeville performances in its theaters and opera houses and, by extension, the women in them.[36]

Early in his sixteen-year sojourn in the islands, Isaac Cooper took part in the kinds of arrangements made possible by the intimacies of the urban colonial world. Soon after his discharge, he took up with a woman named Rubia Ryan. A son, who was named Bruce Cooper, was born to them in 1904.[37] Naming his son after his younger brother indicates that he saw his son as part of the Cooper line. But other than this note, the archive is silent about Rubia Ryan, and it is unclear if Isaac ever had a sustained relationship with his eldest son. A little over two decades later, Bruce Cooper would claim Isaac Cooper as his father in a marriage certificate.[38] That Rubia Ryan fades from the historical record was likely a matter of the fraught and expendable alliances that Filipina women negotiated with American men, but also because another Filipina laid claim to Isaac Cooper.

✵ ✵ ✵

Protacia Rubin was about fourteen years old when she married the thirty-three-year-old Isaac Cooper—around 1908.[39] She was born in 1894, in Nagcarlan, Laguna, and was of Filipino and Spanish ancestry.[40] We have no documentation that sheds light on the everyday interactions of their union—or indeed, if it was a legitimate marriage, although Isaac Cooper behaved as if it was. We can only guess if it was passionate, caring, uncomfortable, abusive, one of convenience, or whether they shared the same feelings. The age disparity between a barely pubescent Filipina orphan and the middle-aged American civil service fireman points to some kind of arrangement rather than happenstance romance. There were few places in Manila where two such unlikely people could have met.[41] An account by an American expatriate who married a cousin of the orphaned Rubin sisters contends that Protacia was married off to Isaac Cooper by her extended family, eager to rid themselves of the financial burden of raising their wards. It alludes to how the sisters felt that they were "sold" to their husbands.[42]

But the Rubin-Cooper union belied the established pattern of American-Filipina relations in the colony, which positioned Filipinas most often as the vulnerable supplicant, or as eventually disposable. Aside from the awkward conditions of their marriage, the disadvantages of her youth, and her financial dependence on her husband, it was clear that Protacia Rubin saw herself as neither inferior nor disposable. Her sparse records shed light on the inventive ways that some Filipinas took the raw material of colonialism and molded it according to their needs and desires. In short, she rewrote the rules of the colony and its ambiguous treatment of the legitimacy of interracial marriage to her advantage. In an intriguing reversal of the common power dynamics of interracial arrangements in the colonies, Protacia Rubin eventually elected to treat her marriage to Isaac Cooper with the same sort of cavalier disregard that so many American men had for their Filipina wives.

That she did this, perhaps, was the bigger scandal than the interracial liaisons that were the open secret of the American civilizing project, or even the scandal of a white American man choosing, unlike so many of his peers, to lend legitimacy to his Filipina wife and their mixed-race children.

There are no signs in the archive that Protacia Rubin would become an unbiddable wife.

The couple set up house at 347 Madrid Street in Manila. Protacia Rubin bore her husband at least three children in quick succession.[43] At least one is lost to history. A son, unimaginatively named Bruce Cooper, was born in 1909. Or perhaps 1911.[44] The unnamed daughter followed on August 23, 1912.[45] (This daughter may have been Isabel Rosario Cooper, or she may have been the other of the two living, legitimate children counted by both parents on that date, on their sister's birth certificate. Or Isabel Cooper may have been born as early as February 22, 1909.)[46] As evidenced by their quickly prolific union, Protacia Rubin did not shirk her wifely duties.

Yet perhaps Protacia Rubin had always had a streak of the rebel in her. Maybe she was driven by pragmatism to marry a man twice her age for the financial security and independence he represented—to finally be able to thumb her nose at relatives who were always quick to remind her of their magnanimity. It could be that her marriage, as uneven as it was on paper, also cultivated Protacia's sense of self and worth. The very young wife of a well-employed civil servant had a certain social status in colonial Manila, even considering how most of these kinds of arrangements ended. It was certainly more than what she had as the orphan ward of her extended family. With Isaac Cooper toiling at the fire department all day, 347 Madrid Street was Protacia Rubin's domain. What is clear is that despite the age gap in her marriage, and its murky legality, Protacia did not act as if these were vulnerabilities.

What we can read in between the lines of ship manifests, birth certificates, pension paperwork, and military transport guidelines is an outline of a story about a man who was committed to his marriage and family, and a woman who decided that the conditions of this commitment were no longer desirable to her. Isaac Cooper went out of his way to claim Protacia and his children as his legal family—which was one thing in colonial Manila, but another thing entirely in the continental United States, where interracial marriages were banned in many states. With the 1916 Jones Act, which was meant to incrementally return sovereignty to Filipinos in anticipation of eventual independence, a policy of Filipinization began to replace Americans with Filipinos in civil service positions. By that year, Isaac Cooper was no longer a captain in the Manila fire department.[47] Many of his fellow expatriates were returning home, having lost their livelihoods to Filipinos.

Unlike his fellow veterans who left their Filipina inamoratas in the islands upon returning home, Isaac Cooper brought his wife and three children, with another one in utero, to the United States.[48] As a military veteran, he used the army transport to move his household, which he was allowed to do as long as his relationship with them could be proved "permanent" through certification and "habitual" residence.[49] In other words, Cooper had to claim his wife and children, provide legal evidence of this relationship, and list them as legitimately bound to him in order to use this benefit. The legal workings of what it meant to return to the United States with a Filipina wife and their mixed-race children were uncertain at best. Nativist sentiment was spurring anti-immigrant legislation targeting immigration from Asia, adding to the racist stew of American social life. But because of the peculiar category that Filipinos occupied in the 1910s—they were neither subject to the Asian exclusion laws nor considered citizens of the United States—they constituted an unevenly defined group that slipped through the legal cracks.[50] The fact that Isaac Cooper had married a brown woman—a colonial ward—and had mixed-race children with her was not of itself unusual: that he was bringing them into the United States as a legally recognized family was altogether another thing.

What was it like for them to travel on a military transport across the Pacific as a clearly interracial family? The 192 or so other first- and second-class passengers with whom they traveled were themselves a mixed group of single men and families with children. The manifest does not reveal if other families had the mixed racial makeup of the Cooper family.

The voyage from Manila, through Nagasaki and Honolulu and on to San Francisco, was significantly shorter than the one that Isaac Cooper had taken in reverse a little over a decade and a half before.[51] They left Manila in late March, arriving in San Francisco on April 19, 1916. Protacia Rubin, now twenty-two, was pregnant with her fourth child. I wonder if they—or she—stuck to their quarters, or if the energy of three young children cooped up in small spaces drove them to brave the stares of their fellow passengers. What were they thinking about the new life they would build—where they would live, how they would support themselves? The family was literally, and figuratively, at sea.

From the urban chaos and vibrancy of Manila, the Cooper-Rubin family disembarked at the busy port of San Francisco and took an overland journey over the Rockies, through the Southwest, eventually arriving in Phoenix, then Maricopa, in Arizona. A few years before Isaac Cooper and Protacia settled there with their brood, Arizona had become one of twenty-eight states prohibiting interracial marriage between whites and Asians.[52] But because of the privileges of white men, and because they were not petitioning the city registrar for a marriage certificate, it is likely that the new family living at 1635 East Adams evaded close scrutiny.[53] In this way, the interracial sins of empire traveled from the outpost to its heart.

The only glimpse we see into their intimate lives during this first year is a family tragedy. Protacia Rubin was thrown from a buggy in August 1916, shortly after arriving in Maricopa.[54] Injured and traumatized, she went into labor prematurely. Her fourth child, a son, died three days later.[55] Protacia almost died herself.[56] The death certificate, a state document, is a stark record of this loss, experienced during a time of magnified strain and change.

I think of how Protacia must have felt the loss, amplified by being a new arrival with no friends of her own in an unfamiliar and perhaps hostile environment. The document fails to capture the grief of a family already coping with displacement and alienation. It cannot account for the silences in a home that might have expected instead the plaintive cries of an infant. It has no room for the bewilderment of the young Cooper siblings, or the ways in which loss might translate to resentment or blame.

❋ ❋ ❋

While a war had caused Isaac and Protacia's orbits to collide in Manila, another war would once again impinge on their family. The war that had been raging in Europe finally pulled the United States into its orbit in 1917. The draft that required men between twenty-one and thirty to enlist soon included those under forty-five, which meant that Isaac Cooper might once again be a soldier. In 1918, just two years after their arrival in Arizona, Protacia's forty-three-year-old husband registered for the draft.[57]

505

ARIZONA STATE BOARD OF HEALTH
BUREAU OF VITAL STATISTICS

PLACE OF DEATH

County...........................

District...........................

Town Or City...........................

No. *520 W Jefferson* St.

(If death occurred in a Hospital or Institution, give its NAME instead of street and number.)

State Index No. *194*

County Registered No. *1716*

Local Registrar's No. *4207*

ORIGINAL CERTIFICATE OF DEATH

FULL NAME *Infant of Isaac I Cooper*

PERSONAL AND STATISTICAL PARTICULARS	MEDICAL CERTIFICATE OF DEATH
SEX *M.*	COLOR OR RACE White Indian Black Chinese Mexican	SINGLE MARRIED WIDOWED or DIVORCED	DATE OF DEATH *Oct 29* 1916 (Month) (Day) (Year)

DATE OF BIRTH *Oct 29* 1916 (Month) (Day) (Year)

AGE ....yrs....mos....days If less than 1 day hrs. or *2³⁰* min.

I hereby certify that I attended deceased from *Oct 29* 1916 to *Oct 29* 1916; that I last saw him alive on *Oct 29* 1916, and that death occurred on the date stated above at *2¹* ....M. The DISEASE or INJURY causing death was as follows: *Mother thrown from buggy 3 days previously caused premature birth and death of infant* (Duration)....yrs....mos....days

OCCUPATION (a) Trade, profession or particular kind of work *None* (b) General nature of industry, business, or establishment in which employed or (employer)

BIRTHPLACE (State or country) *Phoenix*

NAME OF FATHER *Isaac I. Cooper*

BIRTHPLACE OF FATHER (State or country) *Wis*

MAIDEN NAME OF MOTHER *Protacia Rubin*

BIRTHPLACE OF MOTHER (State or country) *Phillippine Isle*

THE ABOVE IS TRUE TO THE BEST OF MY KNOWLEDGE

(Informant)...........................

(Address)...........................

Was disease contracted in Arizona?...........................

If not, where?...........................

CONTRIBUTORY...........................

(Duration)....yrs....mos....days

(Signed) *Dr. Mada Blasse*

Oct. 30 1916 (Address) *520 W. Jefferson St.*

*In deaths from VIOLENT CAUSES state (1) MEANS OF INJURY, and (2) whether ACCIDENTAL, SUICIDAL, or HOMICIDAL.

LENGTH OF RESIDENCE At place of death....yrs....mos....ds. In Arizona....yrs....mos....ds.

Former or Usual Residence...........................

PLACE OF BURIAL OR REMOVAL	DATE OF BURIAL OR REMOVAL
7 mi. West	*Oct 31* 1916

UNDERTAKER *Vare & McLellan* ADDRESS

Filed *Oct 30* 1916 *N. K. Beauchamp* Local Registrar

Filed *Nov 6* 1916 *Q. B. Nichols* County Registrar

Death certificate, Cooper infant. FamilySearch.

We don't know what ultimately caused Protacia Rubin to leave her husband. Perhaps she never felt at home in Arizona and had always been on the verge of returning to more familiar surroundings. Perhaps the possibility of his departure, leaving her to fend for herself, was the last straw. Her feelings about the United States or the legitimacy of her marriage may have been affected by a controversial case in Arizona that received media attention the same year that her husband was registering for the draft, in which a South Asian man scandalously married the daughter of one of his white tenants.[58] It is conceivable that Protacia Rubin feared her husband's looming absence following these tense racial events. Neither their marriage nor their children were enough to anchor her in the United States.

Family legend has it that she reached out to others for help in leaving her husband, because he refused to pay for her passage home. According to one account, Protacia Rubin's desire to leave her husband happened after her infant's death. She allegedly wrote to Manuel Quezon, then the Philippine representative in Washington, DC, to plead her case: "I am a Filipino woman, and I want to go home!"[59]

In 1919, Protacia Rubin left for Manila. Yet Isaac Cooper unquestionably continued to consider her his wife as late as January 1920, when he declared himself to be the married head of his household in that year's census. Protacia Rubin left behind her son Bruce but took with her at least ten-year-old Isabel Cooper. Perhaps she may not initially have seen this separation as permanent, or perhaps Isaac Cooper refused to let all his children go.[60]

Once out of Isaac's orbit, in almost shockingly short order after she arrived in Manila, Protacia Rubin most scandalously, and likely bigamously, married another American soldier. World War I had brought her second husband—Thomas Bernard Ryan, a third steward in the U.S. Army who hailed from St. Louis, Missouri—to the colony around the same time that she returned.[61] At twenty-nine, Thomas Ryan was much closer to Protacia's age, and they soon set up a household in Manila. She did not communicate her defection to Isaac Cooper in a timely manner, if at all.

Back on familiar home ground, Protacia Rubin remade herself. She started going by another one of her names, Josefina or Josephine, marking a new interlude in her life. By November of that year, Isabel Cooper became the older half sister to Josephine Margaret Ryan.[62] At this point, Isaac Cooper had heard the news that his wayward wife had effectively built a new life: by the time he filed for his military pension as an invalid, he no longer claimed Protacia as a dependent.[63]

Isaac Cooper continued to hold on to his son for a few years, raising him until adolescence. His daughter would grow up in Manila, in another man's household, with an increasing number of half siblings. While Isaac Cooper finally moved on, he was indelibly marked by his time in the Philippines. His body bore the marks of his service—at age fifty, he was living in one of the national homes for disabled volunteer soldiers in Los Angeles.[64] He continued to work—this time as a hospital steward—to support himself and his son.[65] His children by Protacia-now-Josefina would continue to remind him, through their own choices and misadventures, that the grander movements of empire and war manifested themselves at the intimate scale of the family

and the individual. Isabel Cooper would not see her father for close to another decade, when she visited him in Los Angeles in the mid-1920s. By then,
the precocious daughter that he had last seen when she was ten was already
Manila's darling and a scandal in her own right.

※ ※ ※

Isabel Cooper did not inherit her proclivity for transgression and scandal
from her father. While she would occasionally look to him for advice, what
is clear from the choices she made is that Isabel Cooper was her mother's
daughter. Josefina Protacia Rubin-Cooper-Ryan was the living text of a
woman's creativity under conditions of despair and desire. Like her daughter
would decades later, she constantly remade herself using the resources available to her and according to her own needs and aspirations.[66] She was more
adept than most at the reinventions that colonial society pressed on its subjects. What emerges from the record is a portrait of a woman who was, at
heart, a survivor. Protacia, the unbiddable wife, and Josefina, the scandalous
and opportunistic bigamist—provided the blueprint of feminine survival
that Isabel Cooper would draw from again and again.

If the general was prudent, he would have known that the "moonbeam delicacy of its lovely women" he so admired concealed four centuries of Filipina anger, cunning, and survival.[1]

❀ ❀ ❀

He should have asked Isabel Cooper about her mother.

1 MacArthur, *Reminiscences*, 36.

Misfiled in an archive, a letter, signed "Chabing Cooper (Belle)." Chabing was the stage name that Isabel Cooper used in her later Hollywood career. This 1951 letter is the last one I find written in her hand. It is a window into her life as an aging actress in Los Angeles, and into her most significant Hollywood role, but also into her past relationship with MacArthur and the stories she continued to tell about that interlude.

The letter's subtext is another story entirely. It captures the lingering legacies of colonial desire in Isabel Cooper's life.

A photograph is enclosed.

Chabing Cooper poses outside on a lawn next to a sunny sidewalk that stretches out into the distance behind her. In the letter, she says this is near where she lives.[1] She leans against a white post, smiling and looking straight at the camera lens. Her dimples are apparent. She wears a long, fitted, off-the-shoulder white dress, holding a red hibiscus and a pale rose. Her body is at a slight angle to the camera. The picture is blurred, her pose, studiedly casual. The sun is bright, casting a harsh shadow on one side of her face. Her eyes squint a little at the photographer. Or perhaps that is the effect of her smile.

She is around forty in the photograph, but can pass for younger, which is both the point and the problem detailed in the letter. By this time, she had been working in Hollywood for almost a decade.

The letter is a late surprise in my research.[2] It is dated January 24, 1951, and addressed to Drew Pearson, the journalist who had earned the ire and enmity of Douglas MacArthur in the early 1930s for his willingness to publicly lambaste the general. Most of Isabel Cooper's other letters to Pearson are from the previous decade, years after she provided him with a counterpunch to the general's libel suit, seeking his help in connecting her with influential

Chabing Cooper in Los Angeles, circa 1951. Courtesy Lyndon B. Johnson
Presidential Library.

people in Hollywood. This letter is separate from their other correspondence, in both its archival home and its late date. It was initially closed to researchers as a condition of the donor's deed of gift, but opened upon review in 1989. It was then inexplicably filed apart from the other MacArthur/Isabel Cooper materials in a folder labeled "Ronald Reagan" in the Lyndon B. Johnson Library's collection of Drew Pearson's personal papers.

I think about the arbitrariness of archival categories, of boxes, folders, and files. I wonder about how many people have actually read this letter, or have seen the photograph of the smiling, hopeful Chabing Cooper. I am struck by the power of the archive to guard and sift, but also by the obstinacy of the materials themselves to somehow endure and emerge. Archives can be tombs as much as they are sites for exhumation.

❂ ❂ ❂

The letter is at turns tinged with panic, excitement, hope, and dry humor. In two back-to-back pages, Chabing Cooper relates the news about her latest role and how gossip about her past might threaten it. She also narrates a very selective version of her relationship with General Douglas MacArthur, replete with truths about colonialism and the lies that made it palatable. The letter shows how Chabing Cooper had a way of writing herself into dramatic story lines—perhaps a by-product of her profession. By this time, Pearson is familiar with her style and with her tendency to build a scene.

Addressed to her "good friend always," the letter reports that Chabing has finally landed a significant film role. For an aging, mixed-race woman in Hollywood, this was truly an accomplishment. She has been cast in a supporting role in I Was an American Spy, an Ann Dvorak vehicle. The film is based on the life of Medal of Freedom recipient Claire Phillips, an American entertainer who operated a Manila nightclub catering to Japanese soldiers during World War II, and her exploits as a clandestine agent for the resistance.

That it was MacArthur who recommended Phillips for the medal, prompting the film that casts his former mistress in "an excellent part," is a piece of delicious historical irony that is not mentioned in the letter. However, she confides to Pearson that the MacArthur episode of her life is resurfacing: her "association" with the general, especially in a film about World War II in the Philippines, about women who diverted soldiers, has too many links to remain buried.

She writes at the beginning of filming, voicing her suspicion that one of a "number of Filipinos on the set" might have passed on her story, which was "known to some people in Manila." As a result, Mr. Diamond, the producer, interviewed her about her past with MacArthur, "intending, so he said to use it for publicity for [herself] and for the picture." Chabing's next sentences are muddled, but telling. She seems to assure both herself and Pearson that Diamond "only wants to tell the story of how kind the General was to me. I do not believe he knows any more about me." Yet she follows that declaration with "and he stared at me." The nature of that gaze is evident in the way it pulls against the two sentences before it. In the negative space between lines of neat cursive, Isabel Cooper depicts the entangled desires she, as a mixed-race, aging actress with a murky past, constantly navigates. It also recalls an incident almost a decade before, when she tells Pearson about a casting director from RKO harassing her after a dinner meeting: he "took me home but not without some advances. I tried to laugh about it at first—but he became very serious & although I haven't seen him since that night, three weeks ago, he still telephones and threatens in a mild form."[3] She is trapped by the vulnerabilities of her past and present.

The story she narrates is almost comical, except for the stakes for a woman living a precarious life in Los Angeles. The reason Isabel Cooper is reluctant to divulge details to Diamond about that "sensitive subject" has less to do with its potential for rendering her vulnerable to harassment, or harming her reputation, but rather her fear of having her age found out and losing the role because of it. Because she is playing "an 18 or 19 year old servant girl," the interview had her furiously calculating how young she would have had to be in the fictional timeline of her first meeting with MacArthur so as not expose her present-day age as more than twice that of the character she is playing.

She tells Pearson about her improvisation: "I told him I started on the stage in Manila at the age of five which is true and the General first saw me when I was seven—took an interest in me asked me how I would like to attend school in Washington (which is true except the age) and later perhaps become a ward of his aging mother." Her explanation likely disappointed Diamond, who was perhaps hoping for a more exploitable or sensational story. She reports to Pearson that she even showed Diamond a few school compositions that the general corrected to corroborate her story, prompting Diamond to order his secretary to contact the publicity department.

I imagine Isabel Cooper in the producer's office, across from his desk, fumbling for a plausible tale that will keep him interested but not endanger a longed-for role; her horror when he picks up the phone to his secretary to demand the publicity department; the temptation of how the publicity might mean badly needed income. I think about how she holds on to her old school compositions, offering them as evidence of the shape of the general's kindness.

Her letter ends with an entreaty to Pearson for his advice, given his own tangled history with MacArthur, and her invaluable assistance in that history. It also ends with a somewhat startling and theatrical statement: "Maybe if MacArthur ever saw anything in the papers about me and his name linked with it he'd have me shot."

There is no evidence of a reply from Pearson.

A lone article in the *Lubbock Evening Journal* captures the fantastical story Chabing weaves about her relationship with the general.[4] She relays a story of a MacArthur who was so struck with the five-year-old "daughter of an officer on his staff" and her "vivid personality and flashing dark eyes" that he sent her to the United States for her education and "paid all the bills." The story Chabing crafts lingers on MacArthur as a benevolent father, recounting treats of "a big ice cream soda at a shop near Dupont Circle" on Saturdays. She notes that she has not seen the general since 1937, when she was fourteen, fabricating a more acceptable Hollywood age for herself. The writer paints a girl with fond memories: "He was the most wonderful man I ever met. . . . He opened up an entire new world to me."

I Was an American Spy is not the hit that Chabing Cooper hopes. It is her penultimate credited role.

The letter and its photograph, the not-quite-right narration of her relationship that becomes part of the film's press, and the stories they tell directly and obliquely are artifacts of imperial intimacy. Aside from the nearly screwball energy of Chabing's tale of her encounter with the producer, it is the inadvertently narrated story—part truth, part fabrication—that lingers. The claims she makes public in the article are believable. The story of the kindness of the general, his paternal interest and tutelage, how this sort of thing just *was*. The almost-breezy nature of the anecdote she shares with Pearson and the reporter, and the matter-of-factness in the way she relays it underscore the banality of how a young Filipina might encounter an older American soldier in Manila. It was, after all, also her mother's story, twice.

The letter in Chabing's looping hand and its accompanying photograph capture how Isabel Cooper mastered a number of different gendered roles, both onstage and off, in the margins of empire and in its center. It pulls three men into close proximity with each other through her, but also gestures to the broader male gaze that tracks her over the course of her life, and her awareness of that gaze. The relationships she has with men—MacArthur, Pearson, Diamond—continue to touch her life, providing material and an audience for her versions of her history.

These intimacies are the intangible stuff that binds empire together.[5]

Onstage at five (*which is true*). Encounter with the general's kindness at seven (*which is true except the age*).

The letter and the article conjure the five-year-old who first set foot on-stage in Manila (though more than a decade before she really meets the general), and connects her to the forty-year-old actress still hoping for her breakout role after a lifetime of performing, who grapples with a history that keeps rearing its head. I think about the distance between the two, measured not only in time and space but also in the currency of innocence. From an early age, Isabel Cooper had to learn to deal in that particular illicit tender.

American empire meant that Filipinos could never claim innocence, not even a five-year-old. Americans wrapped that mantle around themselves. In much the same way that the United States peddled a genocidal war that saw any Filipino boy under the age of ten as killable under the banner of pacification and benevolence, it asserted the virtuousness, the goodness, of what it forcibly bestowed on its "little brown brothers." Despite evidence to the contrary, in the imperial calculus, Filipinos were somehow culpable for their own colonization. *They were asking for it.* As the carnage and carnality at the heart of empire were laid bare, its continued wish for innocence also persisted. Beautiful cities rose, teachers were shipped over to tutor the natives, roads were built, and civilization paved over the body count.

In similar fashion, Isabel Cooper's recollection of her five-year-old self singing and dancing onstage and her recharacterization of her relationship with the general as patronizing and innocent covers over a much uglier historical reality. Her lie about her age when meeting MacArthur and the nature of the tutelage he offered her is believable because so much of it was built on American insistence about the righteousness of its mission in the Philippines.

He opened up an entire new world to me.

Yet Isabel herself was evidence of the peculiar erotics of empire in the archipelago.[6] Her letter illuminates the ways in which she had learned to work alongside colonizers' desires to continue inflicting discipline (and themselves) on Filipinos, and their simultaneous yearning for absolution. No matter the claims and attempts of its administrators, progressive reformers, and the white women who came with them to wash their colonial wards clean of their sins of savagery, American imperialism created a world where disreputable behaviors and habits flourished. The movement of the imperial frontier to the Philippines fashioned the islands into a modern demimonde. It wasn't as if Spanish empire—four hundred years of being in a Catholic convent—had not cultivated its own perversions under the shroud of piety.

The libinal is woven into empire's design. But the American flavor of imperialism claimed righteousness as a pillar of its singular mission of uplift. That was its particular colonial kink.

Colonial Manila was a strange amalgam of a city being made comfortable for family-friendly imperialism and the illicit arrangements that made bourgeois sensibilities blush.

A five-year-old girl on Manila's stages, especially one of mixed race, could never be apprehended as innocent, no matter how Chabing tells her story. She would already have been caught in the city's confused webs of desire, her body a visual reminder that American colonial segregation stopped behind closed doors. Singing and dancing onstage placed the "half-caste" problem in the public eye. Isabel Cooper and her siblings were part of the first generation of American mixed-race children on the islands, numbering into the low thousands by the time she was a small child.[7] This new category of mestizo—not born of Spanish colonialism or Chinese migration—belied American assertions of moral superiority.[8]

The existence of Isabel Cooper and other mestizos was evidence that sex, and lots of it, defined the colonial encounter. It was illicit but ordinary. While some mestizos were born of legitimate marriages that were often eventually abandoned by American men, many were the progeny of relations between American troops and Filipinas employed as launderers or housekeepers by the soldiers. Others were the "offspring of Canson's Santa Ana bailerinas and American fathers, some of them prominent in the community," and while not exactly proving that "racial prejudice [did] not affect mating habits," certainly confirmed that racism worked through sex.[9]

In that way, the Americans were nothing special, much to their chagrin. Just a little over a decade into American imperialism in the islands, the abandonment of American mestizos by their fathers was taken up as a cause célèbre by churches and civic groups. By 1914, around the time that Isabel Cooper began treading the boards at age five, an American Mestizo Association rallied to care for "children of mixed American-Filipino blood," who were seen as vulnerable prey for disreputable Filipinos or Chinese.[10] The uncertain social position and perceived sexual vulnerability and allure of the "American mestiza" generated anxiety that Asian men might also cross the color line by entering into relationships with partially white American women. That, clearly, was a privilege reserved only for white men.[11]

Thus when Isabel Cooper at forty or so tells the tale of the general who wants to be her guardian—of his kindness—it is a kindness steeped in the twisted carnality of race, sex, and empire.[12] That she defines his offer as wardship and care is revealing. Colonial wardship was a tarnished thing. As colonial wards, Filipinos served as capitalism's necessary reserve labor army while buttressing fantasies of racial superiority and benevolence. In the occupied archipelago, interracial intimacy was the perverse form of this wardship. A five-year-old mixed-race child performing onstage, no matter how innocent her act, was already wrought up in these troubled undercurrents.

There are no photographs of a young Isabel singing or dancing onstage. I imagine a precocious child working the charm of innocence on an audience, delighting some and making others anxious. As a denizen of the stage and early film world in Manila, Isabel Cooper came to understand these entangled desires of empire—and how they would define her life. Her early stage career capitalized on these colonial seductions.

"Dimples," the stage persona that Isabel Cooper cultivated in her teens, captured the undercurrents of innocence, sex, and racial desire that played out in Manila. The traces of this history seep between the lines of the letter she writes decades later.

❊ ❊ ❊

The girl who would become Dimples returned to the city of her birth as it was undergoing a renaissance. By the time Protacia Rubin arrived in Manila in 1919 with her daughter, World War I had ended and Isabel Cooper was on the cusp of adolescence. The United States itself had been a late entrant to the conflict, and the European war had been relatively incidental to Philippine life.[13] The continued occupation by the United States, however, meant that there was a constant flow of military personnel and colonial bureaucrats in and out of the islands—one of whom Protacia Rubin rather precipitously married.

The "Washington of the Orient," with its thriving downtown shopping district, was probably more cosmopolitan in Isabel Cooper's young eyes than Maricopa, Arizona. The city was being made modern for bureaucrats, businessmen, teachers, and their families, all of whom cut their teeth on colonialism but wanted the comforts of home.[14] Its waterfront parks and parkways, neoclassical government buildings, streets with trolleys, sewer systems, and electric lighting showcased the progressive empire that the United States styled itself to be. There were more opportunities for people from all walks of life to rub shoulders, thanks to the power of profit. Strolling on Calle Rosario, peeking in the windows of Clarke's or the Silver Dollar Saloon, having lunch at Tom's Dixie Kitchen on Plaza Goiti, Filipinos and Americans mingled in public.

If the Philippines was the progressive colonial laboratory of the United States, it was also its demimonde. Manila was both the colonial administration's showcase for urban planning and the archipelago's red-light district. The second decade of American occupation in Manila had not softened white American colonial attitudes toward race mixing: intimate encounters were carried out in illicit spaces. Reputable women, Filipinas and Americans alike, looked down on the cabarets and dance halls that flourished outside city limits. At the end of the Paco tranvia line, the infamous Santa Ana Cabaret continued to offer its clientele entertainments of the more risqué variety. Now patronized by luminaries such as the Filipino president of the Senate, Manuel Quezon, and the American governor-general, Francis Burton Harrison, men "danced and set their tables on both sides of the hall," blurring the lines between business and pleasure with their interest in the Filipinas who entertained in these spaces.

Taking the tranvia line home, Isabel Cooper and her family would have seen colonial men heading to these places to dance and drink after work.[15] Perhaps her own stepfather frequented them from time to time.

Even in a city as cosmopolitan as Manila that had long seen mestizo Filipinos, reminders of the common reality of interracial sex were unsettling because they threatened the colonial racial order. As a member of an interracial American household, and of mixed race herself, young Isabel Cooper occupied a social space that was not quite respectable.[16] As Isaac Cooper's legitimate daughter, she had avoided the fate of some of her mixed-race peers. As Thomas Ryan's stepdaughter, she had the advantage of his income as a soldier. But as Josefina Ryan's daughter, she bore the mark of her mother's choices.

On the edge of adolescence and already showing signs of the striking beauty she would become, Isabel Cooper was poised to enter the city's demimonde class. Living in Calle Herrán in the Paco district of Manila, she would have attended Paco Intermediate School, a public school in her neighborhood, at least for a time.[17] But this kind of education was not the kind of schooling fated for her—no matter what fantasies the general lived out in correcting her school compositions years later.

She was roughly ten when she returned to Manila with her mother. If Isabel Cooper had first been onstage at five, returning to the stage at ten—or soon after—all but sealed her fate.

❉ ❉ ❉

And 1919 was a formative year for Isabel Cooper. She left her father, brother, and her home in Arizona and traversed the Pacific. She discovered her mother could make life-changing decisions. She was obliged to make room in her life for her mother's new husband, and soon after, for more siblings. All these changes left their mark.

The year 1919 marked her return to a city immersed in heady conversations about the Filipina, conversations she was old enough to absorb. The kinds of ideas taking shape in popular periodicals such as the *Philippines Free Press* and the *Graphic* were expressed through a bewildering mix of beauty pageant photographs, editorials about the dangers of educating women, reports on Filipina singers and musicians traveling to perform in Europe, and arguments by early feminists on the importance of equality.[18] The feminist (and antifeminist) ideas being debated on the islands were not unique—the question of women's suffrage was also coming to a head in the United States and other countries. In the Philippines, which was wrestling with ideas about nationhood and independence, the woman question was shot through with political, social, and cultural anxieties about Filipino identity.

A young woman coming of age in the city was surrounded by these energies.

The stage and, increasingly, the screen took up these vexed conversations. Just a few years before her birth, entrepreneurs had put up the first theaters across the city.[19] In those early days, movies were just the "incidental attraction." The main draw was still the "stage show," where "no respectable woman" would venture.[20] This vibrant creative medium came into its own during her time away. By the time Isabel Cooper returned from her brief sojourn in Arizona, Manila had transformed from a city that showed movies to a city that also made them.

On the screen in 1919 was the first feature-length film of pioneering filmmaker José Nepomuceno, *Dalagang Bukid* (Country maiden).[21] Nepomuceno had taken a story popularized through the musical dramatic form of the *sarswela* and made it into a sly filmic commentary on Filipina sexuality. Its star, Atang de la Rama, a twelve-year-old also known as the Queen of Kundiman who plaintively sung the Tagalog love songs onstage, reprised her stage role on film.[22] Because it was a silent film, during its first run in the Empire Theater in September 1919, Atang, costumed in an evening gown, sang the theme song of the film live. Winking at the sexual innuendo of the broken clay pot onscreen, Atang's rendition of "Nabasag ang Banga" (The broken pot) titillated audiences with its allusion to her character's loss of virginity.[23] The audience response to Atang's seasoned stage performance had Nepomuceno deciding that Atang would accompany all showings of the film.

The success of *Dalagang Bukid* ensured that audiences would see its sequel a month later, shoring up the nascent Filipino film industry as an arbiter of public opinion, but also as a promising and suspect medium of modernity.

I imagine a young Isabel Cooper seeing Atang de la Rama's saucy performance, noting the audience's delighted reaction, absorbing the magic of Tagalog paired with the promise of Hollywood glamour—of something uniquely Filipino in the making. At the very least, she would have heard about it—this was the social world she occupied, and Atang, just two years older, was talked about. At ten years old, flipping through the pages of the *Graphic* or the *Philippines Free Press*—perhaps not really digesting the nuances of opinion pieces on the rise of the modern girl or the modest Filipina, but seeing photographs of glamorous Hollywood stars interspersed with coverage of local celebrities, Americans and Filipinos alike—a young, impressionable girl would come to understand that there was a captivating alchemy and power to the stories told on the page, the stage, and the screen.[24]

Isabel Cooper learned her first lessons on entertaining a crowd, of titillation, of what kind of sway a Filipina actress could wield, from performances like Atang's, as well as Hollywood's arrival in the archipelago. While educational reforms had opened up opportunities for more girls to acquire schooling, including a campaign targeting the precipitous drop in the numbers of girls in school after the elementary grades, Isabel Cooper's curriculum for life came from the stage and screen. An uncle that she had become reacquainted with operated the hand-powered projectors in a local cinema.[25] If she was anything like Atang de la Rama, who had snuck into Charlie Chaplin films years earlier, Isabel Cooper would have persuaded her uncle to smuggle her into the theater. She also reconnected with her mother's extended family, some of whom had formed an orchestra. Through them, she became fluent in a uniquely American repertoire.[26]

By this time, Manila's theater scene rivaled those of other cosmopolitan cities.[27] While Teatro Libertad catered to Filipino tastes with its traditional *sarswela* performances, the Zorilla Theater began to present American plays, making it a destination "even for Americans."[28] Bodabil—that decidedly Filipino take on vaudeville—thrived with the arrival of Luis Borromeo, who would take a young Isabel Cooper under his wing.[29] Under the keen eye of Borromeo, who had cut his teeth on the North American vaudeville circuits, bodabil unabashedly and indiscriminately borrowed from Filipino and American repertoires.[30] He was known as the Jazz King for popularizing the genre in the islands. He soon started his own troupe of vaudeville performers in two of Manila's bigger venues, putting *sarswela* stars and early film actors under contract for his shows at the Olympic Stadium.[31]

Just as he spotted Atang's talent, he would see Isabel Cooper's potential.

By about age twelve or thirteen, Isabel Cooper dropped out of school and started treading the boards in Manila as a full-time performer.[32] She became reacquainted with a stage life that was much changed from her childhood and learned to fill in time between the film screenings that now competed for the audience at the same theater venues. I imagine her rushing out onstage in a line of chorus girls as the films rewound.

And as bodabil came into its own in the islands—getting more risqué along the way—Isabel Cooper, aka "Dimples," became the headliner, with her own slew of devoted fans.[33] The showier entertainments of vaudeville spawned three theaters in the city, the Palace (formerly the Sirena) on Ronquillo, the Savoy on Eschaque in Isabel Cooper's neighborhood, and the Rivoli in Plaza Sta. Cruz. Isabel Cooper was the Rivoli's star.[34]

❋ ❋ ❋

The next time she appears in the archive is through the reminiscences of a longtime colonial persona, Lewis Gleeck, who recalls what life was like for the American bachelor of this period (a de rigueur visit to the Santa Ana Cabaret that might result in an evening with a bailerina for five pesos, "which included breakfast, shower, and a rubdown").[35] He lists the notable stage performers of his youth, drawing on the fervid memories of compatriot A. V. N. Hartendorp, someone who had clearly thought of the Philippines as his sexual playground. The same Manila appears fictionalized in the first published story of Filipino writer Nick Joaquin, who writes about the dreams and disappointments of vaudeville life, drawing on his cousin's experience as a jazz pianist and his own childhood spent in and out of the Rivoli during Dimples's heyday.[36] In the sepia-toned memories of these men, Dimples was one of the big vaudeville stars that emerged in the early 1920s.

She had a recognizable act: performing to "sailors on shore leave, local residents, foreigners and Filipinos" in the Rivoli and Savoy, she coyly delivered the lines of "Has anyone seen my Kitty?" This "memory of her," "pert and cute," ambling across the stage "to the uproarious delight of the U.S. Navy in the front row" was woven into the "sounds and smells and quaint glamor of the old Manila."[37]

That "Dimples" stuck as her stage name—given to her by Borromeo—was not just because of her distinctive dimples, but because the name hinted at her "pert and cute" signature style that played at innocence.[38] At thirteen or so, like many of her fellow stage performers, Isabel Cooper knew what was up.

She had few illusions about where a girl like her belonged. Someone like her—mixed-race, with a Filipina mother possibly bigamously married to another American soldier—embodied the fringes of respectable society, that part of empire that its idealists would rather sweep under the rug. She lived

ANG GUSALI NG PELIKULA'T VAUDEVILLE NA
MARARANGAL

VAUDEVILLE

ARAWARAW

ITATANGHAL NG

RIVOLI AMUSEMENTS CO.

ANG

ISANG SAMAHANG GANAP AT MA-KABAGO SA BOONG KAPULUANG PILIPINAS

ANG AMING MGA "STAR"

DIMPLES —— MIAMI
VITANG COWPER
FARIAS —— MILLIE —— BEBE

PARITO 'AT PANOORIN ANG 'AMING MGA'
PALABAS 'AT KAYO 'AY MASISIYAHAN

Dimples at the Rivoli. *Liwayway*, October 27, 1923, 1. Courtesy Lopez Museum, Manila.

in a society where her value and worth were always measured with the instruments of racial and sexual desire. Like her mother and other Filipinas living in the colonial Philippines, she was seen as a sexual object, available for the most inconstant kinds of affection and the most fleeting of commitments.[39]

Onstage at least, she could turn the colonial gaze to her own ends. Singing the lines to the 1922 Tin Pan Alley song, Dimples was the unsettling progeny of empire's sometimes conflicting and sometimes aligned desires.

"Has Anyone Seen My Kitty?" was the perfect material for someone nimbly straddling the role of coquettish ingenue.[40] Shuffling, turning, and posing to the upbeat music and playing to the audience, Dimples lisped the suggestive lyrics about a girl's lost cat, playing up its double entendres. Repeat audiences came to expect her practiced choreography, impish facial expressions, and the suggestive lyrics delivered in a teasing sing-song, "I sit all night and sigh, / 'Cause it's lonely in my flat, / Come Pussy, Pussy, Pussy. / Nice Pussy, Pussy, Pussy; / Anybody seen my cat?" The sailors in the front row, who lingered to watch the acts again and again, hooted and hollered when she hit the chorus. Onstage, Dimples, sly and seasoned, delivers the coup de grâce: "Won't you please help me find my lonesome cat, / I know she's doggone lonesome."[41]

❋   ❋   ❋

Dimples's stage ascendance, marked by this bawdy Tin Pan Alley tune, coincided with the arrival of a new face in the archipelago. The dashing brigadier general and West Point superintendent Douglas MacArthur was shipped off to the Philippines by Chief of Staff John Pershing that same year. The new commander of the Philippine Division arrived with his bride, the socialite heiress Louise Cromwell, and her two children from a previous marriage.[42]

Decades later, when Isabel Cooper recalls her meeting with the general for the eager producer, she fabricates an encounter that due to her fictional age could only have been innocent except to the most perverse. In this tale, she modifies her age when meeting the general only because she does not want to appear older than she was: "The General first saw me when I was seven—took an interest in me asked me how I would like to attend school in Washington (which is true except the age)." This meeting does not occur when she is seven or thirteen.

While it is possible that Isabel Cooper first met the general sometime between 1922 and 1925 (when she was in her midteens), her occupation as an actress would already have placed her firmly in the demimonde. She would have been considered approachable: young enough that a comment about coming to Washington for schooling would not be out of place, but old enough for it be a veiled invitation for other kinds of tutelage. Years later, in his memoirs, MacArthur characterizes his view of educational work in the Philippines as "one of the most romantic chapters in Philippine history": perhaps this romance had to do with the access American men had to young Filipinas.[43]

There was already trouble in the MacArthur marriage upon arrival—with or without which the general might have sought his comforts elsewhere. Louise Cromwell could not bear provincial life in the islands, nor, it seemed, her spit-and-polish husband, for very long. A man—particularly a soldier—in Manila would have found ample opportunity, time, and place to take up with a vaudeville star. Perhaps when nurturing his career connections and becoming close friends with future president Manuel Quezon, who frequented the cabaret and other entertainments (and made a point of abolishing segregation in them), he might have met Dimples.[44]

There is, however, no evidence for an early meeting that the older Chabing Cooper writes about, other than the coincidence of being in the same city during the same time that his marriage unravels and Dimples becomes famous for playing at innocence. While he may have been in the audience as she sang about a lost kitty, and she would have heard of the newest young general, their trajectories would not definitively collide until his return to Manila later that decade. By 1925, when her first movie came out, Douglas MacArthur had left for the United States once again.

❊ ❊ ❊

The presence of a much lower-ranked American soldier in Isabel Cooper's family affected her life more immediately. Thomas Ryan's marriage to Josefina not only cemented the kinds of dynamics between Filipinas and American soldiers that would shape Isabel Cooper's outlook; it also expanded her family. At home, Isabel Cooper was pushed into the role of much older sister by the arrival of half siblings Josephine Margaret in late 1920, followed by Rosemarie Ruby in 1922. Her mother occupied with raising small children, Isabel Cooper, unsupervised, had the run of the city.

Her mother's marriage proved once again to upend expectations about who was caring for whom. The larger colonial project positioned Filipinos as childlike wards who needed supervision and discipline, and Americans as the authority who would provide this kind of care. Yet, like many of his peers, Thomas Ryan fell ill with tuberculosis in the tropics and came to depend on his bride to nurse him, and likely on his stepdaughter to support his growing family. As the family breadwinner, Isabel Cooper became more and more entrenched in stage life: her family relied on her stardom and her ruination.

❈ ❈ ❈

Still in her early teens, Isabel Cooper was thrust into the unsettling and precocious persona of someone between childhood and womanhood, who was both Filipina and American. The allure of "pert and cute" hinged on precisely this ambiguity and flexibility, which allowed the audience to pin their own fantasies on the body singing and dancing onstage. Her manager, Borromeo, understood the pull of Dimples's act and cannily played on her youth to conjure illusions of innocence that her latent sex appeal winked at.

Working hard at the act of innocence, Isabel Cooper went down the path furthest from it. She knew that she was not the most talented or beautiful among the other hopeful chorus girls that vied for a place onstage.[45] When she started out, Borromeo had not particularly set her apart from the other girls: she paid her dues, night after night, on the chorus line. On the unforgiving boards of the Savoy and Rivoli stages, Isabel learned the craft of bodabil. Exhausting two-a-day schedules ground her down but also built her stamina to deliver performances while "tired, or fagged after nightly wriggling, dancing, and singing."[46]

There was no room for inflated egos or a lack of pragmatism on bodabil's stages: Isabel Cooper knew she didn't have the standout voice talent of someone like Katy de la Cruz, who was Borromeo's "Queen of Jazz." If she wanted her stage career to last, she had to cultivate a unique stage personality. Each theater had its own signature acts: the comedy duo of Chuchi and Zelima at the Savoy, the Sirena's chorus line pageantry, and the slapstick act of the Charlie Chaplin–like Canuplin. Supplementing these acts were the bodabil singers and dancers, like Dimples, who performed jazz, the melancholy kundiman, and romantic American ballads.[47] These acts were a dime a dozen—Dimples became a headliner because she turned her innocent act into the quintessential modern American ingenue during a historical moment that was obsessed with Filipina womanhood. Young and modern Dimples Cooper came to epitomize the New Filipina, that promising and alarming vision of womanhood in a Manila grappling with its identity.

By the middle of the swinging 1920s, Dimples was a household name. Her dark bobbed hair, with its signature curl, her red lipstick, and the flapper

Dimples needs no introduction to local theater-goers.

Dimples in her vaudeville days. Image from *Graphic*, May 4, 1929. Courtesy Rizal Library, Ateneo de Manila University.

dresses she wore had become as familiar to her fans as her trademark poses and those flashing dimples.

The Washington of the Orient had its newest star.

✤ ✤ ✤

That Isabel Cooper called MacArthur "Daddy" is one of the more titillating details about their relationship. But this moniker was not just a pet name, one that captures the dynamics of their significant age difference. It also described the intimate valences of the relations between empire and colony, despite Governor-General of the Philippines William Howard Taft's early description of Filipinos as "little brown brothers."[48] In writing her letter to Drew Pearson long after her Dimples stage days had waned, Chabing Cooper puts into play the familiar roles and tropes of colonial desire, reminding him that the scandal of empire is only ever swept under the rug for a little while, that no one in its convoluted, painful hold could ever be innocent.

nine

A TRAVELER'S TALE OF VAUDEVILLE IN THE ORIENT

On my travels to our new possessions in the Pacific, I had the pleasure of meeting fellow Americans and partaking in the little corners of American life that have been cropping up across the Orient. Manila has certainly come into its own in the ten years since I have been a visitor to the islands, and is a surprisingly pleasant mix of modern amenities and quaint tropical trappings. It is proof positive that the humble labor of bringing civilization to the dark outposts of the world yields fruit.

For the traveler seeking entertainment, this Pearl of the Orient offers an array of diversions. Americans have made their mark on the stage here. I asked the advice of Mr. John C. Cowper, the director of the Savoy Nifties, and known as the dean of the Philippine variety show, and of Lou Borromeo, one of vaudeville's newest impresarios, about where to find

This text is based on early variety programs and similar articles about the Manila vaudeville stage, such as John Maynard's "Impressions of the Manila Vaudeville Stage," *Philippine Magazine*, October 1929; and Domingo H. Soriano, "The Dancing Girls Talk of the Patrons," *Graphic*, May 7, 1930, 44. See also Dimeglio, *Vaudeville, U.S.A.*; Stein, *American Vaudeville*; Gleeck, *The Manila Americans*. The description of Dimples's voice and performance comes from Carter, "The General's Dimples." One of the songs that Carter claims was MacArthur's favorite was "Are You Lonesome Tonight?," which was a quintessential Tin Pan Alley tune written in 1927 and recorded several times that year. Sheet music for the song was also published in 1927, which was likely how Isabel Cooper encountered it. In 1960, Elvis Presley recorded the most popular version of the song.

Manila's best entertainment. I pride myself on being somewhat of a connoisseur of the amusement market. I have seen acrobats, jugglers, variety acts, comedy skits, magicians, and strange novelties—from rank amateurs to headliners like Will Rogers in the Ziegfeld Follies. On my voyage to Manila, I caught an array of entertainments in San Francisco, Honolulu, and even Shanghai.

Eager to see what the Philippine stage had on offer, I took in the sights and sounds without prejudice. It was a mixed bag to be sure, but there were some notable highlights.

At the Savoy and the Rivoli, Mr. Cowper and his associates have improved the stage sets and costuming, and have nurtured local talents along.

One particular standout was Katy de la Cruz, a local songstress introduced as "the Sophie Tucker of the Philippines," who regaled a rapt audience with her signature ballad, "St. Louis Blues," followed by some jazz standards. I was electrified by her masterful scatting—Filipinos have surely taken to jazz and made it their own, much as they've lent a local flavor to vaudeville. A rare stage presence, this Queen of Jazz had the audience roaring with delight at her naughty humor and banter with her piano accompanist (gossip has it that they are an item). It is rumored that she is the highest-paid act in the local "bodabil" shows. She well deserves star billing.

Among the more recent rising stars is one of Mr. Borromeo's protegés, the young Dimples Cooper. Miss Cooper's appeal is that of the ingenue, and choreographer Buster Dunson has worked with her to better show off that indefinable "it" factor that she surely has in spades. While her vocal talents fall short of Miss de la Cruz's, her throaty rendition of Lou Handman's "Are You Lonesome Tonight?" had more than a few fellows sighing. The attractive star certainly knows how to play to young men in the audience with her flirtatious interpretations of the newest Tin Pan Alley selections.

On the whole, the singing was a pleasant surprise, the dancing less so. However, the Philippines stands out for the loveliness of the girls onstage. While the performance itself was mediocre, the attractiveness of the diminutive and exotic Malay beauties is incomparable. Their looks are a recompense for the sometimes-indifferent ambitions and undeveloped talent some of them possess. However, it should be noted that among the chorus line are natural dancers who have taken up the direction of Mr. Cowper, Mr. Borromeo, and other vaudeville bosses with some enthusiasm and success. Miss Cooper was said to come from the chorus line herself—perhaps others will follow in her footsteps.

The space between the documented and the undocumented leaves room for the imagined.

. . . 1904

Dear Bruce,

I hope this letter finds you Lizzie and the children in good health. I am writing because you have a namesake now in the Philippines. Your nephew Bruce Cooper was born this past year. He has a good appetite and a booming voice & would keep his cousins Herald and Vivid in good company.[1] I wrote to you about his mother Rubia some time ago.[2] It seems my life as a bachelor has come to an abrupt end.

1   Vivid Irvin Cooper was born to Bruce Cooper (Isaac Cooper's younger brother) and Lizee Parfrey in April 1904 ("Minnesota Births and Christenings, 1840–1980," FamilySearch, https://familysearch.org/ark:61903/1:1:FD78-NCQ). A son, Herald Clifton, was born to them in 1901 ("Wisconsin Births and Christenings, 1826–1926," FamilySearch, https://familysearch.org/ark:61903/1:1XR5Q-XSW). Another son, Floyd Cooper, was born to them a year after Herald but died in infancy ("Wisconsin Death Records, 1867–1907," FamilySearch, https://familysearch.org/ark:61903/1:X2BJ-4XY).

2   It is unclear if Isaac Cooper was in a common-law marriage with Rubia Ryan, but their son, the second Bruce Cooper, had his name and continued to claim him as his father into adulthood ("Philippines Marriages, 1723–1957," FamilySearch, https://familysearch.org/ark:61903/1:1FNQP-SIV).

. . . 1916

Dear Bruce,

We will shortly be taking the voyage back home. My wife Protacia and our three children, with another on the way, will arrive with me next month on April 19, weather willing. Our transport will dock in San Francisco, after which we plan to take a train to Arizona, where a friend has told me he may have work for me at his farm. Our departure from Manila has been sudden. . . .

. . . 1919

Isaac—

I am not coming back to Arizona. It holds too many terrible memories for me, and it never felt like home, as I tried to tell you again and again.

This is hard to write. I have met someone else, and we are now married. I am building a new life here. I consider our marriage over. If you will allow Bruce to come to Manila when he is older, I would be grateful.

~~Protacia~~ Josefina Ryan

. . . 1921

Dear Father and Bruce,

How are you? I am well, and though you may not wish to hear it, so is the rest of the family. I have some good news for you. I have been hired on as a regular at the Rivoli! Mr. Borromeo, my manager, says that I have talent and that he'll help me improve my singing so that I can have an act of my own. I sure do practice enough in front of the mirror, if only to drown out all the crying babies in the house. Oh, how I wish you could come to see me! Maybe someday you will. My dream is to be a movie star in Hollywood, like the divine Gloria Swanson. Mr. Borromeo tells me that he thinks I might be the one to do it.

... 1929

Darling,[3]

I feel so cherished by the by care you are taking to ensure my safety and comfort on this voyage. I will do as you say and not stay ashore in Singapore and drink only soft drinks. I love the thought of my fierce soldier roaming the shops in Shanghai and accosting a girl to have her fit a fur coat for me. Then I became dreadfully jealous of her, because she was in the same place as you. You are so generous to your Baby Girl. I confess I am relieved by your descriptions of <u>not</u> enjoying the nightlife at your various stops. Perhaps that is jealous and petty of me, but as I am also lonely here without you. I think it is only fair that we both suffer apart. Your story of the gambling clubs in Hong Kong and the Chinese flappers did make me laugh.

I am imagining boarding the ship that will take me to New York, and I imagine you waiting on the dock for me, just as I waved you away when you sailed from Manila. I can't wait to see you again. I hope you don't send TJ in your stead. It will be the best start to our life together and our happiness if <u>you</u> are there to greet me.

My heart aches, as yours does, and I am desolate with loneliness. . . .

3 No letters from Isabel Cooper to Douglas MacArthur are known to exist.

Not a flicker remains of Isabel Cooper's early films.

One could blame the humid tropics for eating away at celluloid, but the destruction of Manila by heavy artillery near the end of World War II, flattening large swaths of the city, was the main culprit. The devastation of the city that had come to be known as the Pearl of the Orient and the Washington of the Orient came at the hands of the occupying Japanese forces and the atrocities they committed, but also at the command of General Douglas MacArthur, who insisted on returning to the Philippines' capital on his way to Japan.

Amid its casualties—rape, bayonetings, mass murders—the memory of an earlier war waged against Filipinos by Americans (*kill everyone over the age of ten*) retreated.[1] Overwritten by the spectacle of MacArthur's dramatic theater of liberation, the memory of U.S. soldiers "pacifying" the Filipino natives was buried.[2]

The loss of three films, all shot between 1925 and 1927, pales against the staggering calamity that Filipinos in Manila confronted after the monthlong battle in their city. But these three films shed light on how an even earlier spectacle—of sex and scandal—laid the groundwork for historical amnesia about U.S. empire in the Philippines well before the celebratory commemorations of American rescue and liberation.

Here is the story of two kisses, the scandals attached to them, and the woman in their midst. It hinges on how making intimacies public through the Filipina body as a visual spectacle obscured the imperial violence and its sly but no less brutal partner, the civilizing mission. It is a story pulled from archives that insist on the distractions of sex and scandal, but here, read awry, obliquely, out of true, arrives at some other conclusion.

Seven years after Protacia Rubin packed up her belongings and her daughter and sailed back to Manila, Isabel Cooper is a favorite of gossip and scandal. A rising star onstage, she cultivates and revels in the attention. If the combination of innocent youth and carnality sets her apart from her fellow hemline-raising peers, her casting as the modern Filipina/American beauty catapults her into the spotlight.

Chorus girls are a dime a dozen on Manila's early bodabil stage. While Dimples is beginning to stand out as an act, stage work is hard on the body, and the audience demands to be entertained in new ways. When Vicente Salumbides, with the whiff of a recent trip to Hollywood still clinging to him, walks into the Rivoli in 1925, she takes note.

The young, charismatic, aspiring director is looking for a woman with a modern look for his film *Miracles of Love*.[3] He has ambitions for the film—it will herald a Filipino Hollywood. To be shot by inventive cinematographer José Nepomuceno, it promises a fast-paced modern romance, and needs a fast-paced modern girl. Dimples, with her mestiza looks and Tin Pan Alley repertoire, fits the bill.

Other girls before her have been plucked from the vaudeville stage to act in films—the stage and screen cross-pollinated their stars. Dimples is in the right place with the right face at the right time for "the glory days of the 1920s" in Philippine silent film.[4] She starts going by "Elizabeth Cooper" for her screen name, perhaps to drive home the point that she is cosmopolitan by way of being half American. But everyone continues to refer to her as Dimples.

Salumbides's movie calls for a captivating beauty whose face on a magazine cover could mesmerize a young doctor, but also an actress who could carry intense emotion for the film's close-ups, a camera angle Salumbides had learned from his apprenticeship in Hollywood. Isabel Cooper has a face made for the movies: big expressive eyes, a wide, mobile mouth, the charming gap in her front teeth, those dimples. Her skin, pale, picks up the light. Salumbides (who intends to play the doctor) and Nepomuceno plan to debut the use of Hollywood makeup and costuming designed to work with motion picture cameras, along with pacing and editing that has not yet been seen in Filipino movies. Paired with their modern "American" star, the new look of Filipino film is on its way.

❋ ❋ ❋

I imagine a young Isabel Cooper, thrilled by the interest shown by Salumbides, flattered to be chosen for a lead role in a film.

I think about how her home life is a stark contrast to the upbeat, comedic romance that she is filming. There, Thomas Ryan has taken ill with tuberculosis, and Josefina Ryan is caring for him along with her two young daughters. The sounds of his constant coughing fill the house in Paco.

I wonder if the hard life of the stage or the movies' promise of glamour are an escape, a choice, or both.

❋ ❋ ❋

Miracles of Love is a star-making turn. The story is light and humorous—a romance with two beautiful young people in love, comedic moments of mistaken identity, and the timeless theme of children acting in defiance of parental pressures and social boundaries. The plot turns on Salumbides's besotted doctor being mistaken for someone answering the family's ad for household help when he comes to the house to meet the object of his obsession. Seizing the opportunity, he disguises himself as a houseboy in her family's home and gains her confidence while she evades her parents' schemes for her to marry a wealthy old suitor. In the end, the young lovers elope in a funny, fast-paced chase scene. Theatergoers are enchanted. It is the first time that Filipino audiences see a film produced by and starring Filipinos that has the same kind of visual quality as American movies. As Salumbides promised, Elizabeth Cooper becomes the face of Filipina modernity.

For her part, Dimples refines her pert and cute stage act to more fully inhabit "Elizabeth Cooper." Used to projection and exaggeration in her singing and dancing numbers, she learns to broadcast emotion for silent film without the help of lyrics and live accompaniment. She adapts her facial expressions for the whirring camera and Salumbides's demanding eye. She learns to develop her character according to a longer story arc instead of an audience's immediate reaction.

The reviews single her out, much to her delight: "Elizabeth Cooper introduced to the screen a new type of American Beauty—to go along with the Spanish mestiza and the less popular kayumanggi (brown maiden)."[5]

Isabel Cooper has hit upon her turn on stage and screen. The modern American-style costumes she sports in the film make her a fashion icon. Mirroring her character in *Miracles of Love*, she graces magazines as the model of modern American beauty.

She would never return to the anonymity of the chorus line. She and her mother pile up her earnings on the bed and throw the bills into the air—a celebration and a relief.[6] Yet her rising fame sharply diverges from the downward spiral of her mother's life. In a bid to get treatment for his tuberculosis,

Dimples in magazines. *Manila Movies*, March 21, 1931, 20. Courtesy Tommy Ko personal collection.

Thomas Ryan sails back to the United States but dies at sea.[7] He is buried in the Presidio in San Francisco. Josefina Ryan is left in Manila, along with their two young children and another one on the way.[8]

The house in Paco enfolds a sometimes-untenable multitude of emotions in 1925.

A girl, sixteen or so, on the edge of dreamed-of fame and womanhood, is tethered to her widowed mother and two half sisters.

A woman, thirty-one, perhaps mourning, perhaps unmoored.

❋ ❋ ❋

In the midst of the turmoil of her family life, Isabel Cooper becomes the poster girl for the New Modern Girl in the Philippines and adds fuel to the heated national debates about the role of the Filipina.[9]

Her first sin was to be the female half of the first on-screen kiss in Philippine film. Her second and greater sin was to be the symbol of the modern Filipina—that fraught figure—while committing the first.

The best and only image I find of this national scandal is blurred and secondhand, a film still that survives by being printed in Salumbides's 1952 book about Philippine film. The filmmaker's archives, along with a recorded interview, were destroyed in a fire at a researcher's house in the 1970s. What remains of the iconic scene is this. A young girl, her skin incandescent in the sun. Her hair is swept off her face, which is in profile, tilted up. Her front elbow is drawn back, emphasizing the arch of her back, and angling her body to the camera and the audience.

The man she is kissing, who is kissing her, fades into the gray stone wall of the background. He is darker in complexion, clad in a sweater. We can see a small, pale hand stealing around his waist. He leans over her. He should be the dominant figure in the scene, but it is she who commands the eye.

Her costume absorbs all the light, along with her skin. She is modestly dressed, yet immodestly displayed.

It is incendiary.

José Nepomuceno is the architect of the infamous scene. Ever the pioneer and provocateur, he wants to push the boundaries of Filipino film. Nepomuceno had commented slyly on lost innocence years before with Atang de la Rama and her broken clay pot. With the fresh success of *Miracles of Love*, and a new, recognizable muse by his side, innuendo will no longer suffice.

He wades straight into the heated debates that swirled around the Filipina in the 1920s. Anxieties about Philippine modernity and national identity coalesce through debates about her dress, her demeanor, and her morality.[10] Manila intellectuals, religious leaders, social notables, and politicians passionately argue about women's education and suffrage. The terms of the Philippines' longed-for independence are filtered through moral panics about young women's décolletage, smoking habits, and other signs of loose behavior. Movies, and Hollywood, particularly their representations of women, are an easy target for politicians, educators, and religious leaders looking to blame "foreign ideas" for corrupting the Filipino people.[11] Even Filipinas who argue for suffrage or educational equality preach that "well-bred women" should distance themselves from the corrupting influence of Hollywood "film actresses" and the way that they dress and dance.[12]

The kiss that shocked Manila. *Ang Tatlong Hambog* (1925). Image from Vicente Salumbides, *Motion Pictures in the Philippines* (Manila, 1952).

In this morass, Nepomuceno wants to feature Elizabeth Cooper, new symbol of a modern Filipina/American beauty, kissing on the movie screen. It would be the first Filipino kissing scene on film.[13] He knows the daring move will confirm him as the father of Filipino cinema and seal his renown as a pioneer. He convinces her to do it. For her, it would be a different trajectory.

Isabel Cooper is already That Woman. At sixteen, she bears social opprobrium as the price of success. She is inured to audiences leering at her onstage. Kissing her costar, though not a part of her everyday repertoire, is the inevitable endgame of the persona she has cultivated.

The story line of Nepomuceno's film, *Ang Tatlong Hambog* (The three braggarts), revolves around three men courting the same girl. They try to outdo each other to impress her. One shows up in a car, the next in a *kalesa* (a horse-drawn carriage), and the third and most humble suitor on a *carabao* (a water buffalo).

Aside from the promised kiss, the film is a vehicle for Nepomuceno's inventive filmcraft: realistic fights, scenes featuring the grandeur of the Philippine landscape, and a distinctly Filipino comedic touch.[14]

But everyone comes to see it for the kiss. (I think about the world that Isabel Cooper walked through, and who she is in this world, and wonder if this is her first kiss. Later, I find out that perhaps it isn't, that she had a rumored affair with the son of a sugar planter. I wonder at the way this secret is exposed, the detail about the loss of her virginity artfully dropped by a cousin's husband who makes a name for himself writing about her, published after her death in an American business journal, of all places.)[15]

Isabel knows it will be uncomfortable to kiss Luis, though he was nice enough.

The small crew watching makes it awkward, the loud whirr of the camera distracting. Don Peping's constant directions about how to angle her body make her feel more self-conscious.

It was strange to kiss outside, in broad daylight. And stranger still to kiss on the grounds of a church.[16] She makes the sign of the cross before the film starts, just in case.

She sweats in the light blouse and saya she is wearing. She wonders how Luis, in his infernal signature sports sweater, is doing.

He moves closer, his expression grave, ardent. She stifles the urge to giggle.

She forces herself to relax, dropping her arms to her sides gracefully as he presses his lips to hers. Her eyes close. They hold the pose, barely breathing or moving—until Don Peping is satisfied. It is the classic Hollywood kiss, re-created Filipino style.

No one actually kisses like this, she thinks.

They do it one more time.

One version of the story—the one that is published a decade later to commemorate the film's debut—depicts Isabel Cooper's apprehension when she sees the preview of the film. In this telling, she begs Nepomuceno to edit the film and cut out the kiss. He persuades her to persist, that she is riding on a wave of change. The scene will be historic and she, Elizabeth Cooper, will be the symbol of modern Filipino womanhood.[17]

In this version, he is the visionary and she, merely his unimaginative and reluctant instrument.

❀ ❀ ❀

The story could be read another way. That Isabel Cooper understands fully how the spotlight turns harsh for women like her; that her reputation, and not her costar's or director's, will be subject to public ruin beyond even what living in the demimonde already demands. Manila is a small city, after all, and she has to live in it. Perhaps she understands that she is clinging to a wish for an innocence that she has never been accorded. She realizes this and goes ahead with the kiss. Don Peping's argument for being a revolutionary figure in Philippine history is incidental in this version. In this version of the story, Isabel Cooper, as young as she is, decides that she will hazard her career on notoriety. Maybe she doesn't even hesitate at all, and the story just wishes she did.

She really doesn't remember what came before the kiss. In the dark of the theater, the flickering figures on the screen draw laughter, appreciative murmurs, and the occasional gasp.

Then it is there. She and Luis, drawing toward each other.

She's not yet used to seeing herself projected on the screen. It is still strange not to be in her body during a performance, to feel the warped boards of the stage under her feet and attend to the marks laid out on it. It feels distanced from the audience—she cannot calibrate her act according to their mood.

She wonders if it is the size of the kiss, projected on the screen, that feels obscene, rather than the kiss itself. She wonders if she will ever get used to sharing such private moments—fantasies though they are—with an audience.

As Nepomuceno hopes, his movie titillates and offends. He is nothing if not deliberate about how to market his new film. A still of the kiss is used for the display in the theater lobby, drawing both anticipatory and disapproving stares from patrons, never mind that both camps pay to watch. The kissing scene features in the newspaper movie ads as well. It dares a response. It dares people to come see the film.

Conservatives are scandalized and do not hesitate to air their opinions. Even the friars at the Guadalupe Church chime in and refuse to have their premises used for future filming locations.[18] But people still come to see the film that the *Manila Times* describes as "a high class photo-drama . . . action . . . a beautiful romantic story."[19] At the theater, when the scene plays, some audience members "howl . . . in glee while others hoot."[20]

In some ways, it is the continuation and climax of her stage act.

While she may not have been able to imagine the vehemence of opinion the film generates, she is pragmatic enough to adapt. As the face of the kiss, Isabel Cooper is in the middle of the storm. She has, as Nepomuceno predicted, become the Filipino New Woman.

A few months later, Vicente Salumbides once again taps her to be one of three female leads in *Fate or Consequence*. The movie, another romantic comedy, is about "three girls loving the same man" who forgets "his love for one in his temporary infatuation for the other."[21] Salumbides is ready to turn the controversy of the kiss into box-office gold.

Isabel Cooper, aka Dimples, aka Elizabeth Cooper, has truly arrived.

Variety star, 1926. Collection of Juan Martin Magsanoc.

The spectacle of the immodest, modern Filipina takes up a lot of attention. Everyone has an opinion and feels authorized to police the dimensions of this fantastical figure. The obsession over Filipinas engaging in public intimacies cathects moral outrage and anxieties over the meaning of Filipino national identity. But it also displaces and conceals the ongoing and foremost structural cause of this identity crisis—U.S. empire's continuing presence in the Philippines.

Passing judgment on Isabel Cooper, as the New Filipina, behaving outside the bounds of propriety is easier than taking too close a look at Isabel Cooper, mixed-race actress, embodiment of colonial rule's enduring and perverse desires.

* * *

In May 1927, Isabel Cooper leaves the country. She is at this point famous enough for the gossip rags to generate speculation about her absence: media coverage has her marrying a fellow passenger she meets on a transpacific jaunt, or visiting family in the South, or perhaps even running off with a confidence man.[22] She has learned the lesson that in her business, publicity and speculation will only add to her mystique, and the wilder and more fantastical, the better.

Isabel Cooper, however, is headed to Los Angeles, leaving behind her mother and half sisters. Like other Filipina actors before her, she is drawn to the glamour of Hollywood. Described as "the local Mary Pickford," she has attained enough success to try to find roles on Broadway or in Hollywood.[23] It is not an uncommon trajectory, but one often met with little success: "none has succeeded farther than mob scenes, maid and valet parts" because of Hollywood's indifference to "talents from this neck of the woods."[24] Isabel Cooper, riding high on her success on Manila's stage and screen, feels she might break that pattern. Conveniently, her father is living in Southern California. The eighteen-year-old actress takes advantage and strikes out for the boulevard of broken dreams.[25] She arrives via Hong Kong and San Francisco, listing her father, whom she had not seen in years, as her contact.[26]

Elizabeth Cooper, as she goes by in this brief sojourn to the States, promotes her trip with savvy and sends a story to be published in the *Graphic* during her long absence. Knowing that she has a public to cultivate, she tantalizes them with her presence through scenes in print that appeal to their own imaginations about dazzling and scandalous Hollywood life.

Failing to land a movie deal that would star her as the romantic lead, Elizabeth Cooper inserts herself into her own Hollywood plot. Her account,

"Meeting the Stars in Hollywood," reveals a profound understanding of the fantasy relationship she had constructed with her fans both onscreen and onstage. In this story, she narrates a familiar plot of an ingenue in the metropole, but casts herself as worldly yet innocent. Elizabeth Cooper's report from Hollywood cultivates her audience's interest, even as she is offstage, offscreen, and off-island.

Assuming the role of a fan in Hollywood, she confesses her excitement upon meeting a "leading lady" of a film: "I didn't know whether to run or shout or jump. Wonder if you know how that feels."[27] Her tone is confiding, letting her audience know that like them, she, too, can be starstruck—as well as teasing, letting them know that she knows how they feel about her. In what is essentially a letter to her public, she reveals that Hollywood people seem to know her as "the little Filipina girl from the land of romance," which tells her readers that her vaudeville and cinematic fame has reached the metropole, even from as far away as the Philippines.

Not-quite-artlessly, she points out how her distinctive attractiveness stands out in Hollywood, enough to be stared at on a streetcar:

> The boys and girls stared at me—which set me thinking something must be wrong with me, either my dress was attractive or loud or my hair, which I always dressed in curls, was conspicuous. As you know, in the States, they are all bobbed and it is very very seldom that you see a girl with long hair. You must not think that I'm trying to throw bouquets at myself when I say that these people liked me—it must have been my hair or dimple which showed every time I smiled.[28]

Describing her body in detail—including her signature feature—Elizabeth Cooper generates a clichéd fantasy of being discovered, of having a certain attractiveness and difference that is visually apparent. Persuading her audience to envision the young ingenue, already garnering attention with her unique looks, she invites her readers to accompany her on her journey from starring on Manila's vaudeville stage to the glamour of Hollywood, bringing them on the streetcar with her and taking them through the rituals of Hollywood casting.

The account ends discordantly with a graphic narration of sexual assault: Elizabeth Cooper describes being subjected to the casting couch. In sharing this detail with her Manila audience, she transforms a traumatic event into a thrilling drama. She is suddenly the central figure in a familiar cinematic scene of a heroine under duress. Describing her audition for an "Oriental type," which is scripted as a scene of a villain kissing the heroine, Elizabeth

Cooper highlights her body in detail: "He took down my hair and stood me up against the wall and started demonstrating. And that demonstration I'll never forget. He wrestled me and treated me so rough—gee, he was rough. He grabbed my hair as if it were the tail of a horse and held my arms tight and fairly shouted, 'Give me a kiss!'"[29]

Generating a graphic scene of attempted rape, she recasts herself from the scandalous kisser of *Ang Tatlong Hambog* to the classic damsel in distress of the silent film era. Unlike her kissing scene in Nepomuceno's film, this scene is decidedly violent: she describes her body and her body's treatment in vivid language, positioning the audience at home as witnesses to her victimization in Los Angeles. Unable to actually get herself cast in a Hollywood film in 1927, Elizabeth Cooper instead writes a visually arresting scene as a substitute for a celluloid appearance.

Thus the first piece of Isabel Cooper's writing we have is a carefully wrought narration of both her cosmopolitanism and her insistence on being a modest Filipina girl, which also doubled as savvy self-publicity. Her audience at home could continue to admire her body (described in great detail), delight in her Hollywood adventure, rage at her attacker, and reframe her as modern yet modest—at least compared to the "carefree" American girls: "Petting, to them is nothing at all. To smoke and drink, is the sport. The young people are thrill-mad."[30]

The scandals of Hollywood, of a kiss forced on her, of dissolute American youth, are meant to mitigate her own disreputable behavior. The spectacle she offers of the ingenue subjected to wickedness in the big city is also an implicit comparison to the Philippines, which she (and others) romanticize as somehow being innocent of these depravities. The irony, of course, is that it is not.

Rumors fly regarding Isabel Cooper's whereabouts in this period. A few months after printing her account of her Hollywood experience, the *Graphic* mentions her "triumphal return," heralded by "the Rivoli theater hoist[ing] her name in big electric letters."[31] The newly arrived star, "good looking enough to have a place on the Manila stage, versatile enough to be a dancing and singing attraction all in one," is ready to entertain her fans once again. Gossip swirls around her, with the same article breathlessly reporting that her family's home is listed for sale. Apparently, no one could track down her mother to corroborate speculation of Isabel Cooper taking yet another trip abroad, or being linked to an alleged embezzler.

Isabel Cooper is indeed back, living on Calle Herrán as a single working woman, unchaperoned. By the time her daughter returns, Josefina—now going by Josephine—has once again uprooted her young family to travel to the United States.[32] Two additional Ryans have been added to the fold, born well after the death of Thomas Ryan.[33] They sail on to the United States, on the ss *Empress*, likely to claim whatever pension is allotted to Josephine as a military widow. Her eldest daughter is on her own.

In October 1928, Isabel Cooper's stage career is flourishing, but the fickle entertainment industry has deemed that her early star turn on film had "failed to register," and her attempt to break into Hollywood "failed likewise to make much of a hit."[34] Her star is still shining brightly, if a little tarnished: the writer explains how stage actors sometimes have trouble transitioning to filmic roles. Hollywood has debuted its first talkie, and not all the stars of the silent era adjust to these new developments. No film roles present themselves upon her return. Her previous champions, Nepomuceno and Salumbides, have moved on to other, younger stars.[35]

Most of Isabel Cooper's livelihood now centers on the "cruel" and hard life of live stage performance. She remains a draw at the Rivoli and the Savoy, cultivating and commanding a loyal following.[36] She introduces new numbers to her repertoire, two of which will become the general's favorites.[37]

She continues to work her charm onstage and on the pages of the tabloids. Interviews that quote her shed light on her appeal and her insecurity: "I think they are very nice to me. I always try to single out faces behind the footlight while acting. They like me, don't they?"[38]

Perhaps the lack of a family to chaperone her precipitates what happens next. Or maybe it is the media speculation harping about her wilting film career. Or perhaps she is tired, or wanting to be taken care of, or lonely. She has been working for half her young life in a grueling trade.

❋ ❋ ❋

Just the week before the tepid review of her film acting career appears in the *Graphic*, the publication notes a different kind of rising star in the islands: the return of a military career man. Douglas MacArthur, fresh from his divorce, has been assigned as commanding general of the Philippine Department. He is the subject of a breathless "Who Is Who in the Philippines" profile.[39] "The youngest general in the United States Army," the self-professed "great admirer of the Filipino people," his star is rising just as Isabel Cooper's is beginning to fall.[40]

He would soon single out one particular Filipino person for his great admiration. Where a year before, Elizabeth Cooper had written about the unwanted embrace and violence of Hollywood's casting couch and the "carefree" young people for whom "petting is nothing at all," Isabel Cooper writes nothing about her most scandalous role.

* * *

Rumor has it that she catches his eye at a boxing match at the Olympic Stadium. MacArthur signals his interest through a note delivered by an aide. This particular account was relayed to a MacArthur biographer by Allen Cooper, who claims in 1978 to be Isabel Cooper's brother but who leaves only an archival trace of his existence.[41]

Regardless of how Isabel Cooper and Douglas MacArthur come to each other's attention, they soon have an arrangement. As her mother's daughter, Isabel Cooper has witnessed the benefits of liaisons with American men, particularly for Filipinas who occupy the margins of respectability. Repeating a pattern established by Josefina Ryan, Isabel begins to host the general at her home on Calle Herrán. As historian Carol M. Petillo notes wryly, "The relationship was not long a secret from Manila gossip."[42]

I think about the roles she has had, the way her body has been cast as material for spectacle—sometimes distracting from and other times unmasking the deeply rooted desires of empire. I think about the moment that Isabel Cooper made this choice, and I wonder if she felt that it was inevitable—that the memory of empire was so intimately a part of her blood that it would always surface somehow.

Dimples Cooper, fresh from a brief circuit of performances in Japan and Shanghai after a longer sojourn in the States, is once again gracing Manila's stages. Our very own Mary Pickford is here to stay for good, even as it's rumored that she's developed a taste for life in New York and Los Angeles. Friends of the star say that on her return voyage, Cooper was proposed to no fewer than three times by fellow passengers (including the globe-trotting heir of an American railroad company!), as well as a humble crew member. All were bespelled by her beauty and charm. Ever the object of the audience's love, it's clear that Miss Cooper's attractions extend beyond the stage. In the meantime, she is headlining once again at the Savoy, for her loyal followers.

The more uncharitable of her competitors—it isn't a stage family without a little drama—might have mentioned the possibility that Miss Dimples was enceinte, *and had to go away to take care of the problem. Once that seed was planted (so to speak) it was hard to shake off.*

Buntis daw siya: nagpalaglag. Pagkatapos, pumunta siya sa States para magpagaling.

Rumor has it that Miss Cooper is ill with tuberculosis and has retired from performing. She has retreated to her family home in Paco, which has been closed to visitors.

Dimples is back onstage with numbers she has learned from the Hollywood stars themselves. A friend of the actress has shared that she is eager to show Manila's audiences the newest dance crazes, and is working to prepare routines for her loyal fans.

ALLEGED EMBEZZLER and CHARMING INCOGNITA LEFT ON EMPRESS MARCH 24

Tony Ossorio, Is Alleged To Have Carried ₱160,000; Manila's Sweetheart, Luxuriating In Cabin 117, Carried "Isabel Rubin" Alias

W HEN the Empress of Asia of the Canadian Pacific Steamship company pulled out from Pier 7 on March 24, it carried on board two very interesting Manilans. These were Antonio "Tony" Osorio, clubman about town and a member of the well-known Osorio family of sugar fame; and Elizabeth "Dimples" Cooper, vaudeville star and, according to Florrence Loh, Manila's sweetheart. Tony is now about to be extradited for embezzling about ₱160,000.00. Dimples, who up to last Tuesday when a Graphic reporter identified her passport picture at Malacañang, was known to the authorities and to the steamship officials as "Isabel Rubin", is now travelling in parts more or less known, perhaps, still under the same alias.

Rumor has it that Osorio has been preparing for a trip to Europe, where Mrs. Osorio is sojourning, but the date known by friends was April 30. His disappearance on the twenty-fourth, therefore, raises...

Antonio "Tony" Osorio, clubman, sportsman, man about town, who is being extradited from Singapore for the alleged embezzlement of ₱160,000.00.

Your Checks Here Give A Complete Check!

Every centavo you spend is accounted for by the checks you draw on this bank. There cannot be any mistake in paying bills. There cannot be a double payment for that check acts as your legal receipt.

This Bank cordially invites you to make this your headquarters. You'll appreciate the service we offer.

PEOPLES BANK & TRUST COMPANY
"Your Bank"

N. E. MULLEN,
President.

Vivacious, dark-eyed, entertaining Miss Cooper (Dimples), who secured a passport from the governor general's office under the alias "Isabel Rubin"

...ed surprise leading to an investigation of the records and accounts of the Osorio interests of which he was a trusted employee. As such, Antonio Osorio was an employee of his brother, Miguel J. Osorio. As such, he had complete access to the papers of the two sugar mills controlled by the Osorios. In fact, he was conferred the power of attorney by his brother.

The investigations showed that Tony had cashed several letters of credit drawn in his favor at three different banks, namely, the Bank of the Philippine Islands for ₱50,000.000; the China Banking...

Corporation for ₱30,000.00; and the International Bank for ₱80,000.00. Immediately after the discovery of the losses, representatives of the Osorio interests filed the corresponding complaints in the office of the city fiscal who in turn requested the governor general to easier the extradition of the fugitive.

Following cablegraphic instructions from Governor-General Stimson, the American consul at Singapore caused the arrest of Tony Osorio on April 6. Assistant City Fiscal Jose Ma. Paredes and a representative of the Osorio interests left on the President Gar...

Charming incognita, *Graphic*, April 14, 1928. Courtesy Rizal Library, Ateneo de Manila University.

Our favorite smiling star has a new look! Dimples Cooper has been spotted out and about with a shiny new bob, having shorn off her wavy tresses in Hollywood. She returns with a racy new wardrobe sure to be the envy of the town. Seems Manila's current "It Girl" has brought back some pasalubong from her latest jaunt stateside.

"Ang Ating mga Tala sa Bodabil," *Graphic*, July 9, 1927. Courtesy Rizal Library, Ateneo de Manila University.

PART ONE

1

SCANDAL AT THE MAJESTIC THEATER

Daytime, exterior street scene. People walk by the front of one of the new movie theaters in the city, the Majestic.[1] They gawk at the large movie poster featuring Dimples kissing another actor on the lips. There is a mix of reactions, but most stare at the scandal-ous picture in disapproval, clucking amongst themselves.[2]

Onscreen.

> "WHAT A JADE!"
> "MASAMANG BABAE!"

This chapter is written in the style of a silent film, based on a short passage in Petillo, *Douglas MacArthur*, recounting how MacArthur met Isabel Cooper. The account is based on the author's 1978 interviews with Cooper's cousin Mercedes Sotelo and Allen Cooper, Isabel Cooper's younger brother. In Allen Cooper's 1947 marriage certificate, he claims a Josephine Rubin from Portugal as his mother and Isaac Cooper as his father (possibly to evade antimiscegenation laws). Josephine Cooper counts him among her children (as a nine-year-old) in 1928, when she left with him for the United States. There is no evidence that Allen and Isabel corresponded. His name does not appear in any of the other government records of Isabel Cooper's family. MacArthur and Isabel Cooper met after Allen Cooper left the Philippines, which throws his recollection of their meeting into doubt.

1 Parcja, in "Roles and Image of Woman," 211, notes that the film which made Isabel Cooper a household name, *Ang Tatlong Hambog*, played at the Majestic.
2 "What Price a Kiss?," *Philippines Free Press*, July 6, 1929.

Back to scene.

A long line begins to form for tickets to see the next showing, as the previous showing ends, and the audience files out. Some audience members go right back in line.

2

A NIGHT AT THE RIVOLI
DIMPLES, A VAUDEVILLE PERFORMER IN EVENING DRESS FIT FOR STAGE

Backstage at the Rivoli Theater in Manila, around six o'clock in the evening, just before showtime. Discovered, Dimples, a mestiza performer, getting dressed and applying makeup. There are other chorus girls and sundry performers in the background doing the same. They are all in high spirits. A fellow chorus girl brings a copy of an entertainment/society paper to Dimples, who is putting the finishing touches on her face. She opens the page to the large photograph of Dimples in a fitted dress, posing demurely but winking at the camera. She congratulates Dimples on the publicity, and shows the photograph to the other girls, who gather around. The stage manager pops his head in to warn the girls that they are up next, and they all line up.

Onscreen.

  "PRESENTING THE MANILA FOLLIES!"

Back to scene.

The girls finish lining up, and walk out onstage.

3

Onstage at the Rivoli. The girls file onto the stage and do a chorus number, showing lots of leg.[3] Some men in the audience front row holler their approval: they are dressed as sailors on liberty. The chorus girls file out, and the number transitions to a solo featuring Dimples.

3 Felix R. Domingo, "Bare Knees and Bobbed Hair," *Graphic*, May 4, 1929, 4–5.

Onscreen.

"RIVOLI'S STAR, MISS DIMPLES COOPER!"

Back to scene.

Dimples walks slowly across the stage, smiling, flirting with the audience. She walks to the microphone, and the spotlight shines on her. She begins to sing.

Onscreen.

"JUST A LITTLE LONGER
LET ME HOLD YOU CLOSE TO MY HEART."[4]

Back to scene.

This time the camera is closer, focused on her face and its expressiveness as the number ends.

Onscreen.

"HOLD ME FAST WHILE WE KISS, AND THEN
IT'S THE LAST TILL WE MEET AGAIN."

Back to scene.

The ballad transitions to a more lively number. The chorus girls file back in to join Dimples, and they perform a choreographed number, with Dimples always featured in the middle in a clear starring role. Raucous audience reaction to Dimples's performance features officers seated in the rear, away from the rank-and-file soldiers. One in particular, General MacArthur, a new arrival to the city, looks intrigued. He whispers something to the fellow on his right.

4

AN INTRODUCTION AT THE OLYMPIC

Evening, interior of the Olympic stadium. There is a seated crowd watching the boxing match and each other. Dimples is seated

4 Lyrics for "Just a Little Longer" (1926), in *The Complete Lyrics of Irving Berlin*, ed. Robert Kimball and Linda Emmett (Hal Leonard, 2005), 231.

strategically where she can be seen. She is dressed as a modern girl, emulating American movie stars. She gets many admiring glances from the mostly male fans. The boxing match is almost incidental to the action. It is like another kind of stage for her. A few men approach her for autographs, and she is happy to oblige.

T. J. DAVIS, A MILITARY AIDE IN UNIFORM
ASSISTANT TO THE GENERAL

Enter T. J. Davis, who approaches Dimples. He bows stiffly.

Onscreen.

"MADAM, I'VE BEEN SENT ON A RECONNAISSANCE MISSION!"

Back to scene.

Dimples smiles demurely at him. He gestures over to the section where the general and other officers are seated. Around them, the audience cheers at the offscreen boxing match.

Onscreen.

"MY SUPERIOR OFFICER WOULD VERY MUCH LIKE TO MEET YOU!"

Back to scene.

She smiles modestly, noncommittally. He passes her a note, which she accepts but does not read. She thanks him and dismisses him without a reply. She does not acknowledge the section where the general is seated, but sits quietly, smiling to herself. She continues to greet and smile at other audience members who approach her.

INGREDIENTS FOR COCKTAIL

Juice and crushed flesh of one-half ripe mango
2 oz. Spanish brandy
Juice of one kalamansi

Shaved ice

Fill a cocktail shaker with all ingredients.
Shake and pour into tall glass with shaved ice.
Garnish with slice of mango or slice of kalamansi.

Enjoy on the veranda while visiting with uniformed American officer.
Chaperone optional.[1]

---

1 "While he [MacArthur] was still in Manila, Aunty [Mercedes] would occasionally be called over to help entertain the General, and she claims she invented
   what was to become the General's favorite drink." In Carter, *Then and Now*, 160.
   The Douglas was made up of "crushed mango, Spanish brandy, and crushed ice,"
   in Petillo, *Douglas MacArthur*, 161. I have embellished it a little here. Prohibition-
   era rules did not apply in the Philippines. Thomas Carter claimed that it was his
   wife, Isabel Cooper's younger cousin Mercedes Sotelo, who made up the drink.
   She was occasionally called upon to provide a semblance of chaperonage during
   the general's visits to Calle Herrán.

Choosing names is the first act of creating.—Gina Apostol, *Insurrecto*

April 1940 in Washington, DC, is beautiful. Isabel Cooper, having briefly left the city after the end of her relationship with Douglas MacArthur, is once again in the capital.

At first glance, the 1940 story the U.S. Census tells is peculiar: it lists Isabel Cooper as working a forty-hour week as a milkman. But Ethel V. Barfield, the fastidious recorder in charge of sheet 17B, catches her mistake and crosses it out, transferring the information to the next line. Her error is understandable: there is a blank space where the occupation of Franklin Kennamer's wife should be recorded, but she doesn't have one. Isabel Cooper, the former darling of the Manila vaudeville stage and erstwhile mistress to the former chief of staff of the United States Army, is now a housewife. At thirty-one (according to this document), the script of her life seems to be somewhat rewritten. Now Isabel Kennamer, she is married to a lawyer close to her age and living in a rented apartment in northwest Washington.[1]

It is an out-of-character interlude and short-lived.

❋ ❋ ❋

I think about how this slice of her life was captured on official state documents, and how an elusive historical figure can be corralled into becoming legible on occasion. As I gather together the sparse traces of her life for the years immediately following the MacArthur debacle, the facts chronicled in these records become unreliable and evade certitude. Insofar as they capture anything about the woman who now calls herself Isabel Kennamer, it is an early tendency to renarrate who she is.

Where one might think to find definitive proof of age or certainty about her marital status, becomes instead an opportunity for Isabel Kennamer to muddy the waters. Some might call it lying. As I sift through the archives, I begin to think of it as a mode of creativity. Even with so little material to work with, no stage, and no audience, she turns to reinvention.

I wonder who does the talking when the census taker knocks on the door at the apartment on Park Street that spring. The census notes that Isabel Kennamer was born in the Philippines (true), is thirty-one (most likely true), and is white (not completely true). I wonder if the lie about her race is strategic—especially in segregation-era Washington—wishful thinking, or something she or her husband really felt was accurate, or accurate enough.[2] There are no laws on the books in Washington, DC, preventing interracial marriage, unlike Maryland where they marry in 1938, which prohibited whites from marrying Blacks and Filipinos. Claiming whiteness, in this case, allows Isabel Cooper to legally marry Franklin Kennamer. A few years after the census, Isabel Cooper would trim down her age and claim a distinctly different racial identity.

This moment captured by the census is also oddly deceiving. It is a moment of stillness in a life defined by restless mobility, constant performance, and occasional high drama. The few years prior to and following this vision of domesticity are anything but tranquil. Without MacArthur's financial support, life after the Chastleton's stifling embrace is precarious for a former actress whose talents are unknown outside Manila.

Isabel Cooper is itinerant after her role in the journalist's showdown with the general in 1934. With the windfall of the $15,000 settlement, she first relocates to Oklahoma. In the 1940 census, the Kennamers both list their 1935 residence as Oklahoma City, where Franklin Kennamer's family hails from.[3] If indeed she and her future husband met taking classes in Georgetown as her relationship with MacArthur was unraveling, then their relocation to Oklahoma is reasonable.[4] Soon after, however, she departs for Manila.

Her trip home coincides with MacArthur's return to familiar tropical haunts. He sails back to the Philippines on October 1935 at the invitation of President Manuel Quezon, who asks him to serve as the chief military advisor to the commonwealth government of the Philippines upon finishing his tour as chief of staff.

There is no record of their crossing paths during the months when they share yet another capital city. In any case, the general has moved on after meeting a wealthy socialite and world traveler, Jean Faircloth, on his voyage to Manila. She would, soon after the death of his mother, become his second wife.[5] MacArthur does his courting in the Philippines and continues his romance with colonialism in slightly altered terms. If Isabel Cooper was entertaining any thoughts of a reconciliation with the general, the talk about his romance with the very eligible Jean Faircloth ends them.

Isabel Cooper's trip home underscores a few stark truths about the place of women like her in a world crafted by men like him. Unlike MacArthur's, her homecoming is not met with fanfare. It is ironic but unsurprising that he likely feels more at home and welcome in Manila than she does.

A faded undated snippet from newspaper coverage of her visit to Manila lingers. In it, the story goes, the former stage star has turned into an oil painter, her stay in Washington chaperoned by her brother. She is, the article claims, a trained and exhibited artist who had gifted one of her pieces to then–Senate president Manuel Quezon during his stay in Washington.[6] There is no mention at all of MacArthur.

The fame and infamy she enjoyed from stage and screen a scant decade prior have long since faded from the public's fickle memory. Her own pioneering roles as endearing ingenue, modern Filipina beauty, and groundbreaking icon of scandal are overrun by a new crop of eager young stars and brash filmmakers. The city that once could not get enough of the New Filipina has moved on.

She returns to the United States in February 1936.[7] Seven months later, the Manila *Literary Song-Movie Magazine* reminisces about Dimples Cooper "at the height of her artistic triumphs," as if to say that her star has dimmed.[8] There is no mention of MacArthur, just the obituary of her Manila career.

Once she leaves its shores in 1936, Isabel Cooper never returns to the land of her birth. MacArthur would, of course, return *again and again and again*.

❊ ❊ ❊

While it would always bear the imprint of her imperious past lover, Washington is also Isabel Cooper's home. By the time of the census worker's visit, Isabel and Franklin Kennamer have been married for a year and a half.

Franklin Kennamer is a few years younger than his wife, at twenty-eight. He is an alumnus of Georgetown University's law school, and they may have met on its campus or nearby, if indeed she took classes to escape the Chastleton.[9]

... the General first saw me when I was seven—took an interest in me asked me how I would like to attend school in Washington (which is true except the age) ...

The two lines on the census yield little, but leave ample room to speculate about what drives a young, white attorney from the Midwest to marry a mixed-race former mistress of a powerful political player. I think about how the two might have met, in their midtwenties, and who made the first overtures. I wonder how long the specter of the general was a party to their relationship. I think about how their marriage is something woven into the larger fabric of U.S. empire in the Philippines and the kinds of peculiar mobilities and arrangements it enabled.

Josefina Ryan dies in 1938, the same year that Isabel Cooper decides to marry.[10] It is unclear if her half sisters are taken in by a guardian. Josefina's death, the dizzying whiplash movements of her life, and the uncertainty and insecurity she left behind might have further shaken her eldest daughter's views about the lives of women on the edges of empire. I think about how Isabel Cooper may have married Franklin Kennamer to stave off the tribulations she witnessed in her mother's life, which she felt manifesting in hers. Whatever attachments she may have felt for her husband cannot be extricated from the marks left on her family by colonial "love."

In a few years, her brief marriage becomes source material for Isabel Kennamer to refashion herself. The two lines the Kennamers occupy on the 1940 census record their marriage. Her correspondence with Drew Pearson, a short newspaper mention of her divorce, and the divorce petition track its dissolution.

❀ ❀ ❀

The late 1930s and early 1940s are times that are ripe for reinvention. The miseries and deprivations of the Depression inspire innovation, and the looming storm clouds of war add to the intrigue in the air. In Washington, the Kennamers witness the political reactions to the grim developments in Europe and listen to debates about American military intervention. The increasing belligerence of Nazi Germany tests the United States' nominal isolationism. Japan flexes its muscles in China. It seems only a matter of time before the conflicts on the far side of both oceans will land on American shores and the territories it occupies.

Having formerly lived in close quarters with a man whose life was intertwined with global militarism and American intervention, perhaps Isabel Kennamer notes what these signs portend. The tensions of global events saturate the nation's capital, filtering down to her own small life, to her daily routine as a wife.

The lull of her domestic everyday pulls against the past drama and scandal of her three decades. Around her the engines of war and Hollywood become increasingly entangled. She is surrounded by the tensely held breaths of anticipation, while caged up in a new apartment and an unexpected life.

In a letter to Drew Pearson a few years later, she confesses that she is a longtime fan of his radio show, *Listen America*.[11] Pearson continued to report on power brokers in Washington long after his skirmish with the general. I think about Isabel Kennamer, listening to the sound of Pearson's voice over the airwaves, perhaps occasionally recognizing the names he drops as people she might have met during her Chastleton days. The radio provides the illusion of an intimate connection as her life becomes more distant from the centers of power. Perhaps it also reminds her of how far her life has fallen short of the promises the general made when she left Manila. But it is also a window into increasingly turbulent global currents.

Pearson's show is a savvy mix of news and entertainment, reflecting the increasing mingling of politics and the movies that the European war is beginning to shape. The conflict across the Atlantic spawns films that make their way past censorship boards—from outright propaganda to a comical spoof of Hitler à la Charlie Chaplin. I imagine the lonely housewife heading to the movies to escape, and instead encountering the grim shadows of impending war.

The Hollywood of pure entertainment—with fantasy and epic romantic fare like *The Wizard of Oz* and *Gone with the Wind*—begins to give way to war, leading to clashes with an industry code designed to restrict political and social content. Hollywood directors fight on the cultural front lines: Alfred Hitchcock's 1940 *Foreign Correspondent* ends with its protagonist, a New York crime reporter in Europe, exhorting Americans to "keep those lights burning there! Cover them with steel! Ring them with guns! Build a canopy of battleships and bombing planes around them!" United Artists' *That Hamilton Woman*, a 1941 Vivien Leigh vehicle, which might otherwise have appealed to Isabel Kennamer because of its story about a courtesan who became the wife of a British ambassador, is described by its director as "propaganda with a very thick coating of sugar indeed."[12]

Isabel Kennamer's two worlds—the business of film and Washington politics—collide when passionately isolationist senators launch an investigation into Hollywood anti-Nazi films for propaganda that might "influence public sentiment in the direction of participation by the United States in the . . . European War."[13] The hearings drag into December 1941.

By the time Isabel Kennamer appears in the historical record again, the United States has entered the war, provoked by Japan's attacks in Hawai'i and the Philippines. The debate about the nation's role in the global fray comes to a swift end.

When the Philippines was targeted as part of the coordinated strike, Isabel Kennamer's now-remarried former lover finds himself in the midst of a defensive and losing scramble in the land of her birth. Douglas MacArthur errs disastrously in his return to active duty as the commander of the United

States Army Forces in the Far East. Ignoring the orders of his Washington superiors to execute the agreed-upon war plan, his decision leads to the decimation of his air force. Within weeks, Manila is declared an open city, and MacArthur orders a retreat to the Bataan peninsula, leaving the capital to incoming Japanese troops.

These global upheavals coincide with personal ones for Isabel Kennamer.

When Bataan falls in April 1942, and MacArthur retreats to Corregidor under the high drama documented on the front pages of newspapers, Isabel Kennamer begins to question her marriage. When Corregidor—the last stand of the American military in the Philippines—follows a month later, she is on her way to Los Angeles. As MacArthur is ordered to Australia, leaving many American soldiers to the mercies of the invading Japanese army, Isabel Kennamer uproots herself from the city that had been her home in the United States and makes her way to Hollywood for the second time in her life. It is unclear if this move is made with her husband, or if she strikes out on her own. Franklin Kennamer also finds work as an attorney in Los Angeles around the same time.

It is a perplexing time to be on the move, but perhaps the upheavals of the war give her permission to shake up her life. All around her, the war upends lives, speeds up decisions to marry, breaks apart families, drives unlikely people to unlikely jobs, and spurs new kinds of mobility. Isabel Kennamer is no Rosie the Riveter, but for her, as for thousands of women, war begets radical choices.

She uses the resources she has at hand: favors owed from her former life as MacArthur's mistress, the ambiguity of her mixed-race identity, the nearly blank canvas of her fleeting marriage, the lessons imparted by her mother's own inventiveness, and her not-insubstantial experience of playing to an audience of men. Parted from MacArthur and parting from Kennamer, she makes use of the detritus of these relationships to cultivate new ground.

Fifteen years after her first attempt to become a Hollywood ingenue, Isabel Kennamer tries again. This time, she has more of an arsenal—which she needs, because Hollywood does not look kindly on aging starlets, and the bit parts for a mixed-race woman in her early thirties are few and far between. The movie industry calls for connections who might introduce her into the mogul-controlled studio system. While her own family is as far from the Hollywood scene as one could imagine—her younger brother Bruce (the ex-convict) is married and working as a steward, and her father Isaac has remarried and is living in rural northern California—Isabel Kennamer now has people who owe her.[14]

Months after leaving her life as a Washington housewife, she writes to Drew Pearson for the first time since his triumph over MacArthur. It had been almost eight years since the journalist had heard from her. In August 1942, having "been in Los Angeles for some time now," "idle," Isabel Kennamer—now going by Belle Cooper—pens a letter to Pearson, with the flattering entreaty: "I can't think of anyone with more influence than you have to help me."[15]

With this letter, she starts down the path of reinventing herself, a way of life for Hollywood dreamers. Drew Pearson is a willing accomplice.

Their correspondence reveals a woman used to fashioning herself according to male desire, and fluent in its manipulation. Her opening gambit is a study in self-deprecation strategically paired with expressions of admiration designed to elicit Pearson's sympathy. Characterizing herself as someone Pearson, a public persona of some note, has "probably forgotten," she nevertheless holds out hope that her request won't annoy him. It is, of course, very unlikely that Pearson would have forgotten a woman attached to Douglas MacArthur, one whose illicit affair with the general provided Pearson with leverage against his libel suit. Belle Cooper's diminution of her own starring role in that multimillion-dollar drama, however, reminds Pearson of his debt to her. Their roles—and his obligation—established she then asks him if he knows "anyone out here who could give me bit parts in the movies." She ends the letter with one final stroke to his ego, noting his popularity in Los Angeles due to his new NBC radio broadcast *Drew Pearson Comments*, which had gone from a duo to a solo show: "I hope you'll forgive me but I like it better with just you alone now."[16]

With their mutual adversary constantly in the news about the war in the Pacific theater, Pearson is quick to remember and act. In the course of the following month, he writes back to Isabel Cooper, suggesting a couple of contacts: Nat Goldstone, an agent, and Sam Hahn, general counsel for the Scripps League of Newspapers. Writing to Hahn separately—seemingly about a different political matter—Pearson casually includes a request to his friend, possibly embellishing Belle Cooper's story along the way for his own purposes:

> Meanwhile I have a matter which might interest you, and in which I think you could be of considerable service. You may recall that way back in the dim, dark ages you were of invaluable service to Bob and me when General MacArthur sued us to the tune of $1,750,000. You may also recall that a certain lady appeared on the scene and was instrumental in the settlement of that suit. That lady is now [in] Los Angeles and I can tell you, in strictest confidence, that the White House is not averse to have her get a job and live in some degree of comfort.

It happens that she is out of a job at the moment and is looking for something in Hollywood. She has been on the stage for many years, and as you know is a Urasian [*sic*], so that she would fit in pretty well in spy and saboteur parts involving the Japanese.

Whether or not it is actually true that Franklin Delano Roosevelt even knew of Isabel Cooper and her MacArthur entanglement and was invested in her success is beside the point. It is unlikely. But Pearson's confidential aside builds mystery around her, hinting at powerful behind-the-scenes backers who might prefer that the nation's top general not be distracted by a loose cannon. In a sense he borrows from her book. His willingness to vouch for Belle Cooper gestures to a feeling of indebtedness. At the end of his letter to Hahn, he puts a price on the depth of his obligation by offering to reimburse Hahn for any funds that he might advance to Isabel Cooper over the course of his assistance.[17]

Belle Cooper, with a fresh audience, starts anew. Within her first year in Hollywood, she recasts herself away from Isabel Kennamer, the white, married, thirty-one-year-old housewife described in the 1940 census.

Sam Hahn's letters to Drew Pearson describe his impressions of Belle Cooper, which, despite the seamy history with the general that Pearson alludes to, reflect someone much more diffident and unassuming.

I imagine how Belle Cooper comports herself in the two-hour lunch she has with Sam Hahn to give him a favorable impression of her modesty. This is, after all, a woman he knows to have been involved in a high-profile affair, who was instrumental in the humiliation of her former paramour, and who now wants to enter the dissolute world of Hollywood. I think about the care that she puts into choosing what to wear, how to do her makeup, how to walk, and how to modulate her voice.

After lingering over a long lunch, Hahn's letter to Pearson describes a "charming little Eurasian lady" who is "much depressed and somewhat disillusioned with Hollywood." His protective instincts respond to the persona she plays: a damsel in need of assistance, but not yet desperate enough to take a loan he offers on behalf of Pearson. Her gentle rebuff prompts Hahn to declare her a "lady in a million."

This meal is her first audition. It is also an occasion where she directs the scene, obliquely. Belle Cooper walks the tricky tightrope of someone who has not yet acquired Hollywood manners but who also knows to guide the action for her own purposes. She divulges that among her talents, she can dance—and confesses that at a low point in her past she had done "distasteful" kinds of dancing in a Reno nightclub.[18] Emphasizing that she would rather not do that sort of work in the future, she manages to convince a jaded Angeleno that she is now Belle Cooper, that biddable and modest lady, attending to the desires of men like him.

Her lunch audition bears fruit, and Hahn leaves as a new champion of Belle Cooper, the charming Eurasian lady. During the course of their meeting, Isabel Cooper brings up a personage of some import at the *Hollywood Reporter*, who has had some success in placing "similarly situated" friends of hers, as a possible contact that Hahn might exploit on her behalf. It seems she is not quite convinced of her lunch companion's connections. As a result of her subtle suggestion, Hahn conveys to Pearson that he might write a letter of introduction for her. He also states that he will tap his pool of contacts at various studios on behalf of his new charge, including Louis B. Mayer.

Less than two weeks after this meeting, Sam Hahn marshals his resources to arrange for studio photographs of Isabel Cooper, in order to help professionalize her search for movie roles. They are lovely. Isabel Cooper is luminous. The planes of her face catch the light. She is believable and compelling, even when costumed to project the kinds of types a mixed-race actress might be expected to play. She sends a set to Pearson.[19] Hahn then pulls strings for her to meet with Harriet Parsons, the daughter of Louella Parsons, "the Hearst movie journalistic czar." He also contacts RKO public relations on her behalf, along with making arrangements for her to make a personal appearance at the Beverly Hills Theater for a publicized performance.[20]

Belle Cooper is so convincing that Hahn embraces his role as her agent more wholeheartedly than she does hers as an aspiring actor. He is initially more persistent than Isabel Cooper is with regard to her future career. Despite Pearson's and Hahn's efforts on her behalf, there are no parts to be had. Months in Los Angeles may have also made clear Hollywood's enduring disdain for nonwhite actresses. She relays to Pearson that Nat Goldstone, the agent he recommended, "looked down" on her and "yawned" in her face during their meeting.[21] She interviews with an executive of Universal Studios, but it does not yield anything immediate, despite her impression that he was "encouraging in his comment on [her] chances."[22] Hahn notes that in subsequent visits, she "looks well but not too cheerful."[23] He conveys his frustration to Pearson about her consistent failure to take advantage of the opportunities that he sets up for her: "She has failed to visit Betty Parsons at the Paramount Studios. Miss Parsons called me twice about it because she made the appointment for an interview as an accommodation to me." Hahn tells Pearson that he worries that Belle Cooper is "not sufficiently forward"

Studio photograph, hula pose, seated. Jose Reyes Studios, circa 1942. Courtesy of Drew Pearson Papers.

Studio photograph, cheongsam, standing. Jose Reyes Studios, circa 1942. Courtesy of Drew Pearson Papers.

to succeed in Hollywood: she balks at a Beverly Wilshire Theater appearance for the American Legion because she does "not have the proper costume for such an occasion." He then contacts another client to provide costumes for Belle Cooper.[24]

Belle Cooper's not-insignificant talent in pulling together the efforts of these men across a continent is a testament to the success of her self-casting as an ingenue of sorts. While she may have sabotaged the success of her early days in Hollywood, she soon carves out a makeshift career.

None of the letters from this early period mentions the war raging in Europe or Asia, although this war eventually provides the first foothold for her in parts for local color in films that proliferate about the Pacific theater. Two months after Isabel Cooper first contacts Drew Pearson for help with her career, she writes that she is being considered for a role in a Cecil B. DeMille production, as a Japanese girl.[25]

As she begins to find small roles, she also crafts a new public persona. She becomes single, further muddies the waters with regard to her racial identity, and loses a decade. As she shakes off and takes on new skins, animating and discarding roles in real life where roles in the movies are scarce, Isabel Cooper hearkens back to her mother's tactics for survival. The next decade of her life has the agitated feel of incessant costume changes, with little time to breathe.

✷ ✷ ✷

I imagine Drew Pearson bemused as he reads a letter from Belle Cooper, discovering that she has been married all along.[26] This little bombshell further unfolds in another report of her Hollywood progress. She is in production on her first film and perhaps is beginning to shed the damsel-in-distress role she had projected earlier. Her next step, it seems, is to divorce Franklin Kennamer, claiming that she hasn't lived with him for "nearly two years." She tells Pearson that she is enlisting Hahn's paid help in the matter to expedite a divorce. According to her, Hahn stated that "it was the law here for the husband to take care of the divorce fee" but that she would "rather pay for it [her]self." She confesses that she has "been wanting to divorce that guy for a long time but [hasn't] had the money to do so."[27]

Sam Hahn files Isabel Kennamer's petition for divorce just as her Hollywood career, such as it is, gets off the ground. It is a straightforward divorce, involving no children or community property. She charges Kennamer with "cruel and inhuman" treatment that caused her "extreme mental and physical pain and anguish" as justification for the dissolution of their marriage.[28] There is no evidence for her claims in the court paperwork—the use of this language was common prior to the no-fault divorce. Kennamer, who had also relocated to Los Angeles for his job on the Securities and Exchange Commission (either alongside or in pursuit of his errant wife), does not respond to the court summons or contest the divorce. A year passes with no reply. With the outbreak of the war, he enlists in the Marine Corps.[29] The legal machine rolls on without him, and an interlocutory judgment of divorce is granted on March 5, 1943.[30]

The petition for divorce generates a moment of publicity. A short piece titled (to her chagrin) "Kennamer" in the *Los Angeles Herald and Express* announces her divorce, followed by a subheading in smaller print, "Film Actress Divorced from L.A. Atty." She is shown in a photograph just above the short column, wearing a skirt suit, hands demurely clasped, legs crossed, and smiling widely. An excerpt from the court proceedings allows her to frame herself as an object of obsession of her "always jealous" former husband. With Franklin Kennamer absent, her claim that he "falsely accused" her "of having affairs with other men" becomes the official script of their marriage.[31] It is an eye-catching anticipation of the charges MacArthur's biographers would use to malign her, but this time, spun into a narrative of her desirability.

She uses the bit of publicity to further recast herself, even with its teeth-gritting "Kennamer" headline. Alongside fleshing out the unhappy version of her marriage, the article also describes the mixed-race ex-vaudevillian—a "23-year old exotic actress" and "dancer" of "Scotch-Irish-Malayan" descent—as embarking on her U.S. film career. Only three things are absolutely true in the announcement: she is divorced, she had worked as a dancer, and she can finally claim to be a working American film actress.

The timeline for her divorce runs concurrently with the production schedule of her first movie, *So Proudly We Hail*. She finishes filming it just ten days after her petition for a divorce is granted.[32] Her paycheck makes her an official working actress. Sam Hahn's attorney's fee for her divorce—$100—is about half of what she makes in a week for her work as a bit player, a Filipino nurse in the film.[33] She notes in her letter to Pearson that she still owes him for the loans that Hahn advanced to keep her afloat. It is unclear whether she ever pays him back. Her divorce from Franklin Kennamer is finalized on March 8, 1944.[34]

❧ ❧ ❧

The skirt suit pictured in the *Herald and Express* article surrenders a little detail about the rest of Isabel Cooper's life during this time. It appears again, with the same hairdo and smile, in an undated photograph with her half sister Rosemary Ruby "Jimmy" Ryan, a photograph possibly taken by their cousin

Isabel Cooper with her half sister Rosemary Ruby "Jimmy" Ryan. From Thomas Carter, *Then and Now* (1983).

Mercedes Sotelo-Carter).[35] Other than this photograph and the narration of Thomas Carter, the American expatriate who is married to her cousin, there is little documentation of Isabel Cooper's relationship with her half sisters. It is a rare family moment—Isabel Cooper's archives are nearly silent about her siblings. The photograph shows the close resemblance between the two half sisters, down to their matching dimples. They share a seat, leaning against each other. I wonder if they see each other again.

※ ※ ※

The woman in the suit, once again officially going by Isabel Cooper, struggles to build a new life for herself in Los Angeles. She lands other bit parts, benefiting from the vestiges of the war. She continues to write Pearson, and he continues to advise her, "nudging" her to "build a fire cracker" under booking agencies and not rely on them too passively, and even suggesting that she do some consultation with a friend of his who is writing about MacArthur.[36] Just as she rescued him from MacArthur's libel suit, he becomes the well-connected resource she goes to in moments of crisis. She does not hesitate to collect on his debt or press her own demands on him.

She involves him in another personal drama, calling him up in late February or early March 1944, worried about causing "a dear friend of [hers] a great deal of trouble."[37] It is not clear what she has done to embroil her friend in criminal proceedings, but she describes how Milton, her "step-brother by a former marriage of [her] mother's . . . not a blood relation," will have to serve time (fifteen days) unless somehow Pearson and his lawyer connections can help. Perhaps the issue is only resolvable through telephone calls, because there is no written reply from Pearson.

The letter presages a strange interlude in Isabel Cooper's life. Just months after her almost hysterical telephone call and letter to Pearson, and three months after her divorce is official in 1944, she marries Milton Moreno, ostensibly the very same Milton who she describes as her stepbrother, *not a blood relation*, that she had recently incriminated.[38] Stranger still, she marries him again, according to Los Angeles County Court records, in November 1946.[39]

There is no documentation of a divorce in between. In the time spanning the two marriage ceremonies, Isabel Cooper makes another appearance in the press, this time as Chabing Cooper, described by the *Los Angeles Times* as a "dark-haired 25 year-old hula dancer at a night club." She is closer to thirty-seven. The brief article describes her battery complaint against Moreno, a bartender at the Hollywood Tropics. He allegedly climbed into his "ex-wife's" apartment window and assaulted her. She shows her bruised legs in court, adding that her "hula skirt failed to hide her bruises during her dance routines."[40] I think about repetitions and patterns, and whether the "great deal of trouble" she had caused him two years before stemmed from a similar assault.

A month after this incident, the second marriage certificate between Milton Moreno and Isabel Cooper is filed. I think about repetitions and patterns, and whether she turns to marriage to fix them. It is unclear if his abusive behavior continues. There is no divorce document from this second (or third) marriage, but Milton Moreno disappears thoroughly from the archival record after this date. It is not clear how long their second attempt at wedded bliss lasts. On her death certificate in 1960, Isabel Cooper is once again described as divorced, although it is Franklin Kennamer, and not Moreno, who shows up to bury her, and who describes her as a divorcée.

The two marriage certificates track Isabel Cooper's active shaping of her identity through narrations in official state records. While her stated age is consistently at least a decade younger than her actual age, her "color or race" shifts from "Caucasian/Malay" to Filipino over a two-and-a-half-year span (Milton Moreno's goes from "White/Malay" to Filipino). Their second application for a marriage license also ups their count of previous marriages

Remarried, twice. Los Angeles County Court Archives, from Ancestry.com.

from one to two, indicating perhaps that they did officially dissolve their first marriage. She is also more truthful in the second document about her birthplace (not Washington, DC).[41]

Her latest name change—unofficial—to Chabing Cooper also occurs during this period, first used professionally when she plays one of actor Rex Harrison's fourteen wives in *Anna and the King of Siam* (1945), then again in the media report about Moreno battering her. Exactly why she feels the need to change her name, especially because she already has a small body of work under the name Isabel Cooper, is unclear, but I think about her mother's precedent, and the power of naming. In an earlier letter to Pearson, she tells him she is thinking of changing her name (he replies that he thinks it is a good idea, and that he had suggested it to her "some years ago").[42] She chooses Chabing because, she says, "[It is] the name my mother called me when she was pleased with me."[43]

She continues going by Chabing until her last film role.

Choosing names is the first act of creating.

In the decade following her arrangement with MacArthur, Isabel Cooper relentlessly remakes herself. Isabel Kennamer, housewife from Washington, DC; Belle Cooper, ingenue; Isabel Cooper, actress; possibly Isabel Moreno, wife; Chabing Cooper, nightclub hula dancer; Chabing, actress. She shaves at least a decade from her actual age, claims to be white, Malay, Scottish, Irish, Javanese. She moves on from being a mistress to getting married, then divorced, to married again (and again).

Finding herself evicted from a familiar role, and unsatisfied with the one that follows, she invents a plethora of selves in order to survive—sometimes just barely and with bruises to show—in the manifold niches available to women like her. Both distant from and yet intimately bound to the war raging across both oceans, these roles show a woman making do with scant material and doggedly crafting a life and livelihood through ingenuity and manipulation, or what perhaps has been dismissed as "feminine wiles."

Her life was a continual series of departures and arrivals. If someone were to map out her path on this earth, it would be a dizzying line that crisscrossed the globe, sometimes doubling back, sometimes taking an odd detour. She could barely track herself in the world.

She was not a woman who stayed. Or perhaps it was more that she did not know her place.

seventeen

1ST FILIPINA NURSE,
GEISHA, ~~LITTLE SERGEANT,~~
JAVANESE NURSE, UNCREDITED

Empire haunts its mistress. It presses unwanted intimacies on Isabel Cooper, makes demands long after the affair that would come to define her life has ended. In uncanny parallel, the Philippines, fumbling toward independence, finds its colonial bonds to be abiding and resilient, reluctant to release their hold.

War throws these thorny and lingering intimacies into sharp relief. It creates a theater—in the multiple senses of the word—for the dramas of imperial intimacy to play out. Where occupation laid bare the lie of U.S. benevolence, war unashamedly repurposes tropes of rescue and liberation, rendering old things new again.

This moment is ripe for well-loved and conventional roles to resurface: the Philippines, cast as the damsel in distress, and the United States, with MacArthur as the stand-in, as its knight in shining armor. Where the elder MacArthur had been the head of the occupying army of pacification in the islands, the son is understood to be its savior in the new war. Wartime necessities reframe a past encounter rooted in profound violence into a familial bond.

These narratives have traction that play out not only on a geopolitical scale, but also in the everyday lives of people far removed from the combat zone. Isabel Cooper's life during the war years illuminates how imperial intimacy steals its way into unexpected places.

❀ ❀ ❀

Where the details of her personal life are sometimes confused (some of which is due to her own creativity), Isabel Cooper as an actor comes into focus in the war years, and the story this archive yields is one of great irony and familiarity. Her desires and avenues for independence and fulfillment during this historical moment are bound to and enabled by the past. Her relationship with MacArthur, the continuing entanglement of the United States with the Philippines, and the urgency of wartime braid themselves into her life.

The crisis of war wastes no opportunities for plots of sacrifice and heroism to return, reshaping cultural memory about what business the United States even has in a faraway archipelago. Hollywood's new plots are compelling and seductive. They lend themselves to melodramatic storytelling—to cinematic epics of wounded men persisting—of white valor always at the center of action. Where it had entered cautiously into the fray before Pearl Harbor, the war sees the movie industry become one of the United States' best soldiers.[1] Hollywood looks to its heroic battles and figures for the raw material of the silver screen.[2]

For an aspiring actress of mixed race in Hollywood, World War II is a boon. War heightens imperial desires along familiar racial lines.[3] There is an increased demand for mixed-race and Asian actors to provide authenticity to films set in the Pacific and Asia. Even so, the prospects for actors with her look are bleak.[4]

The studio photographs that Isabel Cooper takes are aimed squarely at the kinds of parts that Drew Pearson predicted would proliferate because of the war. She is draped in lei, flirtatiously smiling, ever the welcoming native girl. She wears a cheongsam, flowers in her hair, gazing into the distance. Another series has her in a light *terno* with its butterfly sleeves and a long dark skirt, meant to represent Filipina dress.[5] There are none of her in Japanese dress, what Pearson might have alluded to when he describes "saboteur" parts. But these are understood to be interchangeable types.

She finds roles in films that feature the landscapes and figures of her past. Because the Philippines is a key site of the Pacific theater, and her former lover a pivotal figure in it, the shape of her life in this interval is forged by these tenacious intimacies.

The Philippines, under American jurisdiction at the onset of the war, is attacked by Japan in tandem with Pearl Harbor in 1941. As a place that animates profound suffering and dramatic liberation, the archipelago becomes a common setting for American films.[6] MacArthur, the beleaguered but eventually triumphant hero of the Allied campaign in Asia and the Pacific, haunts the action.

Even as Isabel Cooper works herself free of this particular episode of her past and seeks her own independence as a working woman in Hollywood, these deep-rooted colonial relationships insist otherwise. They tether her opportunities for a nascent self-sufficiency to plots that are woven

FRIENDS AND ALLIES—Miss Columbia (Isabel Cooper) and Miss Philippines (Caroline Cuizon) rehearse scene in patriotic bond show Filipinos will offer at the Victory House.

Miss Columbia, *Los Angeles Times*, 1944.

into the landscapes and relationships of empire and war. They remind her, again and again, of the histories, big and small, that demarcate the horizons of her life.

❀ ❀ ❀

A blurred photograph, accompanying a short article in the *Los Angeles Times* on April 6, 1944, captures the mesh of relationships—past and present—that are caught up in this global conflict. The photograph illustrates a story describing a patriotic bond drive organized by the Treasury War Finance Committee national origins group at the Victory House in Pershing Square. The event features "a score of Filipino men and women in native costume" presenting "a series of tableaux, depicting normal activities on the islands prior to their conquest." The purpose of the drive is to pay for a $300,000 bomber, to be christened the "Spirit of the Philippines," which is "earmarked for General Douglas MacArthur's use in making good his vow to wrest the Philippines from the Japs."

In the photograph, Isabel Cooper is costumed in the drapery of Miss Columbia, standing next to a Filipina organizer, bracketed by American and

Philippine flags. The caption reads "Friends and Allies."[7] I find myself wondering if she stands there smiling, next to Miss Philippines, aware that her participation will eventually touch MacArthur's life, if either of them, a decade after the end of their arrangement, might find ironies in the moment.

There are strange juxtapositions at work in this community event at which a fledgling actress finds herself in the middle of Pershing Square in Los Angeles. Beyond a story of Filipinos being dragged into a war not of their own making, and being called upon to perform their loyalty in a variety of ways, another story filters through. This one is about how friendships and alliances between states are haunted by other kinds of "friendships and alliances" born of colonial desire.

The bond drive's location, Pershing Square, commemorating General John J. Pershing, is a popular site for rallies and recruitment during the war. Pershing notably survived a scandalous rumor of having fathered several "half-breed" children with a Filipina mistress while serving in the Philippines.[8] He was also a former lover of the wealthy and very much married Louise Cromwell Brooks, who later became Douglas MacArthur's first wife.

That Isabel Cooper illustrates this brief account of the patriotism of Filipino nationals highlights the knotty friendships and alliances that once again come into play during this period. Attired as an icon of liberty, she depicts how the intimately entwined players of empire are never quite free of their histories. In this moment, she is obligated once again to serve her erstwhile lover from afar.

As a struggling actress, she is compelled to show up at events like this. It is unclear if the Filipino community in Los Angeles is aware of Isabel Cooper's past with the man for whom they are raising funds. The photograph illuminates the unsettling and continued dependencies between the United States and the Philippines, with which someone like Isabel Cooper, the child of an American soldier and a Filipina, is all too familiar. She smiles, her gaze looking off to the side.

❀ ❀ ❀

In contrast to the scant detail yielded by the black-and-white photograph and her casting as Miss Columbia, the archival record of Isabel Cooper's life in Hollywood hints at a fuller picture of how she navigates her personal landscape of war.

Though Isabel Cooper does not sign up for the war effort other than this strange drafting as Miss Columbia, her early roles in Hollywood are squarely in a war zone.

She starts out playing nurses: a Filipina nurse, then a Javanese nurse, followed by a Japanese geisha. Her first roles say a lot about who is deemed suitable for these kinds of labor, in both real life and fantasy.⁹ These roles draw from the same well that she dipped into for playing MacArthur's mistress a decade earlier, and to the labor of intimacy that women like her perform in peacetime and war.

The roles she lands are in war films that mirror actual events and locations to an almost journalistic degree. It is like following the drum, but on celluloid rather than in the flesh.

By the time she makes her way to Hollywood in 1942, Bataan has fallen and MacArthur has retreated to Australia. These events are the backdrop of the first two films Isabel Cooper is hired for. MacArthur is their phantom lead, his offscreen presence hovering.

Though only a fraction of the screen time for the films, her scenes draw on a backstory defined by the racialized sexual economies of American imperialism in Asia and the Pacific. These are the bit parts of empire.

❋ ❋ ❋

It is years into my research before I feel ready to see her Hollywood films, having spent most of my time researching her early life. I am content with amassing the two-dimensionality of photographs, paper documents, scanned files, and microfiche for a faint outline of her life. There is something safely frozen and inert about them, even as the stories they hold push back against the limits of their forms.

I first see her onscreen through a third party. An artist, Miljohn Ruperto, stages an exhibit on Isabel Cooper, including a silent compilation of all her Hollywood roles. She is in motion, out of context, with no soundtrack, a dizzying panoply of black-and-white and Technicolor scenes.

Still I hold off on watching the body of her Hollywood work.

Instead I track her presence as it materializes in casting lists, daily production reports, budget sheets, shooting schedules, and, rarely, in the tiny print of run-of-the-mill *Variety* film reviews. She unexpectedly appears in a photograph in a production file documenting on-set events during the filming of *The Story of Dr. Wassell*. She is in the background, in clear focus, centered among other women costumed as nurses. She smiles as Cecil B. DeMille blows out the candles on a cake for his surprise birthday celebration. A film historian and librarian who writes a book about Ann Dvorak gifts me with a film still from Dvorak's movie *I Was an American Spy*, where Isabel Cooper plays her penultimate role.¹⁰

On set with Cecil B. DeMille. *The Story of Dr. Wassell*, production photograph. Courtesy Margaret Herrick Library.

I assemble a collection of her films, building as complete a filmography as I can. These films, unlike the few she made in Manila, survive the war.

I begin to watch them slowly, in chronological order.

It is like meeting someone I've heard so much about.

❋ ❋ ❋

I first hear Isabel Cooper's voice in *So Proudly We Hail*, director Mark Sandrich's 1943 drama about the "courage, devotion and sacrifice" of heroic American nurses in the Philippine theater.[11] It is soft, lilting, in character for someone subservient, feminine, and Asian—fitting for someone cast, but not credited, as the "1st Filipino Nurse."[12]

I wait as the film builds the backstories of the main characters, played by the star trifecta of Claudette Colbert, Paulette Goddard, and Veronica Lake.

I strain my eyes to catch a glimpse of anyone who looks remotely like the woman in the studio photographs I hold in my hand.

When she finally appears, I am struck by the way the camera loves her face. I rewind the scene again and again to stretch out the fleeting moment of her American film debut.

Thirty-eight seconds. In her first Hollywood film, the former darling of the Manila vaudeville circuit and deliciously scandal-ridden movie ingenue has thirty-eight seconds of total screen time, speaking eleven words.

❋ ❋ ❋

Isabel Cooper, uncredited 1st Filipino Nurse, is a marginal figure in the film, yet who she is and has been in her life is at its core. The role is perfectly suited to someone who had seen to the needs of one of the highest-ranking soldiers in the U.S. Army.[13] Fittingly, while she is cast as a Filipina nurse because of her ability to speak Tagalog well, she finds additional work on the production as a translator and a technical advisor.[14]

So Proudly We Hail is typical fare for a Hollywood enlisting full force in the war effort, with a twist that it focuses on women in wartime. It is a paean to the real-life story of ten nurses who escaped the fall of Corregidor in 1942. Made and released shortly after the devastating fall of Bataan and Corregidor, it uses military and nurse consultants to add to the film's "true story" claims. Yet while Isabel Cooper has been hired as a consultant, the "fat, pompous man" who is the writer of the film, and whom she cannot abide, has "conversed with everyone but [her]."[15]

The film delves into the gritty realities of the American military's last stand in the Philippines. Mariveles and Corregidor, which feature as the major locations of the film, are key sites that mark the retreat of battered troops. The plot of So Proudly We Hail wraps around the dark months following the fall of Manila but centers on the relationships that the American nurses have with each other and with soldiers in their care or fighting elsewhere. It elevates the romance—whether tragically interrupted or eventually fulfilled—as the stakes of the war. The 1st Filipino Nurse can only ever be a background figure, no matter how foundational she is to the plot of imperial romance. Once the three lead nurses enter the scene—touted as "heroines without mascara"—it is their work and their sacrifices that are legible and important.

Isabel Cooper's brief appearances help establish the deteriorating conditions that the lead characters encounter when they arrive in Mariveles just before the retreat. As the new cohort of American nurses scrub in for surgery,

Filipina nurse. *So Proudly We Hail*, film still. Paramount Pictures.

they are quickly educated on just how dire things have become. Isabel Cooper's main scene begins when a Filipina nurse enters the room, bearing a tray of instruments, and starts to collapse. Another Filipina nurse, played by Isabel Cooper, follows behind her and matter-of-factly states, "It's just exhaustion." She catches her swaying compatriot and helps her gather the dropped instruments. She briefly interacts with Claudette Colbert's head nurse character. Asked where the surgery masks are, she replies, "Masks? We used them all up long ago." Her tone captures the tired pragmatism of someone drained by life in the trenches. The fleeting scene highlights the deprivations of war that Filipinos and others on the front lines had long suffered, and to which the American nurses would soon become accustomed.

The camera lingers on the American nurses, glamorous and dewy even with no makeup, and leaves it to them to embody the harrowing human suffering that the war brings.

There she is, finally.

During the seconds when she flickers on the screen, I wring a sense of what she might have been like "in real life" from her performance. I listen to her quiet voice, study how she moves. I tell myself that this is not Isabel Cooper, but rather the 1st Filipino Nurse, uncredited. Yet the boundaries between the two blur, have always been blurred.

Onscreen, Isabel Cooper's build is slight. She plays the Filipino nurse with an economy of movement. There is a trace of deference in her posture and a quiet tone, but she plays the nurse as capable and otherwise too occupied with the triage of war to genuflect to the new arrivals.

She delivers her lines clearly. Her voice is lightly accented, though it is unclear what accent it is: ambiguous enough to pass for anything. The Tagalog skills for which she is cast do not make an appearance in the final cut of the film. Indeed, the rest of the Filipino accents in the film are all over the place—Filipino Americans playing Filipinos deliver their Tagalog lines with hilariously heavy American accents.

Isabel Cooper's character appears fleetingly in the film a few more times, mostly to serve as background for scenes that flesh out the complex humanity of the American nurses. She makes up part of the crowd when mail is delivered, her face animated as she receives an envelope. (I think about other letters Isabel Cooper has received and written in her life.) Much like her real backstory, she is pushed out of the frame almost immediately as the camera zooms to the film's headliners. The scene is an inadvertent statement about who is relegated to the margins, no matter how central they are to the larger design of empire.

By the time she plays the 1st Filipino Nurse, uncredited, Isabel Cooper has put in more real work than any one of the lead nurses toward the care of the United States' chief soldier, currently embattled in the ongoing war. Now in her early thirties, she has paid decades' worth of dues entertaining American troops and their leaders on Philippine and American soil.

For just over half a minute of screen time, Isabel Cooper works a total of forty-eight days on the film, some of which were half or quarter days, or on standby.[16] She earns $2,027.31 for her film work.[17] In contrast, Colbert, the highest paid of the three leads, makes $150,000 for the picture.[18]

As befitting Isabel Cooper's lowly status in the production, there is no mention of her or any of the Filipino extras in the film's publicity.

When *So Proudly We Hail* debuts, Isabel Cooper once again feels the thrill of seeing her work being viewed by an audience. A lone review of the movie credits her by name, identifying her as a "Filipino Nurse" in tiny print.[19] It is a far cry from the starring roles of her youth, or even her not-so-secret position as MacArthur's paramour, but it is hers.

❋ ❋ ❋

Near the end of the film, as the nurses retreat to Corregidor with the soldiers, the narrator states, "There were about twenty-five nurses there when we arrived. With us, the total came to eighty-eight Americans plus many more Filipino nurses."[20] The last scenes, in which Isabel Cooper's character remains completely silent, follow the on-film revelation that General Mac-Arthur has abandoned the Philippines and has been ordered to withdraw to Australia. The American nurses are prioritized for evacuation, told to pack up, and warned not to share this morale-sinking news with anyone.

The nurses gather in the tunneled network of bunkers of Corregidor Island, where they sleep and tend to the injured and dying. The mood is grim. Isabel Cooper's nurse sits on one of the bunks. As the camera pans right to focus on one of the main characters, we see Isabel Cooper in profile. She opens her mouth, as if to say something, then catches herself.

She, too, has a tale to tell about MacArthur leaving. Or disasters wrought by men of war. But this is not her story to narrate, and the camera lingers instead on Goddard, Colbert, and Lake as the heroines, always, of this plot.

❋ ❋ ❋

The constant and swift transformation of real-time events into cinematic material blurs the line between fact and fiction and illuminates the strange intimacies at the heart of imperial war. Art follows closely on the heels of life, borrowing actors from those who have played the role before. While her involvement with MacArthur had ended a decade earlier, the intimacies of American colonial relationships with the Philippines place Isabel Cooper in curious positions that are reminiscent of her past. She and MacArthur have been long finished, but the durability of the personal connections fashioned by larger geopolitical events puts them in almost constant proximity to each other.

This peculiar effect haunts Isabel Cooper, particularly in her role as a Japanese geisha in *The Purple Heart*, which is shot from October 11, 1943, to mid-January 1944. In this otherwise male-dominated film, her role as a geisha is tethered to her first role as a nurse: they both turn on the work of caring for men in war.

Western notions of the geisha fuel fantasies with which Isabel Cooper is familiar.[21] MacArthur, when he was chief of staff, sat at his desk wearing a ceremonial Japanese kimono. He dressed her in kimonos while they conducted their affair.[22] These twisted and overlapping imaginations about the Orient and its women are part of imperial domination's repertoire. Playing these roles for the camera—roles that were themselves performances oriented for the West—likely strikes Isabel Cooper as yet another uncanny moment of imperial intimacy.

The Darryl F. Zanuck–helmed film features a nearly all-male cast in a spare retelling of a civil court trial in Tokyo of the crew of a B-52 captured after a bombing run.[23] As with *So Proudly We Hail*, the film draws on real-life events: the trial of eight airmen who were part of the April 18, 1942, Doolittle Raid.[24] The film intersperses absurd courtroom procedures with the unspeakable offscreen horrors suffered by the men. It sketches unapologetic caricatures of Japanese people and Axis court reporters while lingering over the noble American prisoners.

Though the film is set in Japan, MacArthur and Isabel Cooper are somehow caught up in it together through the untidy webs of war and imperial desire. In one courtroom scene, the proceedings are interrupted by raucous noise outside. The street erupts in celebration as people shout, "Corregidor has fallen." General Mitsubi, the over-the-top Japanese torturer and plaintiff played by Richard Loo, taunts the defendants: "What do you think of your illustrious General MacArthur now?" Isabel Cooper is not present in this scene, but I'm left wondering how her former lover's defeat resonates with her. She is left to play geisha to a fictional general, and the interchangeability of her real-life role as mistress and her onscreen casting illuminates the banal interplay of imperial desire and patriarchy.

Her role in the film is brief. She appears in a scene at a teahouse, cast as the geisha who hands the general the note informing him of a possible break in the prisoner ranks. Along with two other Asian women, she provides relief from the heavily male cast. In contrast to the stark scenes of the men on trial or awaiting questioning and torture in the jail, the teahouse scene plays to gendered stereotypes of Japanese women as subservient and available. The music is soft, the costuming feminine. The set, while minimalist, contrasts with the austerity of the prison and courtroom.

The establishing shot shows gauzy curtains split over a doorway and pauses over a geisha with an elaborate hairstyle entering the room, note in hand. She kneels next to another waiting geisha, who looks down at the piece of paper she has been given. They both glance over to another part of the room, where Isabel Cooper's character is pulling away from the table where the general and two other men are having tea.

The camera closes up on a three-quarters profile of Isabel-as-geisha as she kneels near the general and his men. The role she plays—a woman in waiting—is reflected in the impassive expression on her face. The other two women school their faces similarly.

Isabel Cooper's geisha receives the note. She glances down at it, then rises to deliver the note, walking mincingly to the general. She says softly in Japa-

Flirting with the general. *The Purple Heart*, film still. Twentieth Century Fox.

nese, "This just came." He thanks her, then, looking more closely at her face, flirtatiously addresses her. She coquettishly smiles back, then retreats to her post. This shift in her expression is dramatic—it is as if she were animated only when addressed by the general, a blank canvas reflecting his desire back to him.

The short scene—she is in the film for less than fifty seconds—establishes Asian women as passive receptacles whose purpose is activated by male interest. It is a durable fantasy, requiring no explanation. It is one the West holds secretly dear even as it imagines itself to be the liberator that saves Asian women from Asian men.[25]

☙ ☙ ☙

The Purple Heart premieres in 1944, crowding Isabel Cooper's other role as Miss Columbia at the Filipino community fundraiser supporting MacArthur's heroic return. *The Story of Dr. Wassell* also opens that year, both films garnering critical and popular acclaim. Unsurprisingly, neither of the films' reviews mentions her or even lists her in the cast (with the exception of the brief *Variety* review), underscoring how films compound the uncredited work of women like Isabel Cooper.

Little Sergeant. *The Story of Dr. Wassell*, film still. Paramount Pictures.

The Gary Cooper–led *Dr. Wassell* also borrows its plot from real life, that of a navy doctor who shepherded nine wounded American sailors through the wartime landscape of Java to eventual rescue.[26]

The major speaking roles for Asian actors are taken up by Philip Ahn as Cooper's noble Chinese assistant, Ping, and Carol Thurston in brownface as another Javanese nurse—the unfortunately named Tremartini—whose love for an American soldier slips into the absurd. In one scene, Thurston performs the obligatory tropical dance for cheering soldiers.[27] The rest of Cecil B. DeMille's massive nonwhite cast give the film its local color.

Cast as "Little Sergeant," Isabel Cooper plays a Javanese nurse tending to wounded American sailors stranded on the island of Java. The role is initially more substantial: it is a named role in the script and studio production paperwork, though not in the final version of the film itself.[28] Perhaps Thurston, in brownface, playing the ridiculous caricature of a nurse in love, took up too much oxygen.

I think about the hopes riding on this credited role, and how they are left on the cutting room floor. Echoes of an earlier sentiment Isabel Cooper expresses to Drew Pearson filter through: "I'd been so disappointed so many times before, I placed very little confidence in this thing materializing."[29]

In the end, the character she plays is completely forgettable, reflecting how the people and landscapes of imperial wars are understood to be incidental to empire. She barely registers onscreen—washed out in contrast to the flashy Tremartini, who is played for laughs as a native woman comically obsessed by one of her white American patients. Tremartini is meant to be funny because the soldiers and the audience are in on the secret that women like her are ultimately for leaving. Her lack of awareness about the one-sidedness of her obsession creates the space for her awkward and frustrated exchanges with the wounded soldier, the object of her unrelenting desire. She refuses to be unrequited.

Meanwhile, Isabel Cooper's Javanese nurse hovers in the background, attending to bandages, checking on patients, helping them dive for cover during air raids. Unlike the flamboyant Tremartini, her presence does not demand love that will never be given in return.

I think about whether Isabel Cooper sees herself in Little Sergeant or Tremartini. Or if she wishes she had the bigger role: she was, after all, familiar with dancing for an admiring audience of soldiers, and with the pale, pale shade of their imperial desire.

Rendered as the living props of a set meant to stand in for Java, Isabel Cooper and the other actors of color cannot be imagined as the subjects of the film. *Dr. Wassell's* dogged focus is on the "real-life" self-sacrificing and humble hero who stands up for the wounded soldiers under his care who are deemed unworthy of evacuation. Their perilous journey through Java is held together by the doctor's belief in the full humanity of "his casualties," something that the Javanese are never accorded.

As the Japanese army closes in, the abandonment of the Javanese people seeps through. Dr. Wassell's heroic stand has its limits. As they race toward a ship that might carry them to safety, the sacrifices made to save the American soldiers elucidate whose lives are worth saving and whose are expendable.[30]

The Javanese nurses working at the makeshift field hospital caring for the soldiers, who cover them during a bombing raid at the risk of their own lives, disappear or die soon after the opening scenes (except for Tremartini). The film doubly erases the kind of violence and trauma experienced by the people of Java—whose home is devastated by a war not of their own making. They operate as rural background as the bombs fall, their homes and villages reduced to kindling, merely checkpoints to be left behind on the escape route.

Little Sergeant, whose brief appearances onscreen are not enough to render her with any kind of complexity, fades away like the good soldier she is. Indeed, one barely notices when she is there and when she disappears. There is more at work here than the uncredited, whittled-away role of Little Sergeant, but that, too, is part of a long and repetitive history of colonial love.

Pulled back into uncanny scenarios of intimacy in Hollywood's doubling of real-life war events, Isabel Cooper becomes witness and collaborator yet again. Onscreen, she finds herself in proximity with empire and its architects, playing roles that she had previously inhabited, more or less, in real life. Between real and reel, the roles remain uncredited, part of the collateral costs of an empire building, defending, and weaving myths about itself.

The sum total of Lolita's lines, in order, with no context, in *I Was an American Spy*:

Naku, we are next, señora. Everyone is going and we sit. Oh, so I do not think the sergeant, he will come.

Si, señor.

He will not come, señora.

Perhaps he cannot. For two days we wait in the sun. It is too quiet. Everyone else has gone to the hills.

You see, señora? Something has happened. It's not good to stay.

Please do not be angry with me, señora. You wish to stay, I will stay with you.

It's about time you're afraid. I'm tired of being the only one sensible.

Huwag mo ako utusan!

Oo, kawawa, no?

In Cavite, señora.

We're both Oriental types, so wouldn't be crowding the American types at all.
　—Chabing Cooper, 1948

In the City of Angels, Isabel Cooper learns quickly that many more wings are clipped than take flight. Behind the soft-focus shine of the Ava Gardners and Gary Coopers—in whose films she appears—often nameless actors toil, competing with each other for time on camera, hoping to catch the eye of the director, often settling for being a blurred face in the background or, at best, voicing a word or two of dialogue. It is barely a living.

Chabing—the name she begins to use—pieces together something resembling a body of work that captures both Hollywood's sexualized and gendered fantasies about imperialism and its adamant relegation of actors of color to bit parts. Again and again, the films she appears in and the roles she plays underscore the film industry's willingness to dabble in the exotic palette of racial fantasy, if only to tell stories that white people love to tell about themselves.[1] She amasses a list of stock racial types in the years after the war. They are predictable roles for a mixed-race woman in Hollywood, whose looks can be made to stretch over the range of racist delusions it holds dear.[2] It is not as if white women did not play these parts—Chabing became all too familiar with speaking roles going to actors in redface, brownface, and yellowface while she was called on to silently lend authenticity to their stilted speech.[3]

It is quite a collection, her trophy case of racial types. It is an ensemble of suspect desires distilled into bit parts. From the nurse and geisha roles that the war generated, Chabing moves on to play a Siamese harem wife, a Native American woman, a Chinese servant, a Chinese American secretary, a hula dancer, another Chinese servant, a Filipina servant, a Caribbean slave girl, and an "Oriental" belly dancer. A few are credited speaking roles with named characters. In lower-budget Charlie Chan films, she has full scenes exchanging dialogue with the lead. In others, she is just another body providing color, being a type.

She is pragmatic about just the kinds of roles someone like her will be able to get. In a 1948 letter to Drew Pearson, she asks for his assistance in acquiring a Screen Extras Guild card, which requires the sponsorship of a top studio executive.[4] Her Screen Actors Guild membership only entitles her to the rare bit part: "I'm sure one or two more members in the S.E.G. won't ruin the movie industry. We're both Oriental types, so wouldn't be crowding the American types at all."[5] Manila's New Filipina, who had catapulted to fame on her American look and style, recasts herself as the "Oriental type."

HULA GIRL, STAGE RIGHT

About halfway through her Hollywood career, Chabing plays a hula dancer. It is perhaps inevitable that she finally plays one on film, because in real life, when not on call for some bit part, she dances what passes for hula (and other exotic numbers) in a nightclub.[6] The role distills the life of someone who dreams Hollywood dreams but is derailed along the way. The nightclub scene in which she is grateful to appear as an extra represents the moment when the lead character hits rock bottom.

My Dream Is Yours is a Technicolor musical crafted for Doris Day.[7] Its plot turns around a talent agent who discovers the golden voice of Martha Gibson (Day) and persuades her to move to Hollywood with no real employment in hand. Feeling desperate after a montage of unsuccessful auditions, Gibson auditions for the floor show at Club Babita, a supper club with stage curtains in tropical prints—a place like that. The seediness of this life is emphasized by the predatory club manager, who, upon hiring Gibson, orders a lackey to give her the special dressing room, the one with no lock on the door. Her talents as a singer set her aside from the nameless other girls milling about at the club, Chabing among them, who are understood to have always been subject to his casting-couch behavior. Gibson is handed a grass skirt and bra, which she looks at askance.

The next scene features Gibson singing and dancing stage center, blonde hair shining under an elaborate flower headdress, clad in a leafy print bra and sarong. She is backed by three hula dancers—wearing the cheap grass skirts and shiny silver bras she rejected, red plastic flower lei, and red flowers in

Hula girl. *My Dream Is Yours*, film still. Warner Brothers.

their hair. Smiling widely, they personify the hapa haole look popularized by Hollywood hula fantasies of the 1940s.[8]

Chabing is the hula girl, stage right. She and her companions shimmy down the stage, gracefully traveling with Gibson as she works the audience with a 1928 Tin Pan Alley tune, "Nagasaki." The lyrics play to American fantasies of Pacific ports of call while the half-life of nuclear devastation in that city haunts Day's breezy rendition.[9] Gibson's vocals skim over the club—"Hot ginger and dynamite / There's nothing but that at night / Back in Nagasaki where the fellas chew tobaccy / And the women wicky-wacky-woo"—and the hula girls gyrate, shaking their hips in time to the beat of Hollywood's hula dreams. Chabing and the other two women weave their way through tables, smoothly navigating patrons, waiters, and each other. Their choreography is practiced and smoothly performed—after all, they were cast straight from the club into the film by LeRoy Prinz, the film's choreographer, who had seen the show at the Seven Seas.[10]

❀ ❀ ❀

The nightclub Chabing Cooper dances in, like the one onscreen, is a familiar landmark in places like New York, San Francisco, and Los Angeles.[11] The

Seven Seas is a watering hole for Hollywood industry players wanting to be seen and entertained, and it peddles many of the exotic fantasies that Hollywood holds dear. Along with jazz, or Cuban- and Spanish-themed music and dance, fantasies of the South Pacific and Hawaiʻi draw middlebrow white audiences hungry for the exotic.[12] Just like the movies, these showrooms and clubs are willing to cast people who look the part, who are willing to endure low pay, groping clientele, and long hours. At the Seven Seas, "across the Chinese Grauman's Theater on Hollywood Blvd. . . . very nice & charming with its tropical atmosphere," Chabing has worked from at least 1946 until 1948, and earns $57.00 a week for her troubles. She shares the stage with two other dancers who offer, among others, a "Hawaiian act," and a Samoan knife dancer named Satini who "used to be in Ziegfield's [*sic*] Follies."[13]

My Dream Is Yours depicts the work that women do at clubs like these as undesirable—exactly what Chabing had described as "distasteful" to Sam Hahn upon first arriving in Hollywood. For Doris Day's character, her nightclub performance is an act of desperation that opens her up to the seamy overtures that the fantasy of hula invites. It is the marker of her failure— *Looks like show business has given me up.* In the scene, the jealous wife of a handsy man throws a drink in Gibson's face. As she is ushered off the floor, the other three hula girls, veterans of the club, distract the audience and cover up the altercation, seamlessly moving her offstage. Gibson is rescued by her agent, who bundles her away to get her big break.

The film moves on quickly from Gibson's brief foray into this disreputable world. Yet for the three nameless women in the club who dance with her, and the other similarly costumed women serving drinks, the scene repeats, even as the camera stops recording. Night after night, they perform for audiences who ignore them, or don't ignore them enough, hoping that a chance encounter or a strategically directed smile might mean an invitation to audition or, at the very least, a "week's worth" of work that can round out rent.[14] In the scene, Chabing dons the maligned grass skirt that she wears in real life. This role is not a stretch. The overlaps between real life and the movies are painful, but they pay.

She ties the rustling plastic snugly around her waist, fiddles with the garish lei draped across her chest. These are familiar, routine gestures, much like the dance she performs. Her hair is pulled away from her face, falling in waves down her back. Her face is powdered, lipstick applied. The crew readies the lights for the scene, and she and the others are positioned onstage. Doris Day finally enters, takes her mark, and the director calls, "Action!"

Chabing raises her chin, flashes her smile, those dimples.

When the scene is over, her life rolls on.

Harem. *Anna and the King of Siam,* film still. Twentieth Century Fox.

HARRISON'S HAREM

Following the trio of war films that launch her Hollywood career, the first role not related to World War II that Chabing plays is as one of King Mongkut's many wives in Darryl Zanuck's 1946 *Anna and the King of Siam.* The film, like Margaret Landon's 1944 biographical novel, draws on Anna Leonowens's deeply embellished account of her time in Siam.

Populating Hollywood's obsessions with the harem, Isabel Cooper appears with fourteen other women to greet Irene Dunne, who plays the intrepid Anna, the British governess who has arrived at the royal palace to teach the king's innumerable children. The wives are barefoot, clad in loosely draped trousers and snug, revealing tops. In contrast, Anna is demurely covered in an elaborate architecture of hooped skirts, a full contingent of crinoline petticoats, and corset. She looks out of place but also manifestly destined to be the center of the action, the purveyor of civilization. On Anna's first night in the palace, the curious wives peer through a window screen at the strange new guest. It is the kind of flattened characterization they will have for the rest of the film.

As one of the king's "thousands" of wives, Isabel Cooper's flitting onscreen presence props up the importance of the king's status (the king is played by a yellowface Rex Harrison)—the more wives, the greater the ruler. For the most part nameless and meant to be indistinguishable from each other, the wives are the artifacts of the "strange and still half-civilized state" of affairs in Siam that Anna's liberated individualism must navigate.[15] As a homogenous mass, almost childlike and, for the most part, leading invisible lives behind palace walls, the harem verifies what is understood to be true of Asian women in the story, onscreen as well as off. *Women do not exist in Siam.*[16] It is an aphorism that Anna is determined to prove false, but the film makes clear that she is an exception to this rule.

Lumped together with the children they bear him, the king's wives are allowed to take lessons with Anna, but they are meant to be a foil to the indomitable Englishwoman, whose refusal to pander and willingness to be "a very difficult woman" stimulate the king's ire and attention. Even the king's two most important wives—his first wife and the mother to his heir, Lady Thiang, and his latest favorite, Tuptim (played in yellowface by Gale Sondegard and Linda Darnell), cannot command the respect Anna does.

The message of the film becomes clearer as it unfolds, as Anna works her civilizing magic on the king. The only women who can exist in Siam are white women.[17] The nameless wives of the king are mere vessels for his pleasure, or surrogates who bear the children that Anna will teach, substitutes for her own dead son.

There are other messages in the film—about empire, about the pale mimicry of brown people yearning for progress and modernity. Inevitably, the wives' imitation of Anna fall short, highlighting the unbridgeable gap between them and someone like Anna. Onscreen, Chabing and the king's harem orbit around the imperious Mongkut, appeasing him, filling the space around the king's table, tasting his food, and receiving instruction from Anna or the king. Silent, decorative, subservient, the king's wives are a constant reminder of the distance between the king's dreams of civilization and the backward tendencies of the Orient. In the end, the story of "Harrison's harem" is also about colonialism's continuing obsession with the sexual lives of other women, upon whose bodies it projects its own narratives of desire and revulsion.[18] Though *Anna and the King of Siam*'s black-and-white depiction of the backwardness of others recalls the Victorian era, the harem's haunting presence is a relic not so much of the past as of Hollywood's unexamined fascination with race and sex.

Chabing, hovering in the background, waiting for the king's recognition or the approval of his hired governess, might be at the margins of this story, but she is at the center of colonialism's unrelenting gaze.

The indistinct chatter that is the extent of Chabing's part in the harem de-volves into what is supposed to pass for the savage speech of Native women fighting over spoils—which happens to be the ball gown removed from the pale, pale body of Paulette Goddard's white slave Abby.[19]

Cecil B. DeMille's *Unconquered*, touted as 1947's "greatest screen spectacle," depicts the "adventures of those patriots who helped build America" and "whose daring drew the map of America across the wilderness . . . in lines of their own blood!"[20] Overwrought publicity aside, its story of a 1763 con-flict between settlers and Indians in the Alleghenies at Fort Pitt was carried out in DeMille's signature epic style.[21] DeMille was supposedly pained by Hollywood's "slipshod Indians," and his film boasted, among its 4,233 extras, 150 "Indians" (53 actual), who were listed alongside "150 copper mugs and bowls" and "40 pieces of Steigel glass."[22] In a ledger, Indians, like wives in a Siamese harem, make up an arbitrary calculus of authenticity.

The film's elaborate sets and colossal cast revolve around the brave co-lonial lieutenant, the white slave girl, and the villainous fur trader in league with the Indians. The meandering plot pulls together a number of settler co-lonial myths: captivity fantasies, the taming of the frontier by white settlers, and the triumph against Native savagery. Inevitably, Abby, who is framed as the white woman everyone wants, is tasked with driving home the vulner-ability of the heroic settler. It is another variation of colonial kink that culmi-nates in the captivity fantasy. *You've seen what they do to white women.*[23]

In the brief scene where Chabing appears, she is once again grouped with other anonymous actors in a larger gathering of Indians preparing for war against the settlers. Here, instead of being in a harem, she is part of another feminine horde who fixates on a white woman's clothes. The description of the angles, action, and dialogue in the film's production reports reads: "Ext. Guyasuta's Camp—Night 25MM CLOSE SHOT Abby's green dress, feminine hands clawing at it—CAMERA BOOMS BACK revealing young Indian squaw standing on log and holding dres [sic] up to herself with group of squaws surrounding her tearing at dress."[24] Unlike the white settler women at the ball who merely gawk at Abby's beauty in an earlier Cinderella scene, or the harem wives in *Anna and the King of Siam*, DeMille's Native women act on their undisciplined desires. They undress Abby, who is left in her petticoats and chemise, disheveled but still perfectly well lit and beautiful. She is tied with a rope, defenseless before a crowd of savage men and women. This, too, is another fantasy of captivity and rescue. Abby is subjected to a horrifying

Native women, tearing at dress. *Unconquered*, film still. Paramount Pictures.

and phallic "dance of death" with Indian men hovering perilously close to her beautiful white body, prodding at her with fire and bayonets. She twists against the ropes, gasping and flinching.

I think about other frontiers, and how DeMille's settler fantasy borrows not only from the eighteenth century but also from distant places to fill in where "real" Indians should be.[25] Playing a nameless Native woman, Chabing brings full circle how the genocidal campaign against Native peoples on the continent was exported to the Philippines. There is remarkably little difference in how both are narrated through Hollywood's dearly held tropes and racial types. Chabing, as one of the "savages" stripping off Abby's clothing, embodies a threat to white womanhood that becomes a justification for genocide.

The white actress who plays a chief's daughter married to the treacherous fur trader has the only Native woman's role with a real speaking part. In contrast to Abby's beleaguered damsel, she unsurprisingly sacrifices herself out of heartbreak because her husband prefers Abby's alabaster beauty.[26] It is a plot that Chabing has already become familiar with. This Native version of *Madame Butterfly* is Hollywood's fate for its caricatured Pocahontas or Malinche figure, *what it does to yellow and red and brown women.*[27]

It takes forty-five minutes and six takes to film the scene where the Native women fight over Abby's green dress. For six seconds of uneven screen time and one day's worth of standing around, Chabing earns $75.[28] It is more than she makes dancing hula at the nightclub, where her body, in another kind of racial drag, performs America's imperial choreography.[29]

CHINESE WOMEN, VARYING TYPES

Unsurprisingly, Chabing's most substantial roles in this period are in low-budget Charlie Chan films. These return her to small speaking parts and real minutes of onscreen time in a series that is established, recognizable, and popular. That she plays Chinese women is not an issue: the lead role of the Chinese detective is played by a yellowface Roland Winters, not the first white actor to take on the part.[30] She plays two separate speaking characters over the span of two years, attesting to the interchangeability of Asians. The roles, along with other bit parts playing Chinese women, are part of her patchwork of survival.

In *The Chinese Ring* (1947), Chabing plays the servant of a Chinese princess seeking Chan's help who is murdered while waiting in his den. The mystery unfolds, and as Chan's investigation gets underway in San Francisco, we encounter Lilly Mae Wong in the princess's apartment. While Chan performs his deductive reasoning procedure in the apartment, Lilly Mae, clad in dark Chinese pajamas, enters dramatically from another room, pointing a gun at Chan and his companions. Chan is unbothered, apparently having decided that her innocent face does not match the threat of the gun in her hand. He reveals the murder of her mistress, and Lilly Mae, aghast, denies any knowledge of it. He questions her further and is satisfied with the information she provides about the princess's activities. Lilly Mae and other members of the supporting cast trail Chan around the apartment as he deciphers more clues.

As Lilly Mae responds to the detective's questions, we get a sense of Chabing's acting once again—absent in the minuscule background parts she has had since her first two Hollywood roles. There is not much she can do with the stock character of Lilly Mae, even with her memorable entrance. She is meant merely to be a foil for Chan's inscrutable genius. But the role, limited as it is, gives her a chance to be in a scene and engage in dialogue with the lead. The ambiguous accent she uses for the scene sounds more Filipino than Chinese, but given Winters's own egregious caricature of a Chinese accent, it is more than serviceable.

The next time we see Lilly Mae, she, like her princess, is a corpse. She has been shot with a poison dart from the open balcony windows. We see only

Lilly Mae. *The Chinese Ring*, film still. Monogram Pictures.

the bottom part of her prone body: Chan lifts her wrist to feel her pulse, then immediately proceeds to investigate.

It is Chabing's only onscreen death. She and the woman who plays the princess have done their job to move a Charlie Chan mystery along. *You know, woman not made for heavy thinking but should always decorate scene like blossom of plum.*[31]

As a decorative flower, Chabing is, according to *Variety*'s review of the supporting cast, "adequate."[32]

Perhaps both Winters and his director, William Beaudine, are impressed by her work: she is shortly recast as Miss Lee, a receptionist, in her second Charlie Chan film in as many years. Perhaps we are not expected to recognize her in a different role, with a different accent.

The convoluted mystery of *Shanghai Chest* turns around an insurance scam and the murders that ensue out of greed. Chabing plays less of a decorative flower than a recalcitrant Chinese American professional. Her take on the role pokes fun at what the audience's expectations might be of a Chinese secretary in Chinatown. The scene with Chan and the intractable Miss Lee opens at the insurance office and starts off with a somewhat sharp comedic exchange. Chan greets Miss Lee in Cantonese, and she enunciates in

Miss Lee. *Shanghai Crest*, film still. Monogram Pictures.

American-accented English. *I'm sorry but I do not speak Chinese.* It is an un-expectedly sly staging that sends up yellowface, language, and authenticity. No one is more Chinese than the white man with scotch tape on his eyelids who can speak the mother tongue, least of all the Filipina playing a Chinese American secretary.

Chabing's Miss Lee is supremely unhelpful and delightfully unwelcoming—playing against type. This Asian woman repels rather than accommodates and has no time for the detective's persistent questions. Once she confirms that he is a detective, she becomes even more uncooperative, claiming to know noth-ing about the business she works for. She successfully stonewalls Chan's at-tempts to find out more about the insurance company she works for: "I don't know anything, Mr. Chan, and I'm just here to answer the telephone."

Miss Lee's refusals are too suspicious, and the audience soon discovers her complicity in the crime. As soon as Chan leaves the office, she picks up the telephone receiver and begins to dial, reverting to the stock character of the treacherous Asian woman.

After the peak of her named roles in the Charlie Chan films, Chabing is called on to play more Chinese women—it seems she has indeed hit her stride representing "Oriental types." She plays a local woman cleaning fish in a street scene in the tortured romance *Singapore* (1947). Her uncredited role reflects the labor of Malays and Chinese who are present in much of the film, tacitly supporting the nostalgic expatriate postwar lifestyle in the British colony.[33]

In the fleeting scene where Chabing appears, she plays one of the anonymous Singaporean natives who constantly haunt the edges of the film. The amnesia-struck Linda Grahame, played by a radiant Ava Gardner, navigates the dirt roads in a pencil skirt and heels, searching for a former servant to find out more about her past. She stops to ask some women for directions, speaking in Chinese. Chabing, sitting next to another woman on the steps of a small house, smiles pleasantly, replies, and returns to scraping fish with a knife. Her companion follows up and points Grahame in the right direction.

Chabing is the "second Chinese girl," uncredited, in the 1950 crime drama *The Great Jewel Robber*. The film tracks the "straight from the headlines" case of a thief who used his Casanova charms to seduce women and rob the rich. Chabing appears as a serving girl dressed in a cheomsang (or something close enough) at a Hollywood party hosted by a wealthy widow about to be hoodwinked by the con artist. She weaves her way around the opulent ballroom, offering a tray of drinks to guests in black tie and fancy dress.

LOLITA, DREAMING

Near the end and apex of her Hollywood career, she once again plays a Filipina. In 1951, despite the fears about the truth of her age that plague her in the early filming of *I Was an American Spy*, which had prompted her to write in panic to Drew Pearson, she wraps the film as one of "the principal actors & actresses."[34] She is hopeful that this performance will generate other roles and holds dear a compliment from the producer about "how happy he was" with her work.[35] The publicity about MacArthur prompted by her earlier interview with the producer is negligible.

The same April that *I Was An American Spy* hits theaters, MacArthur returns to the United States for a victory tour of sorts. He has been ignominiously fired by President Truman, whose aim in Korea is to keep the war from expanding. With no intentions of retreating and his eye on the Republican presidential nomination, MacArthur plays to the public. He gives a dramatic speech criticizing the president at a joint session of Congress.[36] Ever the showman—perhaps he has learned from past teachers—he ends with a melodramatic flourish, quoting an old army song: "Old soldiers never die, they just fade away." The line belies his ambition. His speech is televised. MacArthur is in the air once again.

Despite this historical convergence of MacArthur's return and Chabing's past relationship with him, the film's publicity people focus on the real-life Claire Phillips—"Heroic Actress-Spy of Philippines"—to promote the film. All Chabing has to show, after all, are the faded compositions of her former father figure. Hired as a consultant to the film after Allied Artists purchases the rights to her book, Phillips embraces the spotlight as "Manila's Mata Hari."[37] She is written up in the *Los Angeles Times* and makes public appearances.[38]

The stories of the war's white heroes and heroines are film-worthy, full of high drama, suspense, and suggestive intrigue.[39] The studio's catchphrases for the film tout it as "A Thrilling and Unforgettable Saga . . . Of One Woman's Heroism . . . The Taut, Tense, True Story of a Courageous Girl . . . Who Risked Dishonor and Death . . . To Fight for Her Country's Flag."[40] Phillips's story holds some parallels to episodes in Isabel Cooper's life: Phillips, too, toured as a singer and dancer in Asia as a young woman and had a clientele of officers and civilians during the occupation. Like Isabel Cooper, Phillips learned to parlay sensuality and its promises into survival. But where Isabel Cooper used her illicit relationship with the general for her own gain, Phillips extracted secrets from her Japanese patrons to aid the war effort and, ultimately, MacArthur. Neither Isabel Cooper's real encounters with MacArthur nor those she fictionalized for her curious producer hold up to the shiny medal plot of *American Spy*.

Ann Dvorak is cast as Phillips.[41] Chabing plays Lolita, her Filipina servant. The three women are all about the same age, their lives intersecting peculiarly through the production. As Lolita, Chabing must also pretend to be two decades younger, underscoring her casting as subservient to the filmic Claire Phillips. She observes Dvorak and Phillips becoming close over the course of filming, their friendship cultivated by the story of war and heroism in empire's strange circuits.

American Spy turns on Phillips's exploits as "Madame High Pockets," a code name playing on her use of her décolletage as the hiding place for information. She is the proprietress and hostess of the exclusive Club Tsubaki, where she draws out classified military secrets from lonely Japanese men. In the film, glamorously dressed entertainers sing sultry torch songs to men distracted by tropical cocktails and the beautiful women who serve them. Meanwhile, in the kitchen, members of the resistance, some of whom are Claire's staff, traffic food, medicines, arms, equipment, and highly sensitive information to the guerrillas in the mountains.

The film begins with an explanation for Claire Phillips's motivation: shortly after Manila is attacked in December 1941, she witnesses her husband's death

Lolita doing laundry on the move. *I Was an American Spy*, film still. Allied Artists.

at the hands of Japanese soldiers. She returns to the city and takes on the identity of another entertainer, Dorothy Fuentes, an Italian Filipina mestiza who had died in the attack.

As Claire Phillips's faithful servant, Lolita watches over her mistress and her daughter while Claire carries out her plot of revenge. The majority of her speaking scenes occur in the first twenty minutes of the film, when she, Claire, and Claire's daughter flee Manila after the Japanese attack. They trudge through the countryside, lingering at an abandoned home to rendez-vous with Claire's lover, an American soldier. Lolita is pessimistic, anxious, doubtful of her mistress's happy reunion with her sergeant. She tries to tem-per Claire's unswerving conviction about the integrity of her lover's promise. Chabing infuses them with truth: she is all too familiar with unfaithful sol-diers and their broken promises.

The absence of spirit and hope in the sum of Lolita's lines identify her as clearly unheroic, someone who would not risk everything in conditions that would wilt the most hardy of souls. *It's about time you're afraid. I'm tired of being the only one sensible.* They are at odds with many of the choices that Isabel Cooper has made in her life. But as Lolita, Chabing plays someone afraid and sensible. Her task is to be the foil for the brave, unconventional protagonist. Diminutive next to her mistress, she is costumed in modest skirt and blouse, the uniform of a native working class. She is afraid for all their lives as they follow Claire's desperate flight from Manila, through the jungles, and back again, but her fear and need to survive never overshadow the intensity of Claire's love and desire for revenge. All her scenes in the film have to do with serving her mistress, even in the midst of war. It is as if she has no family or history of her own, and only has meaning or life in relation to Claire Phillips, heroine.

American Spy is based on reality, but it is also steeped in colonial fantasies about the place of natives in heroic tales.

❋ ❋ ❋

I linger over her scenes in this film. They are among the last that she records.

The "excellent," "principal" role she describes in her letter to Drew Pearson is not memorable, although for an Asian actor in Hollywood it is substantial. She is listed on the second page of roles in the opening credits, third down, and before Philip Ahn, a Hollywood regular.[42]

Lolita first appears onscreen listening to the transistor radio reporting on the attack and the evacuation. Claire tells her to turn it off, but Lolita, undeterred, urges her mistress to take action. Her role as the nursemaid to Claire's daughter becomes more apparent when the sergeant stops by the club and makes plans with Claire to meet up once they evacuate the city. The camera zooms in, framing the white family of soldier, entertainer, and adopted daughter. It pans to include Lolita when the sergeant directs her to dress her young charge.

Si, señor.

As Claire's companion during evacuation, Lolita walks country roads and hides out in deserted buildings, all the while caring for Claire's daughter, doing laundry, and feeding them. She is the receptacle of Claire's unreasonably wild hopes, the one who must urge her to move on in order to survive when all signs point to their abandonment. *Please do not be angry with me, señora. You wish to stay, I will stay with you.* Claire is the generator of will and desire, of action, and Lolita merely her faint echo.

The sheer madness of Claire's hopes is vindicated by the arrival of a Filipino guerrilla sent by her fiancé. They leave with him, after a testy exchange where Lolita tells him not to order her around. *Huwag mo ako utusan!* They trek through the jungle, where Claire's fiancé compromises the safety of his fellow soldiers by lingering. A priest awaits them. Claire and the sergeant kiss.

War wedding. *I Was an American Spy*, production photograph. Allied Artists. Photograph courtesy of Christina Rice.

Lolita offers Claire a white camellia for her hair, her sole adornment for the hasty ceremony. Claire and her sergeant marry to the drone of the Spanish priest, interrupted by the shelling of bombs, and a plaintive lone harmonica. Lolita watches as they kiss again. His unit pulls out, heading for Bataan. They kiss once more, and Lolita is left to comfort her mistress as she collapses in despair. When they learn later on that Corregidor has fallen, Claire leaves her daughter with Lolita while she searches for her husband. The two Filipinos in the scene comment on the distraught but determined Claire: *Oo, kawawa, no?* An expression of pity and empathy for the depth of love that only the principal characters are allowed to feel, despite their own desperate straits.

We do not see Lolita again until well after Claire—now widowed and going by Dorothy Fuentes—has established her upscale nightclub. We find out that Lolita and Claire's daughter have been hiding out in Cavite when they make their way to the club. They are a brief reminder of Claire's personal stakes as she continues to draw out information from her Japanese clientele, but they are quickly hidden out of sight in the club's private rooms. We see Lolita one final time, when Claire dangles a fan dance as a lure to delay the departure of a Japanese officer in order to buy time to pass on what she knows about his planned offensive. Lolita helps assemble the makeshift giant fans that Claire uses for a dance that is only hinted at in the film.

There are scenes that do not include Lolita, but which instead hold echoes of Isabel Cooper. Claire defending her virtue, slapping a too-insistent Japanese patron. *I'm no Madame Butterfly!* The echoes of Isabel Cooper's life as a vaudeville performer filter through in the identity of Dorothy Fuentes, reincarnated by Phillips as her secret identity. It comes into view in the glimpse of Fely Corcuera, the Filipina entertainer on the club's staff who sings a traditional Japanese song to her homesick audience. The soldiers are of a different race but are occupying forces just the same. The film strongly hints that, in order to survive, the women of the club may have had to perform intimacies offstage. All these are familiar to Isabel Cooper.

       ❊ ❊ ❊

In the interim, a barely-there role—more of a prop—in *Anne of the Indies*, as a slave girl, sold in the flesh markets in the Caribbean. It is only later that I come across a production photograph that clearly captures Chabing's features and confirms that she was, indeed, in the film.[43]

       ❊ ❊ ❊

When *American Spy* is released, its reviews are tepid at best and derogatory at worst. Despite the allure of a real-life story, and the sensationalist marketing of the film—*the Reader's Digest Sensation that Rocked the Nation!*—it falls flat. *Variety* deems it "rather ordinary" and "spottily directed."[44] *Boxoffice* pronounces the film "replete with cliches" and weighed down by a "lusterless cast" and a "hackneyed" script.[45] Chabing is mentioned with other Asian cast members like Richard Loo, Leon Lontoc, and Philip Ahn as "among those doing assorted types with just mild results" or "only average."[46]

As Lolita, Chabing fails to make an impression, just as *American Spy* fails to live up to the drama of real life. I think about the fervent wish she releases into the world, and her hopes that this role, this time, might be the one. I think about how tired she must be after more than a decade of bit parts and long hours at the nightclub. *Looks like show business has given* me *up.*

She does not write Drew Pearson again after the letter announcing her excitement and fear about *American Spy*. It is unclear if he ever writes her back.

✳ ✳ ✳

Isabel Cooper's last archival traces appear in a letter, as a postscript, and in an eighty-second performance in a black-and-white burlesque film. Her last role comes on the heels of her biggest (if most disappointing) part in *American Spy*.

In 1952, Sam Hahn writes Drew Pearson about a political matter. At the bottom of the typed page, almost as an afterthought, he reports that he is finishing a settlement for "MacArthur's girlfriend," one that will result in a "substantial sum of money." He notes that she is a return client: the case is the fourteenth that he has handled for her.[47] There is no record of how Isabel Cooper dealt with this windfall, what precipitated it, or how long it was able to support her.

About a year later, she makes her last and most confounding film appearance.

It is the kind of performance that charts the edges of her desperation and puts the final weights on a sinking career.

✳ ✳ ✳

It is a decade since Hahn first met Isabel Cooper over lunch at Drew Pearson's request. *The little lady confided in me that she can dance and that she did dance in Reno for a living, although she found it distasteful.*[48] She comes full circle in her final film appearance.

Her last role, billed as Chabing, is in the low-budget exploitation film *The Art of Burlesque*. She performs what passes for a belly dance to what passes for Middle Eastern music.[49] The film, ignominiously going by the alternative titles of *The Professor Misbehaves*, *The Gay Exotics*, *Striptease College*, and *Striptease College Girls*, embodies her fear of performing distasteful dancing for a living.

The fake documentary of a striptease college is no more than a vehicle to show off women in various states of undress.[50] It features scantily clad coeds under the tutelage of a bungling professor training them for burlesque. Some of the actors are professional burlesque performers, at home in dishabille and nudity. Others are less so. The audience is treated to a curriculum of near-naked calisthenics for toning bodies, an anatomy lesson on proper proportions (with silhouettes projected against a screen), an au naturel lesson on the benefits of the outdoors, and a narrator stringing together a plethora of jokes involving bananas, woodpeckers, and cats.

Chabing. *The Art of Burlesque*, film still. Stewart-Raimond Productions.

I think about young Isabel Cooper, playing at innocence on Manila's vaudeville stage. *Nice Pussy, Pussy, Pussy; / Anybody seen my cat?* Or about a time when an onscreen kiss was a scandal to be weathered. The paths Chabing Cooper has taken to this point are predictable and tragic.

Much of *The Art of Burlesque* features a parade of women in the "college" dressed in pasties, sheer gowns, and lingerie. Their educational journey ends with many of the graduates of the program going to France for further study. It is here that we encounter Chabing. By this time, the thin attempt at a plot has been abandoned, the narrator fades away, and the last half of the film is more bluntly voyeuristic, with solo burlesque routines one after another set in a bare Parisian salon.

The different types featured—from an imitation buxom Marilyn Monroe to a statuesque Swedish lass—are white except for two who play to Oriental-ist fantasies. Chabing is one of them.[51] Of all the burlesque performers, she alone does not shed clothing.

She slinks into the room to the strains of music meant to evoke harem fantasies. She is dressed comparatively modestly, with only her midriff and one shoulder bare. The long, flared skirt she wears is fitted to her trim waist and accented by a sequined girdle. She wears a veil that falls from a small headdress and drapes under her chin, so as not to hide her face. Her feet, in silver sandals, peek through as she shimmies around the room.

There is little sensuality to her dance: her arm movements, meant to accentuate her figure and the lines of her body, are stiff and almost frantic. She smiles alluringly, determinedly baring her teeth, on occasion looking directly at the camera. She shakes her hips, circling the space and occasionally pausing for effect with a pose meant to be seductive. She spins around the room, shrugging her shoulders, undulating her extended arms. There is a quality of a marionette to her movements; her flourishes are contrived.

The camera zooms in, cutting her body in half, which exaggerates the jerkiness of her dance. It pans out again, and she beckons to the viewer, knees bent, hips swiveling, with a pulling motion toward her body. She glances at the camera swiftly, batting her eyelashes, flashing her dimples, dipping her chin coquettishly. Her gaze is still compelling.

She performs one minute and twenty seconds of painful burlesque with little grace and an air of desperation. Her arms describe circles in the air. They flap like the wings of an agitated bird.

Finally, she makes her way to the back of the room, where the dancer before her had exited. Her performance over, she shrugs playfully at the audience. In the moment before she leaves the frame, she drops her act. The difference in her posture is stark. It is a mere second, but the honest moment that is supposed to be saved for the wings is captured onscreen.

She does not want to be here. *The little lady confided in me that she can dance and that she did dance in Reno for a living, although she found it distasteful.*

She is tired. She has performed this and other racial types onscreen and off, night after night, to different audiences.

The Art of Burlesque is a fake documentary, but it is perhaps truer to Isabel Cooper's life than any of her other films.[52] In this film, the actresses have roles and are credited by their stage names (Dora Dare, Lotta Class, Miss Dimples). Chabing is credited as herself.

The film is shot in 1953, and released in 1954.[53] There are no extant reviews of her last film appearance, or records of where it was shown.

※　※　※

Her onscreen body—playing racial types in bit parts—constitutes the last traces of her archive. In the final years of her movie career, Isabel Cooper has the spare frame of someone who has been forced to shed her expectations and her hopes. She has always been lean, but her famed dimples now barely register in her hollowed cheeks.

I think back to the studio portraits she had taken a decade earlier, of the soft curve of her face, the optimism in her gaze. That woman has been whittled away by the relentless grind of Hollywood and by the stunted repertoire accorded to women like her.

There are no other roles after 1953. Isabel Cooper's archive is silent until her death in 1960, when a death certificate is filed. It is the last place she is identified as an actress.

In pursuit of Isabel Cooper, I find myself in New York City in March 2014, during a cold snap. A small gallery in Chelsea is hosting a solo exhibit by artist Miljohn Ruperto, an eponymous meditation on Isabel Rosario Cooper.[1] With so little material about her, I have become a jealous collector of her bare traces.

The exhibit grapples with Isabel Cooper's ghost. I am struck by a particular short film that makes up part of Ruperto's multimedia assemblage, and which plays in my head long after I return to Honolulu.

The Reappearance of Isabel Rosario Cooper is minimalist. Shot in grainy, desaturated color that appears black and white, its entirety frames a long corridor, where a faceless, shrouded figure slowly emerges, approaching the viewer. The phantom is just barely visible against the shadows. It makes slow progress. Staring at its barely discernible silhouette begins to play tricks with the eye. Before the specter can be fully revealed, it recedes down the hallway, melting back into the dark recesses of the passage.

Matching the film's visual tone, its lone sound element features a woman singing a plaintive torch song, unaccompanied. I find out later from the artist that it is a version of the 1920s song "Thinking of You." The singer's wistful delivery echoes throughout the small gallery space in New York—*I fall asleep at night. . . .* The mood of the film is despairing, disquieting. It plays on a loop, one of a trio of short films that make up part of Ruperto's exhibit.

Given the patchwork of Isabel Cooper's life, and the particular version of her story that becomes most legible, I am drawn to Ruperto's rich imaginings. He grapples with questions about lost stories, about people who are understood not to matter, and how an archive might be mined, undermined, and reimagined in the process.[2] It is an exercise that others have struggled

The Reappearance of Isabel Rosario Cooper, film still. Courtesy Miljohn Ruperto.

with—the meaning and stakes of piecing together histories from the margins. Jenny Sharpe, mulling over the lost histories of slavery's past, asks, "But what if the story was not recorded from the start? What if the ghosts of the past are spirits that are doomed to wander precisely because their stories have not been told?"[3]

Rife with ghosts, Ruperto's exhibit wrestles with untold stories, with habitual plots and their hauntings. Its mixed and open approach to Isabel Cooper's life contends with not only the question of who she was, but also how the genres that have narrated her carry out the quiet violence of history's work. Perhaps ghosts coalesce to urge a different story into being.

❀ ❀ ❀

A glaring example of stories that ultimately shove Isabel Cooper into a doomed plot (these are part of a long tradition): In 1976, two years before William Manchester published his definitive MacArthur biography, the *National Enquirer* got the scoop.[4] "Passionate Letters Reveal . . . the Sensational Love Affair of 50-Year-Old Gen. Douglas MacArthur—& a 16-Year-Old Filipino Girl" outlines the "torrid love affair" evidenced by "never before published letters."[5]

On the ten-year anniversary of his death, MacArthur was likely rolling over in his grave. The short, four-column article not only told the tale of how the existence of the letters defanged his libel suit against Drew Pearson, but also gleefully included prize passages confessing to his "starving, panting body" and longings that made him feel "ill and faint." The *Enquirer*'s readership is subjected to long quotes that detail MacArthur's fantasies and memories of lovemaking, the article's solution to not being able to reproduce the letters themselves. After touching on the discordant end of the affair, which includes the tale of the libel suit, the article concludes with both their deaths, contrasting MacArthur's "hero's funeral" with Isabel Cooper's "friendless" suicide.

While rumors had certainly swirled in Manila, Washington, DC, and Los Angeles, the *National Enquirer*'s salacious report was the first open resurrection of the scandal of "the beautiful Isabel Rosario Cooper." Other accounts that follow are more or less faithful to this version. In many ways, its repetition in later biographies, film documentaries, news columns, websites, and social media threads contributes to the real disappearance of Isabel Cooper, the flattening out of who she was. She is buried by the sheer volume of depictions as "the girl," "the teenage lover" whose life was defined by her attachment to the general. Her "unsuccessful marriage and divorce" and suicide are implicitly tied to his supposed abandonment.

I discover that she has made it into someone's list of Top Ten Military Scandals.[6] In this, her story follows a familiar pattern where historical figures from the margins come into focus only in that moment when their lives intersect with those who are deemed to matter. These stories of Isabel Cooper that constitute her recurring afterlives are definitive and authoritative in their narration. They contract her life to this one pinpoint moment of infamy as "his 'Dimples.'" While sometimes stretching to include details on the "Queen of Philippine Vaudeville," they inevitably shrink back to tired and comfortable patterns.[7]

In their insistence on binding Isabel Cooper's story to these conventional tropes, they instigate a haunting. Hauntings, Avery Gordon points out, are the materiality of ghosts, of restive spirits *seething* because of unresolved injustice.[8] Isabel Cooper lingers in ghostly form, in imaginings and other vestiges not only perhaps of deep resentments and the fury of violent, unaddressed wrongs, but also because of the slow ruin of a cage.

The sheer sedimented power of these repeated stories constrain her. They have weight, they hold her down, these projections of other people's desire for whom Isabel Cooper has become a convenient, glamorous, and scandalous vehicle. These are the cages that confine her, fashioned by the social limits which colonial and Filipino patriarchies imposed on mixed-race women of a certain class whose ambiguous loyalties and refusal to conform caused anxiety. The bars are soldered by the kinds of stories through which women like Isabel Cooper—those unruly subjects of empire—are always narrated.

The power of haunting, the unruliness of ghosts, regardless, seep through. Over sixty years after her nearly anonymous and lonely death, Isabel Rosario Cooper continues to incite interest and obsession. The woman buried in an unmarked grave in Culver City has a posthumous fandom. Among Isabel Cooper's ghostly, insistent manifestations in writing, visual art, social media, and other unlikely places are attempts to tell her out of plot. They counter the limited ways she has come to be legible, wrestling with her afterlives as a way to think through the absence and erasure of women like her.

✻ ✻ ✻

In 2008, several years prior to Ruperto's exhibit, Isabel Cooper appeared on-stage once again, in a small theater in Minneapolis, this time as a character in a four-woman play. I did not see the play. I encounter its afterlife through a published collection of Asian American drama.[9]

Sun Mee Chomet's play *Asiamnesia* is fittingly about the kind of roles available for Asian women onstage and onscreen. Its all-Asian casting showcases the virtuosity of Asian American actors while simultaneously laying bare the racial stereotypes that limit the roles they are asked to play. It resonates with Isabel Cooper's own struggles as an actor.[10] In Chomet's play, Isabel Cooper returns to present-day Los Angeles, appearing as a character alongside Anna May Wong and Oyuki (a "celebrated geisha and wife of millionaire George Morgan") to illuminate the hard limits on Asian women's roles. They reminisce over a sushi dinner to celebrate the casting of the play's main character, Sarah, in a film.

In the stage directions, Isabel Cooper enters clad in "lingerie with a 1930s bedroom gown," "matching fluffy slippers," and bold red lipstick. The character notes are a familiar condensation of her life:

> Eurasian Filipina actress famous for first onscreen kiss by an Asian woman. Became mistress of General Douglas MacArthur when he was stationed in the Philippines when she was sixteen. She traveled to the United States and lived in Washington, D.C., as his secret mistress. After he refused to make the relationship public, he attempted to send her back to the Philippines but she insisted on remaining in the United States. She went to Hollywood to try to make it, but to no end. She committed suicide in 1960.[11]

Asiamnesia onstage. Courtesy Theater Mu archives. Photograph by John Autey Photography.

While Chomet's characterization of Isabel Cooper, for the most part, hews to this familiar summary of her life, the script itself reveals a woman with her own disruptive desires. Paralleling Manchester's most familiar account of the affair, Chomet's Isabel recounts how MacArthur wanted to keep her prisoner. Isabel declares her desire to go to law school, which is met by a gift of a black negligee and a mandate that her "duty lay in bed." Rather than acquiesce, this version of Isabel rebels: "So I snuck out and found men in every level of politics in D.C. I'm proud to say that I was most influential in the House and the Senate, whispering policy changes into the ears of many a man over nightcaps. Those were my most politically active years."[12] As the unbiddable and insatiable mistress, Chomet's Isabel exceeds her role as MacArthur's paramour, gesturing instead to the dangerous specter of a recalcitrant woman's place in politics.

Embracing the image of a jezebel while undermining it, Chomet's Isabel understands that "politics is the biggest stage in the world."[13] This depiction of Isabel Cooper treads the thin line of caricature, sacrificing complexity while leaving room for her to act on her own desires. Her frustrated ambition to go to law school is instead redirected to shape the nation's most influential political spaces through her sexuality. The play's positioning of Isabel Cooper as closely bound to the centers of power illuminates the profound reach and limits of the intimate.

In a sense, the scene convenes a haunting. The three women are ghostly figures, animated by a need to pass down their stories to Sarah in the hopes that the intervening years have transformed the dismal conditions they encountered. Isabel comments that Anna May Wong, who in real life had come to despise the "pathetic dying" roles she was always called to play, had "at least made it through."[14] There is something to how the three women, clearly damaged by the subtle brutality of Hollywood and the less furtive violence of empire, remember their lives and deaths:

> ISABEL No one was intrigued with us. I couldn't bear being shunned. So, you see, dear Anna, you earned your place in history. You live on. But I ended it, and I'm forgotten. On my gravestone, it read only: "Isabel Rosario Cooper, a.k.a, Dimples. 1910–1960. Freelance Actress."
>
> OYUKI It should have read, "Tortured and Misled by MacArthur: Hypocrite, Misogynist, and Bastard."
>
> ISABEL (in her own world) Yes.[15]

In this exchange, Isabel mourns how her existence is reduced to lines on a gravestone that could not possibly capture her life. Oyuki, increasingly drunk, attempts to recast how the real-life Isabel Cooper's suicide has commonly been framed as the result of unrequited love, but credits MacArthur as its cause once again. In both cases, despair at being "shunned" or abused leads to death, rather than the exhausting work of navigating the incessant, flexible, and intimate violence of empire. Isabel's ambiguous reply leaves room for interpretation and an interiority that cannot be inscribed in the pithy lines of an epitaph. Her *yes* signals to more that remains unsaid or is unspeakable.

The weight behind her vague response is anchored by an even longer history of Asian American women in imperial circuits that flickers onstage.[16] The repartée of the three ghosts ends with Sarah's revelation that the nonspeaking supporting role she has landed is that of Afong Moy. Sarah explains that she was "the first Chinese woman to come to America. She was one of his most successful displays. She drew 20,000 onlookers in six days. And didn't speak a word of English. . . . But the film is mostly about P. T. Barnum."[17] With that, an awkward silence descends. Anna May Wong calls for another bottle of wine, and the scene blacks out.

Conjuring an even earlier ghost of an Asian American woman displayed in the imperial circuits of 1834 New York, the scene layers nearly two hundred years of roles that have literally caged Sarah and her forebears.[18]

Their lives and their afterlives, too, are part of Isabel Cooper's story.

※ ※ ※

A few years later, Miljohn Ruperto's solo show conjures Isabel Cooper's ghost by way of contending with the power of the incarnations that have come to define her. His *Isabel Rosario Cooper* assemblage offers something out of the usual array of plots that reduce her to nothing more than the object of A Great Man's carnal desires. It is a serious and loving treatment of a flawed and shrewd woman, one that approaches her on her own terms. Ruperto's work allows for a different kind of possession by and obsession with Isabel Cooper, one that finds its pleasures not in the titillation of scandal or conjecture, but through the more arduous and unsettling work of deflection and refusal.

The ghost of Isabel Cooper that haunts the corridor in *The Reappearance of Isabel Cooper,* and which hovers over the exhibit in general, does not offer easy or definitive resolution to questions about who Isabel Cooper was. Her ghostly presence, pieced together through film, writing, and photographs, is more opaque than transparent. It is as if to say Isabel Cooper, in declining the clear outlines of imperial love, can only be apprehended through ambiguity, disappointing desires for some kind of truth, or a verdict about her life.

In the gallery's stark anteroom, one of the four white walls is taken up by eight reproductions of Isabel Cooper's black-and-white Jose Reyes Studios photographs, circa 1942, arranged in rows of four across. The photographs—which are the same ones she sent to Drew Pearson—present her in stock poses and costuming meant to signal her exotic appeal to casting agents. A photograph from the thighs up, with Isabel Cooper in cheomsang, gaze averted. Three photographs of Isabel Cooper in traditional Maria Clara dress: a head shot, smiling, looking at the camera directly; another full-body shot, hands playing flirtatiously with the butterfly sleeves; the third, which I find most compelling, with Isabel Cooper seated, gazing directly into the camera, unsmiling. The rest are a mix of head shots, smiling and serious, of her wearing lei, harbingers of her future occupation dancing hula in a Hollywood nightclub.

On the perpendicular wall, a lectern of sorts holds a typed script of a screwball comedy, *Dimples,* which the artist has cowritten with Jean Shin (made available on the gallery website). A patron who bothers to read it might see Isabel Cooper finally cast as a central character—as herself—in a Hollywood film. The script upends expectations through the genre of the screwball comedy—a "funny film noir that has a happy ending."[19] The premise is an often zany, sexually charged struggle between the male lead and a dominant female character that results in a humorous role reversal: "*Dimples* follows Cooper as the plucky protagonist who survives the disastrous romance/scandal of MacArthur, solves derailed romances of other characters, and finds her way to Los Angeles after avenging herself upon the strict 'Daddy' figure of MacArthur (without wasting much of her energy on him)." In the last scene, she looks out the window of the train on her way west, with the sentiment, "If anyone can land on her feet, it's Isabel Rosario Cooper."

The third wall of the gallery antechamber hosts a projection of a live-action color film that imagines Isabel Cooper's endless days at the Chastleton Hotel, presumably waiting for MacArthur. Featuring a silk robe- and negligee-clad Arden Cho as Isabel Cooper, the film captures solitude, confinement, and monotony through its small interior scenes: waiting at the window, gazing out, smoking; dancing alone to music; eating; arranging and rearranging furniture; napping; sorting letters and photographs; preparing herself for her lover's appearance (he never shows) by brushing her teeth and applying full makeup; eating a lonely room service dinner; going to bed. She looks bored, quietly desperate. She is silent for the whole film, and moves slowly: it is as if she must dole out the everyday activities of her life to fill the vastness of the day. The film depicts the caged energy of a woman trapped in her skin and in the room. The last scene, where she is counting on her fingers in the dark before going to sleep and upon waking, is particularly powerful. It is like she is marking time, tallying her days in prison—or perhaps the days she has left. After it is clear that this is another day of waiting, we see her silhouetted against the window, with a fading light in the background, smoking. She turns the lamp out and continues smoking. The loop begins again.

The torch song from the next room permeates the wall, haunting this imagined portrayal of her days of repetition at the Chastleton.

Ruperto's assemblage of Isabel Cooper's life draws on an intensive research process that pieces together more detail than anyone who has written about her in journalistic, biographical, or documentary fashion. Yet while making accessible the material of Isabel Cooper's life, he avoids the ethnographic impulse to provide a definitive frame to the story, choosing instead to unsettle the archive by withholding his interpretations. It is an approach that allows her story moments of refusal: the studio photographs are framed

Arden Cho as Isabel Rosario Cooper, film still. Courtesy Miljohn Ruperto.

as impenetrable, a performance of a role frozen in time rather than authenticating pieces of evidence. There is no convenient caption for how the images might be read—they ask the viewer to cast Isabel Cooper in a role (and raise the question of how ideas about who might play those kinds of roles have come to be). The documentary style of Isabel Cooper's interlude at the Chastleton provides excruciating attention to the mundane details of her confinement, yet the entire film is steadfastly unnarrated.[20] Ruperto's refusal to provide an interpretive frame leaves room for viewers not only to fill the space with their own meaning, but also perhaps to wonder why they are compelled to do so. The repetition of this refusal in the *Dimples* script—which evades the anticipated happily-ever-after resolution of marriage or reconciliation for Isabel Cooper—further troubles the expectations of genre.

The work as a whole—the studio photographs, script, and films—illuminates the contradictions in subject-focused art. The promise and failure of portraiture—of being able to fix on some knowable and definitive aspect of its subject—works in tension with both the artist's and the viewer's own imaginations and desires. Over the two days that I linger at the gallery, I am struck by the deliberation and care with which Ruperto has created this tribute to Isabel Rosario Cooper. The exhibit is not just the culmination of an artist's serious consideration of Isabel Cooper's life and work, but also itself a commentary on the inherited ways that we encounter subjects like her.

The Appearance of Isabel Cooper, film still. Courtesy Miljohn Ruperto.

It is not a restful exhibit. Miljohn Ruperto's third film of the triptych is *The Appearance of Isabel Cooper*, the compilation of her Hollywood roles through which I first encountered her moving figure onscreen. On the fourth wall of the gallery in New York, an entryway covered by a curtain opens to a small room where *Appearance* plays on a loop, paired with the ghostly *Reappearance*. The two films are run on perpendicular walls, the whirr of the sixteen-millimeter projectors a constant accompaniment. Painstakingly assembling the sum of Isabel Cooper's Hollywood screen time, *Appearance* splices together footage of the thirteen films she is known to have acted in. Ruperto's compilation removes all sound and blurs out all the other actors, leaving only Isabel Cooper in focus.

The assembled scenes showcase the range of roles she has played. Some have her in speaking parts, taking up visual real estate onscreen. In other clips, she hovers on the edge of the frame, so much so that if she were not the only image in focus, one would never have known she was there. She is a smiling waitress, serving drinks at a fancy affair to white people; she is a servant, a geisha, a wartime nurse. *Appearance* wraps with the last clip of Isabel Cooper performing her harem burlesque. She flirts with the camera, shimmying and pausing suggestively. There is a poignancy to this last fragment of film, a desperation that seeps into the seductive gesture. The last scene of *Appearance* fades to black. Exit Isabel Cooper as Chabing.

Despite including all of Isabel Cooper's speaking parts, Ruperto's assembled filmography is entirely silent, befitting the focus on Isabel Cooper's body at work, and the ways in which she has always been reduced to her appearance. Isabel Cooper is known secondarily as a working actress, though it is the notoriety of the onscreen kiss that defines her filmic legacy. Many of her roles are uncredited and difficult to track—in some ways, her Hollywood career is ghostly, an insubstantial body that did not reflect the weight of her aspirations.

As I watch Ruperto's compilation of Isabel Cooper's onscreen Hollywood roles, I am struck by the number of movies she managed to work in. As *Asiamnesia* makes clear, Hollywood was an inconstant friend to women of color, preferring them as silent accessories, preferably moribund. The flickering projection of her roles on the gallery wall documents in shorthand a body of work she managed to build despite the limited horizons for actors of color in Hollywood.

❀ ❀ ❀

Every now and then, someone posts a photograph of Isabel Cooper on social media, or a columnist resurrects her story.[21] Every time, she is tied to the general, and perhaps that is inevitable. The persistence of her ghostly figure, the way it returns and beckons, suggests that her ghost is not at rest, that these stories inevitably fail to capture the complexity of this woman and the world she picked her way through. Perhaps the point is that our own flawed desires—for clear motivation, explanations, or a box to understand her story—will always fall short, because her own creativity exceeded the materials she was given.

Pulling from a flawed archive, artists and writers like Ruperto and Chomet refuse to abide by inherited narratives, choosing instead to work with ghosts and the restlessness they conjure. They create other archives when the existing ones disappoint, or suffocate. They open up possibilities for other plots to carry a story, rattling the cages that incarcerate our imaginations. Perhaps the point is that we need not exorcise ghosts but could come to terms instead with their hauntings and their provocations.

twenty-one

*FOR FUTURE ARCHIVES,
APOCRYPHA, AND FICTIONS*

Isabel R. Cooper #56740

CERTIFICATE OF DEATH
STATE OF CALIFORNIA—DEPARTMENT OF PUBLIC HEALTH

LOCAL REGISTRATION DISTRICT AND CERTIFICATE NUMBER **7053**   **11250**

STATE FILE NUMBER		
1A. NAME OF DECEASED—FIRST NAME	1B. MIDDLE NAME	1C. LAST NAME
ISABEL	ROSARIO	COOPER
2. DATE OF DEATH—MONTH, DAY, YEAR	2B. HOUR	
6-29-60	430	

DECEDENT PERSONAL DATA

3. SEX	4. COLOR OR RACE	5. BIRTHPLACE (STATE OR FOREIGN COUNTRY)	6. DATE OF BIRTH	7. AGE (LAST BIRTHDAY)	IF UNDER 1 YEAR	IF UNDER 24 HOURS
Female	White	Philippines	January 15, 1914	46 YEARS		

8. NAME AND BIRTHPLACE OF FATHER	9. MAIDEN NAME AND BIRTHPLACE OF MOTHER	10. CITIZEN OF WHAT COUNTRY	11. SOCIAL SECURITY NUMBER
Isaac Cooper, Unknown	Josephine Unknown, Phil.	USA	Unknown

12. LAST OCCUPATION	13. NUMBER OF YEARS IN THIS OCCUPATION	14. NAME OF LAST EMPLOYING COMPANY OR FIRM	15. KIND OF INDUSTRY OR BUSINESS
Actress	20	Free-Lance	Motion Pictures

16. IF DECEASED WAS EVER IN U.S. ARMED FORCES, GIVE WAR OR DATES OF SERVICE	17. SPECIFY MARRIED NEVER MARRIED WIDOWED DIVORCED	18A. NAME OF PRESENT SPOUSE	18B. PRESENT OR LAST OCCUPATION OF SPOUSE
No	Divorced		

PLACE OF DEATH

19A. PLACE OF DEATH—NAME OF HOSPITAL	19B. STREET ADDRESS—GIVE STREET OR RURAL ADDRESS OR LOCATION		
	6244 Delongpre Avenue	INSIDE CITY CORPORATE LIMITS ☒	OUTSIDE CITY CORPORATE LIMITS ☐
19C. CITY OR TOWN	19D. COUNTY	19E. LENGTH OF STAY IN COUNTY OF DEATH	19F. LENGTH OF STAY IN CALIFORNIA
Los Angeles	Los Angeles	20 YEARS	20 YEARS

LAST USUAL RESIDENCE (WHERE DID DECEASED LIVE—IF IN INSTITUTION ENTER RESIDENCE BEFORE ADMISSION)

20A. LAST USUAL RESIDENCE—STREET ADDRESS	20B. IF INSIDE CITY CORPORATE LIMITS / IF OUTSIDE CITY CORPORATE LIMITS	21A. NAME OF INFORMANT (IF OTHER THAN SPOUSE)
6244 Delongpre Avenue	☒ CHECK HERE ☐ ON FARM ☐ NOT ON FARM	Frank E. Kennamer
20C. CITY OR TOWN	20D. COUNTY	20E. STATE	21B. ADDRESS OF INFORMANT
Los Angeles	Los Angeles	California	821 Market St., San Francisco

PHYSICIAN'S OR CORONER'S CERTIFICATION

22A. PHYSICIAN: I HEREBY CERTIFY THAT DEATH OCCURRED AT THE HOUR DATE AND PLACE STATED FROM...	22B. PHYSICIAN OR CORONER SIGNATURE	DEGREE OR TITLE
	▶ Theo J. Curphey M.D., Coroner	
22A. CORONER: I HEREBY CERTIFY THAT DEATH OCCURRED AT THE HOUR DATE AND PLACE STATED BELOW... Investigation	22D. ADDRESS HALL OF JUSTICE LOS ANGELES	22C. DATE SIGNED 7-14-60

FUNERAL DIRECTOR AND LOCAL REGISTRAR

23. BURIAL, CREMATION	24. DATE	25. NAME OF CEMETERY OR CREMATORY	26. EMBALMER—SIGNATURE (IF BODY EMBALMED) LICENSE NUMBER
Burial	7-5-60	Holy Cross Cemetery	Robert E. Snyder 3787
27. NAME OF FUNERAL DIRECTOR	28. DATE ACCEPTED FOR REGISTRATION BY LOCAL REGISTRAR	29. LOCAL REGISTRAR—SIGNATURE
CALLANAN MORTUARY	7-18-60	▶ George H. Uhl, M.D.

CAUSE OF DEATH

30. CAUSE OF DEATH		APPROXIMATE INTERVAL BETWEEN ONSET AND DEATH
PART I. DEATH WAS CAUSED BY: IMMEDIATE CAUSE (A) Barbiturate intoxication, acute	ENTER ONLY ONE CAUSE PER LINE FOR (A), (B), AND (C)	
CONDITIONS, IF ANY, WHICH GAVE RISE TO THE ABOVE CAUSE (A) STATING THE UNDERLYING CAUSE LAST DUE TO (B) Ingestion of overdose of barbiturates		
DUE TO (C)		
PART II. OTHER SIGNIFICANT CONDITIONS CONTRIBUTING TO DEATH BUT NOT RELATED TO THE TERMINAL DISEASE CONDITION GIVEN IN PART I (A)		

OPERATION AND AUTOPSY

31. OPERATION—CHECK ONE	32. DATE OF OPERATION	33. AUTOPSY—CHECK ONE
☒		☒

INJURY INFORMATION

34A. SPECIFY ACCIDENT, SUICIDE OR HOMICIDE	34B. DESCRIBE HOW INJURY OCCURRED
Suicide	as above
HOUR MONTH DAY YEAR 430 P.M. 29 60	
35A. INJURY OCCURRED ☐ WHILE AT WORK ☒ NOT WHILE AT WORK	35C. PLACE OF INJURY home	35C. CITY, TOWN, OR LOCATION Los Angeles, Calif.

The precarity of her life filters through the text on her death certificate. *Last occupation: actress. Number of years in last occupation: 20. Name of last employer or firm: free-lance.*[1] At the time of her death, Isabel Cooper had been in Hollywood for nearly two decades, although she had not worked actively in films since 1953. While her age was recorded as forty-six, she was closer to fifty.

A fifty-year-old woman of mixed race in Hollywood was as good as dead. In a film industry structured by the power of the studio and enamored of youth, the aging Isabel Cooper was already a ghost. By the time of her death, she had not worked in years.

The document is issued by the Los Angeles County Department of Public Health and describes the death of one Isabel Rosario Cooper on June 29, 1960. She is found in her home, a squat two-story modernist walk-up apartment building just two blocks south of Sunset Boulevard in Hollywood.

Frank Kennamer is listed as the Informant (*if other than spouse*).

The information on the death certificate contains his knowledge of his former wife. *Color or race: White. Age: 46.* Her death leaves the narration of her life to him. It returns her, in some ways, to the woman narrated in the 1940 census.

In the final accounting of her life, Isabel Cooper could no longer lie about her age. What is recorded is closer than the number she had claimed a decade earlier while dancing hula in the Seven Seas, fighting for bit parts in Hollywood. Her race, too, becomes fixed, rather than malleable, a tool that might lend her a leg up for a rare paycheck.

Birthplace: Philippines. Place of death: Los Angeles. The dead woman at 6422 Delongpre Avenue was a long way from home.

Or perhaps, in the end, someone like her would always find home in the heart of empire.

---

1 Carman, *Independent Stardom.*

A passing comment, shared with me by Miljohn Ruperto, that the son of Isabel Rosario Cooper's first husband remembers his father having a long-standing antagonism toward Douglas MacArthur leads me to a conversation in Berkeley in 2019. Frank Burke Kennamer, the son of Franklin E. Kennamer Jr., never met Isabel Rosario Cooper: he was born after she died. But the traces of her story filter through his memories of his father.

These are the roundabout paths that tracking Isabel Cooper sometimes takes me.

Frank Burke Kennamer is a lawyer like his father before him, but his easy, open demeanor, from what he shares about his father, runs counter to the mold. He was eleven years old when his father died in 1972, from what he suspects were the effects of alcoholism and a bad smoking habit. He remembers conversations at the dinner table with his parents, gatherings with his colleagues at their home over drinks, when his father, "never shy about holding forth," would talk about the war. In his "fog-cutter" voice, the elder Kennamer, a conservative Democrat, shared his less-than-complimentary thoughts on Nixon and MacArthur. The son had not realized that there might be a more intimate knowledge of MacArthur that fueled his father's antipathy, until he found out more about the first Mrs. Kennamer.

Frank grew up not knowing his father well. His mother, Betty Yoshiko Sato, was the child of immigrant chili farmers who lost much of their property during the Japanese internment. They married in January 1960, the same year that Isabel Rosario Cooper took her own life. Frank was born the following year. His father was not around much during his childhood. When he died in 1972, he remained mostly a stranger to his son.

Frank shares "a snatch of a remembered fact" from the days after his father's death. The solid writing desk in the living room, his father's domain, is suddenly free to a child's exploration. He remembers pulling open the main drawer where all the pens were kept and discovering a prescription bottle of pills (pink?), labeled for Isabel Cooper. He does not know who this is, and perhaps, he recalls, he might have asked his mother, who is reticent. He remembers finding out from her somehow that his father had been married once before, and that the first wife had committed suicide.

The bottle he clutches in his eleven-year-old fist has been rolling around in a drawer, mixed in with pens and the other detritus lawyers collect, for a dozen years.

❋ ❋ ❋

Barbiturate intoxication, acute. I think about the bottle of pills prescribed to Isabel Cooper and what they are for. Barbiturates are used to treat serious headaches, insomnia, or even seizures. They have a sedative effect and can be habit forming. I think about how acute poisoning might conceal causes of death that are cumulative, that build sediment over time.

According to the coroner's report, Isabel Cooper died of a drug overdose. It is implied that she did so by her own hand. According to a host of others, Isabel Cooper took her own life out of heartbreak and desolation. This suicide has been the fulcrum of the tragic romance that has defined a life that in reality was much more than being a general's mistress. The strange attachment to this explanation diminishes her.

There are many other reasons why an aging, out-of-work actress in Hollywood might take her own life. There are many other causes for despair that might have accumulated as she crossed oceans, lost family to the wide expanse of American empire, and worked in an industry that spurned her again and again. I think about "the rot" of empire—the term Ann Laura Stoler uses to describe the ruination caused by "compounded layers of imperial debris" that eat away at the body and psyche.[1]

I think about suicides willfully misrecognized and attributed to the tragic inevitability of being unloved by the colonizer. Of how much easier it is to swallow that pill than to shine a bright light on the corrosive afterlives of empire.

I think about other reasons someone might take her own life: chronic pain from a lifetime onstage, an injury, or a disease. To me, the likelihood of debilitation from work or an accident (an automobile incident in 1953 that is almost lost in a postscript), or the possible inheritance from her mother of uterine cancer (she is around the same age), is more believable than three decades of holding a torch for a general who spurned her.

I think about how a suicide can be a last act, or a curtain call that demands recognition. How it might be a last resort but also a purposeful exercise of agency, a way for someone with little control or power to decide her own fate, in whatever small way.[2] It is in line with how Isabel Cooper has always invented, always attempted to write herself through unexpected genres.

When I finally get hold of the Los Angeles County Medical Examiner's Office (multiple letters, phone calls, and an in-person visit over two years), I am told that the file containing the investigation of her death has disappeared. An investigation is always required after a suicide. Perhaps, they say, it has been lost in a flood or, since it was so long ago, taken home by a past employee before the present filing system was put in place. It wasn't, after all, a high-profile case. She died in near anonymity. The fact that she has stymied me at the end once again is perfect—it leaves room for speculation, for answers to questions we have yet to learn to ask.

I think about what a suicide note might have contained, or if she left one, and how she might have narrated herself beyond the spaces allotted on a death certificate.

Isabel Rosario Cooper's latest film, Daughter, Unknown, is the actor's most triumphant project to date. Based on the recently discovered diaries of a 1920s vaudeville star, the tightly written script traces the unlikely rise of "Dimples," the child of an American soldier and his Filipina paramour. Ms. Cooper, who plays the lead character, displays her greatest emotional range yet, as she follows the life of the itinerant performer from the stages of Manila to the glittering cities of New York, Washington, DC, and Los Angeles.

The film's journey to the screen has been bumpy. The script, initially helmed by a series of male writers, was finally handed over to the intrepid Ms. Cooper, who showed a deft hand in transferring her acting experience into writing. In an interview with Variety, she notes, "Maybe all those movies where I didn't get a lead role, or even a speaking part, paid off. It gave me a lot of time to talk with the people around the set who weren't on the screen, to understand how they went about their work." Her observations paid off. Ms. Cooper does justice to a story of anguish and grit that revolves around the main protagonist. In her debut as writer and director she displays the remarkable composure and surefootedness of a veteran filmmaker.

While there are musical numbers, the film itself is not a musical or a comedy. The stage performances are appropriate to the story, with Ms. Cooper standing out in particular in a rather somber nightclub hula scene. In keeping with the mood of the scene, she somehow brings an inflection to a jaunty Tin Pan Alley tune that gives it pathos.

The film's driving engine is the rise and fall of Dimples's career, but it also pays some attention to the star's complicated and sometimes scandalous personal life. That it does so successfully, without losing the story's main focus on Dimples, is due to Ms. Cooper's capable direction. The actors playing the three main romantic *interests, all of them well-cast unknowns, are able to keep up with Ms. Cooper's intensity. Ms. Cooper's decision to center the story on Dimples has very rightly put them in their place, accessorizing, but not driving the story.*

Ms. Cooper has described this project as a very personal one for her, and she has fought tooth and nail to have unheard-of creative control. The end product is one that gestures to the fullness of this long-misunderstood performer's life yet leaves room for the audience's imagination to take flight.

ACKNOWLEDGMENTS

This book owes much of its existence to the librarians and archivists who have so generously helped me over the course of my research. I am grateful to those who were able to help me find crucial materials as well as to those whose efforts helped me understand where the gaps in the archives lay: Jennifer Hadley at the Special Collections of Olin Memorial Library at Wesleyan University; Jean Cannon and Elizabeth Garver at the Harry Ransom Center at the University of Texas at Austin; Kevin LaVine, the senior music specialist at the Music Division, Library of Congress; Rita Cacas at the National Archives and Records Administration; Remeě A. Grefalda at the Southeast Asian Collection, Library of Congress; James Zobel at the MacArthur Archives; Laura Hall, Claudia Anderson, Allen Fisher, and Ian Frederick-Rothwell at the Lyndon B. Johnson Presidential Library; Louise Hilton, Kristine Krueger, and John Damer at the Margaret Herrick Library; Crystal Foley at the Richland County History Room in Wisconsin; John Cahoon at the Seaver Center for Western History Research; Christina Rice and the genealogy staff at the Los Angeles Public Library, Central Branch; Celia Cruz, Justin Hingco, and Mar Alcantara at the Ortigas Library; Maria Elena Clariza from the Philippines Collection, Hamilton Library; and the staff at the following archives, museums, and libraries: the Lopez Museum and Library; the Mowelfund Library; the American Historical Collection and periodicals collection at Rizal Library at the Ateneo de Manila University; the New York State Archives in Albany, New York; UCLA Moving Image Archive; the Library of Congress, Manuscripts Division; the Billy Rose Theater Collection; the New York Public Library; the Bentley Historical Library; the Harlan Hatcher Graduate Library Special Collections; the British Library, Music Division; the UCLA Performing Arts Library; the Charles E. Young Library; the Schomburg Center for Research in Black Culture; the Los Angeles Superior Court Archives; the Los Angeles County Medical Examiner's Office; and the Hamilton Library Rare Books Collection at the University of Hawai'i at Mānoa.

For allowing me to create something of my own from their memories or art, I thank Franklin Burke Kennamer, Miljohn Ruperto, and Sun Mee Chomet.

Additionally, various people have contributed to this book in invaluable ways, from sharing their own research materials to translation assistance, playing sheet music, connecting me to people who know people, giving feedback on drafts, and encouraging me to articulate the story in the form it needed to take. My gratitude goes out in particular to Genevieve Clutario, Tessa Marie Winkelmann, Nick DeOcampo, Carolina San Juan, Tanya Wyatt, Teddy Co, Mark Feldstein, Susan Schoonover, Juan Martin Magsanoc, Sharon Aikau-Foote, Andrew Leovold, and Pia Arboleda. This book has also been shaped by conversations long and short with the people whose work I draw from and who I am fortunate enough to count as colleagues near and far, in particular Mimi Thi Nguyen, Nerissa Balce, Hōkūlani K. Aikau, Oscar Campomanes, Gary DeVilles, Denise Cruz, J. B. Capino, Martin Joseph Ponce, Craig Howes, Cynthia Franklin, Vicente Rafael, Robert Diaz, Victor Román Mendoza, Nitasha Sharma, Jana K. Lipman, the late Teresia Teaiwa, Daniel Bender, Ellen-Rae Cachola, Tony Ballantyne, Roderick Labrador, Jason Ruiz, Keith Lujan Camacho, Thea Tagle, Camilla Fojas, Laurel Mei-Singh, Brian Chung, Konrad Ng, Jenny Kelly, Marisol LéBron, and Laura Lyons. I am grateful to my colleagues in my home department, particularly Joyce Mariano, Brandy Nālani McDougall, Karen Kosasa, Noelle Kahanu, Mari Yoshihara, Robert Perkinson, Jonna Eagle, Betsy Colwill, Kath Sands, Dennis Ogawa, and David Stannard, who have had to hear about this project for a long time in one form or another. I am also grateful to the Honors Program and the people in it: Sue Haglund, Sylvia Wu, Siobhán Ní Dhonacha, Jayme Scally, Rebecca Barone, and Angelique Lepordo.

Over the course of the writing, I learned so much from the work of graduate students, many of whom are now colleagues and collaborators: Kim Compoc, Kathleen Corpuz, Katherine Achacoso, Pahole Sookkasikon, Stacy Nojima, Yu Jung Lee, Eriza Bareng, Demiliza Saramosing, Liza K. Williams, Adrian DeLeon, Jeanette Hall, Kyle Kajihiro, Alexis Erum, Yana Chang, Michael DeMattos, Angelica Allen, Leanne Sims, Robert Findlay, Cheryl Beredo, Tomoaki Morikawa, Sanae Nakatani, Jesi Bennett, Logan Narikawa, and Angela Krattiger.

In traveling to different archives and places where I have presented early versions of this work, I have been gifted the hospitality and company of

Charita Castro and Theo Gonzalves; Vreneli Gonzalez-Banks and Michael Banks; Lucy and David McCanne; Caren Kaplan and Eric Smoodin; Keith Lujan Camacho; Simon Jackson; Nathan Cardon; Gary DeVilles; and Juan Martin Magsanoc.

I have been sustained during its writing by the company of Myungji Yang, Daniele Spirandelli, Ty Kāwika Tengan, Colin Moore, Sarah Wiebe, and Jennifer Darrah. Long live the UH Mānoa writing hui! This project would not be possible without the support of the Center for Philippine Studies under the directorship of Pia Arboleda, which provided subvention funding, and the Office of Undergraduate Education under Ronald Cambra.

As always, Kenneth Wissoker is an indefatigable champion and believed in this book even before I figured out how to write it. My gratitude to Joshua Tranen, Liz Smith, and the amazing staff at Duke University Press for their warm support and professionalism, to Karen Fisher for her meticulous copyediting, and to Aimee Harrison for the gorgeous cover that Isabel Cooper would be thrilled by. Much gratitude to the two anonynous Duke reviewers who gave generous and critical feedback along the way. I also want to thank Cathy Schlund-Vials, Sara Jo Cohen, Shirley Jennifer Lim, and an anonymous reader for Temple University Press, who helped me choose what story I was telling and how I could tell it, even if this book found a different home in the end.

Finally, for the home that you make with me, my love always to Inez, Noah, and Evan.

NOTES

1. THIS IS NOT A LOVE STORY

1 Elisabeth Bronfen puts it eloquently: "The death of a beautiful woman emerges as the requirement for a preservation of existing cultural norms and values. . . . Over her dead body, cultural norms are reconfigured or secured, whether because sacrifice of the virtuous, innocent woman serves [as] a social critique and transformation or because a sacrifice of the dangerous woman reestablishes an order that was momentarily suspended due to her presence." Bronfen, *Over Her Dead Body*, 181.
2 See, for example, the plot of the musical *Miss Saigon*.
3 This tale of liberation and rescue is yet another imperial fiction, the moment of the Leyte landing staged for media posterity by MacArthur a day after to accommodate photographers. See, for example, Lumbera, "From Colonizer to Liberator."
4 Rosca, *State of War*, 267–68.
5 On empire's conditional gifts, see Nguyen, *The Gift of Freedom*; see also Rafael, *White Love*.
6 Manchester, *American Caesar*, 144.
7 Manchester, *American Caesar*, 144.
8 Buhite, *Douglas MacArthur*; Rasor, *General Douglas MacArthur*; Petillo, *Douglas MacArthur*. See also Pilat, *Drew Pearson*.
9 See, for example, Ocampo, "Romances in History"; Francia, "A Sad Tale of Conquest and Betrayal"; Konted, "General Douglas MacArthur and His Dimples."
10 See, for example, *The American Experience: MacArthur*.
11 MacArthur, *Reminiscences*.
12 I use the solidus as the separator and joiner of Filipina and American here to signify the tenuous legal categorization of people from the Philippines during U.S. colonization, who were considered wards and thus eligible to travel to and work in the metropole as nationals, but were not considered eligible for citizenship (though some challenged the racial categorizations of the law, or of

Asianness). But many fell into the gray areas created by inconsistent and flex-ible racial categories: Isabel Cooper, for instance, claimed American citizenship through her father but was also of Filipino ancestry.

13 Hau, Tuvera, and Reyes, *Querida*.

14 Cruz, *Transpacific Femininities*; see also Roces and Edwards's introduction to *Women's Suffrage in Asia*.

15 Chuh, *Imagine Otherwise*.

16 Trouillot, *Silencing the Past*; Beredo, *Import of the Archive*.

17 Arondekar, *For the Record*, 5; Spivak, "Can the Subaltern Speak?"

18 Hammonds, "Black (W)holes and the Geometry of Black Female Sexuality."

19 On the absences in the historical record of slavery, see Sharpe, *Ghosts of Slavery*; see also Hartman, *Wayward Lives*.

20 Arondekar, *For the Record*, 3; Muñoz, "Ephemera as Evidence," 10. See also Mendoza, *Metroimperial Intimacies*.

22 Stoler, *Haunted by Empire*.

23 Lowe, *The Intimacies of Four Continents*.

24 Arondekar, *For the Record*, 3. See also how fiction operated as an alternative archival form and practice for Egyptian women excluded from the official rec-ord: Booth, "Fiction's Imaginative Archive."

25 See, for instance, Gordon, *The Hawthorne Archive*.

3. A GENERAL AND UNRULY WARDS

1 *New York, Passenger Lists, 1820–1957*, microfilm Serial T715, microfilm roll 4883, line 1, p. 189, Ancestry.com.

2 As discussed in chapter 6, Isabel Cooper's exact birthdate remains unknown. She claims a variety of them, and the one birth certificate that tracks the birth of a daughter to her parents does not provide a name.

3 MacArthur was posted in the Philippines from October 1928 to Septem-ber 1930. He and Cooper met sometime in 1929.

4 Petillo, *Douglas MacArthur*, 152–53; Manchester, *American Caesar*, 144; Buhite, *Douglas MacArthur*, 14–15. The suite is apartment 354, based on the address of the letters that MacArthur sends to Isabel Cooper.

5 James, *The Years of MacArthur*, 270n116. Petillo, *Douglas MacArthur*, implies this as well.

6 Manchester, *American Caesar*, 144; Petillo, *Douglas MacArthur*.

7 Manchester, *American Caesar*, 145–46. Petillo, *Douglas MacArthur*, also notes Isabel Cooper's dissatisfaction, in less condemning terms.

8 Buhite, *Douglas MacArthur*, 18.

9 Italicized phrase from Spivak, "The Rani of Sirmur," 267, not italicized in the original.

10 Tadiar, *Fantasy-Production*. For military examples of these state transactions, see Moon, *Sex among Allies*.

11 Ballantyne and Burton, "Introduction," 5.

12 See, in particular, Amy Kaplan's first chapter, "Manifest Domesticity," in *The Anarchy of Empire*.

13 Ballantyne and Burton, *Bodies in Contact*, 25.

14 Douglas MacArthur, letter addressed to "Babe," undated (likely September 29 or 30), 1929, Morris Leopold Ernst Papers, Harry Ransom Center, University of Texas at Austin.

15 The letters are addressed to "Miss Cooper" and most are signed illegibly but attributable to Douglas MacArthur. They are housed in the Morris Leopold Ernst Papers. Morris Ernst was the lawyer who represented Drew Pearson and retained copies of MacArthur's letters. No letters from Isabel Cooper are included in Ernst's collection. All correspondence from MacArthur to Cooper referenced in this book is from this collection.

16 Isabel Cooper, letter to Morris Ernst, December 6, 1934, Morris Leopold Ernst Papers.

17 This ambassador happened to be William Cameron Forbes, who had formerly served as governor-general of the Philippines.

18 These quotes are from published partial excerpts in a 1976 *National Enquirer* article, which gleefully shares the indiscretions of the passionate general. Schwartz, "Passionate Letters Reveal." A copy of the article is included among the Morris Leopold Ernst Papers. Not italicized in the 1976 article. The original letters are handwritten.

19 Endearments collected from letters, excerpts of which are also published in Carter, "The General's Dimples," 32, 39. Thanks to Mark Feldstein for sharing this source with me.

20 Douglas MacArthur, radiogram to Miss Belle Cooper, October 18, 1930, signed "Daddy."

21 As quoted in Schwartz, "Passionate Letters Reveal." The source, Dorothy Detzer, had lived some of her life in the Philippines and was more than a socialite; she was an active lobbyist for causes as wide ranging as pacificism and opposing African exploitation. That Schwartz and MacArthur biographers like Manchester label her a mere socialite is telling of how they thought about the role of women in politics.

22 Murray and Millett, *A War to Be Won*, 181.

23 Douglas MacArthur, telegram to Isabel Rosario Cooper, September 1932.

24 Castro, *Queens of Havana*.

25 ss *Morro*, New York, New York Passenger and Crew Lists, 1909, 1925–1957, Ancestry.com.

26 "Will Vaudeville Stars Shine Again?" *Philippines Free Press*, September 10, 1932.

27 Lisio, *The President and Protest*.

28 As with other claims about Isabel Cooper, no evidence is offered by these biographers, though Petillo, *Douglas MacArthur*, claims an interview or letters from one Allen Cooper, who claims to be Isabel Cooper's brother. The only trace of an Allen Cooper I have been able to find is a nine-year-old boy traveling back to the United States with his mother, Josephine Cooper, which would make him an infant when he first came to the Philippines with her in 1919.

29 The breakup telegram is dated September 11, 1934. Petillo, *Douglas MacArthur*, dates the unraveling to September 1, 1934, but it is likely that by May 1934, their relationship had gone sour.

30 U.S. National Homes for Disabled Soldiers, 1866–1938; 1930 U.S. Census; Register and Descriptive List of Convicts under Sentence of Imprisonment in the State Prisons of California, p. 44; California, Passenger and Crew Lists, 1882–1959, NARA M1764-Los Angeles, Selected Suburbs, 1907–1948; all from Ancestry.com.

31 MacArthur, telegram to Miss Bella Cooper, addressed to 1825 "F" Street, N.W., Apartment #3, September 11, 1934.

32 Anderson with Boyd, *Confessions of a Muckraker*.

33 Manchester, *American Caesar*, 150–56. Pearson casts a wide net trying to find any dirt on MacArthur: a December 4, 1934, letter from E. H. Gavreau regretfully informs him that he is unable to find any reference to MacArthur concerning "Earl Carroll's famous bath tub party." "MacArthur, Douglas, #2," box G238, 1, Drew Pearson Papers, Lyndon B. Johnson Presidential Library, University of Texas at Austin.

34 S. S. Hahn, letter to Drew Pearson, May 22, 1934, box G238, Drew Pearson Papers. Thanks to Genevieve Clutario for sharing this research material.

35 Morris Ernst, letter to Douglas MacArthur, December 4, 1934, Morris Leopold Ernst Papers.

36 Drew Pearson, telegram to Morris Ernst, undated, approximately December 1934, Morris Leopold Ernst Papers. It is possible that Pearson moved her around for her own protection, as he reports to Ernst in another undated communication that she is at the Hotel Algonquin as Miss Rosario "Ling."

37 L. S. Tillotson, letter to Morris Ernst, December 15, 1934, Morris Leopold Ernst Papers. Underlined in the original.

38 Drew Pearson, letter to Morris Ernst, December 13, 1934, Morris Leopold Ernst Papers.

39 "Promised Libel Suit Peters Out on Q.T.," *Inside Stuff* 1, no. 6 (February 1, 1935): 3–4.

40 Isabel Cooper retains Morris Ernst as her lawyer, dated December 6, 1934; unsigned General Release from Isabel Cooper to Douglas MacArthur, dated December 1934, Morris Leopold Ernst Papers.

41 Anderson with Boyd, *Confessions of a Muckraker*, 149. There is evidence in the 1940 census that she resided in Oklahoma in 1935, but she also leaves for Manila soon after: 1940 United States Federal Census, Washington, District of Columbia, roll T627_566, p. 17B, Enumeration District 1-387A.

42 The 1940 U.S. Census includes information on Isabel Kennamer (née Cooper) and her whereabouts in 1935.

43 Baldoz, *The Third Asian Invasion*; Mabalon, *Little America Is in the Heart*; Fujita-Rony, *American Workers, Colonial Power*.

44 Ngai, *Impossible Subjects*, 129.

45 *President Jackson, Seattle, Washington, Passenger and Crew Lists, 1882–1957*, arrival February 19, 1936, microfilm roll M1383_212, Ancestry.com.

46 According to a *Time* magazine article that detailed the failure of the 1935 Filipino Repatriation Act, Filipino laborers' sexual skills and prowess, especially vis-à-vis white women, were incentives for them to stay on the West Coast, and contributed to the failure of the program: "RACES: Philippine Flop," *Time*, October 3, 1938, 10.

47 Douglas MacArthur, telegrams to Isabel Rosario Cooper, various dates in 1932, Morris Leopold Ernst Papers.

48 Stoler, *Carnal Knowledge and Imperial Power*, 19. See also McClintock, *Imperial Leather*.

6. THE FARM BOY AND THE UNBIDDABLE WIFE

1 William Howard Taft, the first American governor-general of the Philippines, made famous the commonly used phrase "little brown brothers" to describe the backwardness of Filipinos to President William McKinley.

2 For more on the necropolitics and biopolitics of U.S. imperialism in the Philippines, see Balce, *Body Parts of Empire*; Kramer, *The Blood of Government*.

3 Rafael, *White Love and Other Events*. See also Winkelmann, "Dangerous Intercourse." On queer colonial intimacies, see Mendoza, *Metroimperial Intimacies*; on interracial sex in the colony, see Stoler, *Carnal Knowledge and Imperial Power*.

4 Stoler, *Carnal Knowledge and Imperial Power*.

5 The exception to accounts that do not discuss Isabel Cooper's parentage is perhaps Thomas Carter, *Then and Now*; this book about his marriage into his wife's family makes mention of Isabel Cooper's Filipino/Spanish origins. See also Molnar, *American Mestizos*. The mixed-race population in the colonies was also not only a result of Spanish or American white men and Filipinas having offspring. There were also a small number of mixed-race African American and Filipina progeny as a result of this imperial venture; see Marasigan, "'Between the Devil and the Deep Sea.'" Chinese Filipinos had also long been a result of Chinese migration to the Philippines and nearly four hundred years of Spanish colonialism. See also Chu, *The Chinese and Chinese Mestizos of Manila*.

6 "Philippines, Manila, Civil Registration, 1899–1984," FamilySearch (https://familysearch.org/ark:/61903/1:1:QKJG-P9BW), August 23, 1912, citing Birth, Manila, Metropolitan Manila, Philippines, Civil Registry Office, City Hall of Manila.

7 On her 1960 death certificate, 1914 is listed as her birth year, the information likely provided by her first husband, Franklin Kennamer. In two separate marriage documents relating to her second husband, Milton Moreno, in 1944 and 1946, Isabel Cooper records 1919 and 1921 as her birth years, shaving more than a decade off her age. In 1927, when she first traveled to the United States on the *Shinyo Maru*, she lists 1909 on the ship manifest, which corroborates the date listed on the 1930 U.S. Census. An unnamed daughter was born to Isaac Cooper and Protacia Rubin in 1912, as recorded in "Philippines, Manila, Civil Registration, 1899–1984," FamilySearch (https://familysearch.org/ark:/61903

/1:1:QKJG-P9BW). It is also the same year of birth she lists on the manifest of the *Morro Castle*, upon returning to the United States from a trip to Cuba in 1932.

8 The official end date of the Philippine-American War was 1902, according to the Philippines' new occupying power. Filipino independence fighters continued armed struggle against the United States well into the next decade.

9 "Richland County, Wisconsin, Town History," Wisconsin Genealogy Trails, http://genealogytrails.com/wis/richland/history_towns.htm; Ramos, *History of Crawford and Richland Counties*. Isaac Cooper's mother, Malinda Jane Wright, was a twenty-five-year-old widow with four very young children—two of whom were not biologically her own—when she remarried less than four months after the death of her first husband (*Republican and Observer*, December 7, 1893, p. 8, col. 4, "Cooper"; courtesy Richland County History Room). Her second husband, George Cooper, was twice her age, a Civil War veteran who nonetheless represented security for a newly unattached woman with four young children in rural Wisconsin. Malinda Jane came with a plot of land and a farm from her father as a dowry of sorts. Soon after he married her, George took over the running of the farm (1874 and 1880 Dayton Township, Richland County, Wisconsin, land survey; courtesy Richland County History Room). George Cooper gave the two younger children—Milo and Ella—his last name, but it was perhaps too much to do the same for Malinda's first husband's children by another wife (1880 Wisconsin Census; courtesy Richland County History Room). Isaac was born a year or so after Malinda Jane and George were married, and was followed by Bruce in 1877.

10 Boaz was not a fast-growing place: by the time Isaac was six years old, Boaz had a population of seventy-five. When Isaac was eight, the town of Boaz invested in a two-story school building and hired its first teacher for school-age children like the Cooper siblings (Ramos, *History of Crawford and Richland Counties*, 1015). The two younger Cooper brothers, Isaac and Bruce, were disciplined in their schoolwork—or at least in their attendance. They were not late or absent in 1884 and 1885 ("School Reports," *Republican and Observer*, June 12, 1884, p. 1, col. 3; "Boaz School," *Richland Rustic*, February 14, 1885, p. 3, col. 6). Elijah Bruce went by Bruce. Malinda Jane had three more children after her sons with George Cooper: a daughter, Martha, who died as an infant, and twin boys, George and James, born when Isaac was fourteen. In 1893, Malinda Jane died at home ("Cooper," *Republican and Observer*, December 7, 1893, p. 8, col. 4; courtesy Richland County History Room). Isaac was eighteen, his youngest twin brothers just four. George Cooper, sixty at the time of his wife's death, leaned heavily on his older children to eke out a living.

11 Pérez, *The War of 1898*.

12 Wexler, *Tender Violence*; Hoganson, *Fighting for American Manhood*; Hoganson, *American Empire*.

13 Cooper, Isaac, enlistment papers, United States Army, July 15, 1894–October 21, 1912, Enlistment Papers, 1894–1912, box 271, RG 94, entry 91, Adjutant General's Office, National Archives and Records Administration. See also William McKinley's policy approach to the Philippine islands: "Benevolent Assimilation"

Proclamation, December 21, 1898, in *The Statutes at Large of the United States of America from March 1897 to March 1899 and Recent Treaties, Conventions, Executive Proclamations, and the Concurrent Resolutions of the Two Houses of Congress*, vol. 30 (Washington, DC: U.S. Government Printing Office, 1899).

14 "Filipinos Kill Our Troops," *New York Times*, August 27, 1898.

15 Tens of thousands of Filipinos died over the course of the pacification campaign—excluding the hundreds of thousands of civilians who were the collateral damage of the fighting.

16 William Atwood diaries, August 12, 1899–May 1, 1900, October 22 entry, Michigan Historical Collections, Bentley Historical Library, University of Michigan at Ann Arbor.

17 After Filipino forces turned away from the losing proposition of conventional warfare against the Americans, guerilla tactics defined the Batangas campaign. May, *Battle for Batangas*, 82.

18 General Arthur MacArthur was displaced as the military governor of the islands by an incoming civilian administrator, Howard Taft, by mid-1900.

19 Winkelmann, "Dangerous Intercourse"; Kramer, *The Blood of Government*, 105.

20 May, *Battle for Batangas*, 131–62. As Mendoza, *Metroimperial Intimacies*, notes, the sexual encounters of American men included those with Filipinos.

21 Winkelmann, "Dangerous Intercourse"; *Report of the Surgeon-General of the Army to the Secretary of War for the Fiscal Year Ending June 30, 1899* (Washington, DC: Government Printing Office, 1899). See also Roces, "Filipino Elite Women and Public Health."

22 Kramer, "The Darkness That Enters the Home."

23 Bautista with Planta, "The Sacred and the Sanitary," 157.

24 James A. Leroy, as quoted in Gleeck, *Nine Years to Make a Difference*, 6.

25 Mendoza, *Metroimperial Intimacies*.

26 Gleeck, *The Manila Americans*, 11.

27 Hartendorp, "I Have Lived," 113.

28 As quoted in Gleeck, *The Manila Americans*, 37.

29 Mrs. Campbell Dauncy, as quoted in Kramer, *The Blood of Government*, 196. Legitimating interracial relationships through open courtship and social interaction, as opposed to the outright economic transactions of sex work, constituted a greater threat to the racial hierarchy of colonial society, and more particularly, as Stoler argues, to the social position of white colonial women (Stoler, *Carnal Knowledge*, 39).

30 Charles W. Hack, Journal, typewritten, February 11, 1902, box 1, folder 6, p. 26, Manuscripts Division, Library of Congress. Most of the primary sources I have located on this period are from American colonial archive. For scholarship on Filipinas during this rough period, see Camagay, *Working Women of Manila*; Mendoza-Guazon, *The Development and Progress of Filipino Women*; and Sobritchea, *Women's Role in Philippine History*. See also Roces, "Mixed Blessing."

31 Rafael, *White Love and Other Events*, 240n18.

32 "United States Census, 1900," FamilySearch (https:family/search.org/ark:/61903/1:1M316-SZV); Winkelmann, "Dangerous Intercourse."

33 *Census of the Philippine Islands*, vol. 1 (Washington, DC: United States Bureau of the Census, 1903), 42.

34 Torres, *The Americanization of Manila*, 212. See also Winkelmann, "Dangerous Intercourse," chapter 1; Doeppers, "Manila's Imperial Makeover."

35 Government of the Philippine Islands, Bureau of Civil Service, *Official Roster of Officers and Employees in the Civil Service of the Philippine Islands* (Manila: Bureau of Printing, 1913), 92. Digital copy from the University of Michigan.

36 Petillo, *Douglas MacArthur*, 64–75.

37 "Philippines Marriages, 1723–1957," FamilySearch (https://familysearch.org /ark:/61903/1:1:FNQP-S1K).

38 Bruce Cooper (the first) and Rubia Ryan disappear from the historical record—at least as connected to Isaac Cooper—after Bruce Cooper names Isaac Cooper as his father in a 1927 marriage to Lydia Neill in Manila.

39 The exact date of their marriage, if indeed they were officially married, is unknown. This may have been a more casual common-law affair (as was likely Cooper's first relationship with Rubia Ryan), or solemnized and made legally binding, none of which, by practice, American men were held to if they chose to dissolve the relationships or leave the islands.

40 Josefina Protacia Ryan, arriving in Vancouver, then Seattle, by ship in 1928, lists Laguna, Philippines, as her birthplace: Seattle, Washington, Passenger and Crew Lists, 1883–1957, micropublication M1398, RG085, Ancestry.com. In a 2015 article, I wrongly contended that she was born in Mexico: Gonzalez, "Illicit Labor." While this remains a possibility, the Protacia Rubin listed in that document is likely someone else.

41 Government of the Philippine Islands, *Official Roster of Officers and Employees*, 92.

42 Carter, *Then and Now*, 97. According to Carter, Protacia Rubin's younger sister, Hermogena, was also married off to another American.

43 Some children are named, like Bruce Cooper, and others do not have verifying documentation, including a brother, Allen Cooper, who later claims to be related to Isabel Cooper and who became a key informant for Carol Petillo's biography, *Douglas MacArthur*.

44 Phoenix, Maricopa, Arizona, sheet 10B, NARA microfilm publication T625, 1920 U.S. Census. Like his sister, Bruce Cooper (the second) also foils attempts to fix his birthdate, as he claims an October 22, 1909, birthdate upon arriving in Los Angeles in 1934, rather than the 1911 birth year that is recorded in the 1920 census. California, "List of United States Citizens," S.S. *Taiyo Maru*, October 12, 1934, Los Angeles, Passenger and Crew Lists, 1882–1959, Ancestry.com. Bruce Cooper travels on a U.S. passport.

45 "Philippines, Manila, Civil Registration, 1899–1984," FamilySearch (https:// familysearch.org/ark:/61903/1:1:QKJG-P9BW).

46 Other documents, mostly passenger and crew lists of ships arriving on American shores, list myriad birthdates and birth years reported by Isabel Cooper, beginning as early as 1909 (and as she aged, pushing her birth year forward). Part of the reason that Isabel Cooper's date of birth is hard to pin down is the plethora

of contradictory records (some of which she herself invented), human error, and the destruction of many official records during the bombing of Manila in World War II. She also colluded fully in muddying her birth year, particularly as she got older, when being younger in Hollywood was essential to her survival.

47 In 1915, Isaac Cooper is listed as a captain in the fire department, pulling a salary of P3,000. Government of the Philippine Islands: Bureau of Civil Service, *Official Roster of Officers and Employees in the Civil Serves of the Philippine Islands*, July 1, 1915, 106. By the following year, he is no longer listed. Digital copy from the University of Michigan.

48 U.S.A.T. *Logan*, Voyage No. 51, ship manifest of first- and second-class passengers, March 31–April 19, 1916, National Archives, Washington, DC, Ancestry.com.

49 *Manual for the Quartermaster Corps*, United States Army, 1916, 565. The exact wording: "Certificate is necessary that the person is a permanent member of the family of the enlisted man concerned, habitually residing with him, and has no other home."

50 Baldoz, *The Third Asian Invasion*.

51 U.S.A.T. *Logan*, Voyage No. 51.

52 Mixed-race Spanish Filipinos in the United States utilized their colonial racial heritage to argue that they were indeed white and either eligible for naturalization or not subject to antimiscegenation laws in the United States; Baldoz, *The Third Asian Invasion*, chapter 3. Arizona did not add the category "Malay" to its antimiscegenation law until the 1930s, after courts ruled that Filipinos were not Asian but Malay; Pascoe, *What Comes Naturally*, 92–93. It is unclear why Isaac Cooper chose Arizona to settle his family: perhaps he was used to warmer weather, and Minneapolis, where his father now resided, did not appeal to him. Isaac's father, George W. Cooper, would die on January 27, 1918, in Minneapolis (Ancestry.com).

53 World War I Draft Registration Cards, 1917–1918, Serial Number 9799, Arizona, Maricopa County, Draft Card C, National Archives, Washington, DC, Ancestry .com. The race anxieties that would crop up in California and the West Coast in particular around migrant Filipino laborers and their intimate contact with white women in dance halls had not yet reached a boiling point in mid-1916, when the Cooper family settled in Maricopa, just outside Phoenix.

54 Or a horse plow while farming, according to Carter, "The General's Dimples."

55 Arizona deaths, 1870–1951, FamilySearch. The mother is listed as Protacia Rubin and the father is listed as Isaac Cooper: U.S.A.T. *Logan*, Voyage No. 51, lists three children traveling with the couple.

56 This claim is made by Carter in "The General's Dimples," 36.

57 Isaac J. Cooper, age forty-three, listed as a retired Civil Service fireman with Protacia Cooper as nearest relative (World War I Draft Registration Cards, 1917–1918).

58 "Home Life," in *Echoes of Freedom: South Asian Pioneers in California, 1899–1965*, Southeast Asia Library, University of California, Berkeley, http://guides.lib .berkeley.edu/echoes-of-freedom.

59 Carter, "The General's Dimples," 36.

60 A nine-year-old Bruce Cooper is listed as living with Isaac Cooper in the 1920 U.S. Census, Family Search (https://familysearch.org/ark:61903/1:1:MCRG

-7QT), Isaac F. Cooper, Phoenix, Maricopa, Arizona, United States, citing sheet 10B, NARA microfilm publication T625. There is no further archival evidence of her third child. This unnamed and archivally absent child may be Allen Cooper, whom Carol Petillo lists as her source for his sister's relationship with MacArthur.

61 Thomas Ryan, World War I draft card, 1917–1918, Ancestry.com.

62 Ancestry Family Trees, Connolly, Josephine Margaret Ryan, November 6, 1920, Luzon, Philippines, Ancestry.com.

63 U.S. Civil War Pension Index: General Index to Pension Files, 1861–1934, Isaac Cooper, December 27, 1920, Application No. 1444807, National Archives, Washington, DC, Ancestry.com.

64 U.S. National Homes for Disabled Volunteer Soldiers, 1866–1938 (National Archives Microfilm Publication M1749, 282 rolls); Records of the Department of Veterans Affairs, Record Group 15, National Archives, Washington, DC, Ancestry.com.

65 1930 U.S. Census. By the 1930 census, Isaac Cooper identifies his marital status as divorced. Whether this was truly the case (if it was legally necessary and, if so, actually filed) is unclear.

66 Carter, in "The General's Dimples," also claims that Protacia, or Asiang, as she was called by family, went on to marry an American lawyer named Blanco and bore a number of other children. He relates that she died of uterine cancer in 1937, with her niece, his wife, at her bedside. No archival documents track Protacia/Josephine's alleged last marriage, and her official death certificate is dated 1938.

8. "DIMPLES": INNOCENCE (COLONIAL KINK)

1 By the time of the letter, Isabel Cooper is using a post office box for her return address, but she is listed as living at 1510 Allison Avenue near Sunset Avenue in the August 1950 Los Angeles central telephone directory and the June 1952 directory. Prior to that she was living at 6205 Lexington (June 1945 Los Angeles directory): it is likely that was the residence she lived in with her second husband, Milton Moreno.

2 Chabing Cooper (Belle), letter to Drew Pearson, January 24, 1951, "Ronald Reagan" folder, box G263, Drew Pearson Papers.

3 Isabel Cooper, letter to Drew Pearson, February 18, 1943, box G210, Drew Pearson Papers. Thank you to Mark Feldstein for sharing these materials, which were not archived during an earlier search.

4 Patricia Clary, "General MacArthur Helps Girl Become Hollywood Actress," *Lubbock Evening Journal*, January 23, 1951.

5 See Lowe, *The Intimacies of Four Continents*; see also Matsuda, *Empire of Love*, 13, on French imperialism in the Pacific as an "empire of love" that emphasized "enjoyment" and "satisfied exercise of possession and occupation."

6 Balce, "The Filipina's Breast"; for an earlier treatment of sexuality and nationalism in the Philippines, see Reyes, *Love Passion and Patriotism*. See also Nubla, "The Sexualized Child and Mestizaje."

7 Winkelmann, "Dangerous Intercourse," infers the census underestimated these numbers.

8 Four hundred years of Spanish colonialism and Chinese migrant trade had yielded a significant mixed-race population before the arrival of the Americans. See Tan, *The Chinese Mestizos*.

9 Gleeck, *The Manila Americans*, 96, 98; see also Winkelmann, "Dangerous Intercourse."

10 Winkelmann's dissertation, "Dangerous Intercourse," has a chapter dedicated to the American mestizo population; see also McElhinny, "American Mestizos in the Philippines."

11 Koshy, *Sexual Naturalization*; Teng, *Eurasian*; Pascoe, *What Comes Naturally*.

12 Balce, "The Filipina's Breast."

13 Ambeth Ocampo, "The Philippines during World War I," *Philippine Daily Inquirer*, June 26, 2012, https://opinion.inquirer.net/31501/the-philippines -during-world-war-i.

14 Torres, *The Americanization of Manila*.

15 Torres, *The Americanization of Manila*, 179.

16 Onorato, *Jock Netzorg*, 21.

17 Bruce Cooper lists 2141 Herrán Street as Josefina Ryan's address, returning to the United States from a visit to Manila in 1928, and it is used as the home address by Douglas MacArthur a few years later on his letters to Isabel Cooper. Calle Herrán, or Herrán Street, has today been renamed Pedro Gil Avenue after a Filipino statesman. Incidentally, it is also the same street where man of letters Nick Joaquin grew up during this period.

18 Cruz, *Transpacific Femininities*; Roces, *Women's Movements and the Filipina*.

19 Pareja, "Roles and Image of Woman," 28. The theaters were in Quiapo (Cine Orpheum), Santa Cruz district (Cine Cervantes), and Sampaloc (Cine Moderno).

20 Joaquin, "A Movie Album," 170.

21 José Nepomuceno and his brother Jesus had set up the Malayan Movies studio, launching Filipino movies in the islands in the 1910s; DeOcampo, *Film*, 290–92.

22 Atang de la Rama first sang during intermissions in between *sarswelas* as a youngster before she became the main act onstage and on film.

23 Quirino, *Don Jose and the Early Philippine Cinema*, 48–49.

24 Weinbaum et al., *The Modern Girl around the World*.

25 Carter, *Then and Now*, 153.

26 Thomas Carter, in *Then and Now*, 153, documents some family members in the early cinema scene (an uncle who was a projector operator in a theater) and a family orchestra.

27 Lacónico-Buenaventura, *The Theater in Manila*; yamomo, *Theatre and Music in Manila and the Asia Pacific*.

28 Torres, *The Americanization of Manila*, 173.

29 San Juan, "From Vaudeville to Bodabil."

30 Bodabil first started off as comedy skits or song-and-dance routines in between the main acts of full-length *sarswelas* or musical plays, a Spanish dramatic genre adopted and adapted by Filipinos that was both social and political in its aim.

In between the main showcases, variety acts from torch songs to magic acts, dramatic skits, and dance numbers took the stage to entertain the audience. They flourished alongside the amalgam of live stage novelties that made up stage life in the islands: American vaudeville, sarswela, "Moro-Moro plays, Chinese theater, children's puppet shows and newly written Seditious Plays" coexisted with "duets, Spanish dances, and magic acts interspersed with short comic and travelogue films." San Juan, "From Vaudeville to Bodabil," 40. See also Burns, *Puro Arte*; Fernandez, "Philippine Theater," 68.

31 "How They Got Their Names," *Philippines Free Press*, November 25, 1933, 38–39. As in the movies, Filipino and American men were the impresarios of this newly arrived theatrical form. Borromeo was soon joined by John C. Cowper, who directed the "dancing babies" of the Savoy Nifties (Domingo H. Soriano, "The Dancing Girls Talk of the Patrons," *Graphic*, May 7, 1930, 44).

32 The 1940 U.S. Census lists Isabel as having a second-year high school education (equivalent to the eighth grade in the U.S., or approximately age thirteen, which lines up with the age when she would have made her second debut on the stage).

33 Felix R. Domingo, "Bare Knees and Bobbed Hair," *Graphic*, May 4, 1929, 4–5.

34 Rivoli Theater would later be known as the Tivoli.

35 Gleeck, *The Manila Americans*, 176.

36 Joaquin, "The Way We Were." The short story was published in 1937, originally titled "The Sorrows of Vaudeville" but changed to "Behind Tinsel and Grease," in the *Sunday Tribune Magazine*.

37 Gleeck, *The Manila Americans*, 171.

38 "How They Got Their Names," 39.

39 Isabel Cooper had no illusions that she would join the ranks of the coeds at the university or the Filipinas who were featured as society beauties or accomplished classical singers or musicians in the *Graphic* and the *Free Press*, like her cousin Mercedes Sotelo, who eventually married Thomas Carter, who in turn wrote about Isabel Cooper in his memoir of being an expatriate in the Philippines. Sotelo freelanced as a journalist, worked as a law clerk, and attended law school, in contrast to her more worldly cousin.

40 A link to an audio file of "Has Anybody Seen My Kitty," with appreciation to Susan Schoonover for her music sleuthing skills: Sheet Music Singer, http://sheetmusicsinger.com/1922songs/wp-content/uploads/2018/11/Has-Anybody-Seen-My-Kitty.mp3.

41 H. Pres. Porter, "Has Anybody Seen My Kitty," c. 1922, sheet music from British Library Music Collection, with appreciation to Tanya Wyatt for its retrieval.

42 Rumors circulated that Pershing had an affair with MacArthur's wife while the latter served in the war, and that he had MacArthur shipped off to a makeshift assignment in the Philippines for his own reasons.

43 MacArthur, *Reminiscences*, 24, 282.

44 Joaquin, "Manila," 257–58.

45 Domingo, "Bare Knees and Bobbed Hair."

46 Soriano, "The Dancing Girls Talk of the Patrons," 45.

47 Pareja, "Roles and Image of Woman," 47–48.
48 The phrase was used in a paternalistic but nonetheless racist fashion. See Miller, *Benevolent Assimilation*, 134.

11. THE NEW FILIPINA, KISSING

1 Welch, "American Atrocities in the Philippines."
2 Lumbera, "From Colonizer to Liberator"; Campomanes, "Casualty Figures of the American Soldier."
3 Pareja, "Roles and Image of Woman," 210.
4 Nick Joaquin, as quoted in Pareja, "Roles and Image of Woman," 47.
5 S. A. Pilar, *Archipelago*, as quoted in Pareja, "Roles and Image of Woman," 211.
6 Carter, "The General's Dimples," 36.
7 FamilySearch (https://www.familysearch.org/tree/person/details/LYZB-J46).
8 While at this point we leave behind Josefina's story, it is worth noting that well past her second husband's death in August 1925, she continued to use his name for herself and for progeny that were born long after his ability to have fathered them: in October 1926, Catherine Melba Ryan was born, followed by Mary Nazarena Magdalena Ryan in 1928. It may be that she recorded their births late, or just kept Ryan's name while continuing to take up with other men. Carter alleges that she takes up with yet another American after the death of Thomas Ryan. At this point, her son Bruce Cooper was old enough to have made his way to Manila, though the exact date of his arrival is unclear. "Philippines, Manila, Civil Registration, 1899–1984," FamilySearch (https://familysearch.org/ark:/61903/1:1:Q26N-13QH), Catherine Melba May Ryan, September 7, 1926; Birth, Manila, Metropolitan Manila, Philippines; "Washington, Seattle, Passenger Lists, 1890–1957," FamilySearch (https://familysearch.org/ark:/61903/1:1:KDZ4-K6W), Josephine Margaret Ryan, 1928.
9 Weinbaum et al., *The Modern Girl around the World*; Roces, "Gender, Nation and the Politics of Dress."
10 Cruz, *Transpacific Femininities*; Roces, "Is the Suffragist an American Colonial Construct?"
11 Manuel Roxas, Speaker of House of Representatives, as quoted in Maria Paz Mendoza-Guzaon, *My Ideal Filipino Girl*, 1931 (no publisher), American Historical Collection, Rizal Library, Ateneo de Manila University, vi.
12 Mendoza-Guazon, *My Ideal Filipino Girl*, 32. See also Cruz, *Transpacific Femininities*.
13 Jose A. Quiriño, "How Don Peping Turned the Queen of Zarzuela into Our First Movie Star," *Woman's Home Companion*, January 27, 1982, 48–49.
14 Pareja, "Roles and Image of Woman," 211–12.
15 Carter, "The General's Dimples," 36.
16 Pareja, "Roles and Image of Woman," 20.
17 Luis F. Nolasco, "La Historia del Primer Beso de Cine en Filipinas," *Literary Song-Movie Magazine*, September 1936, 79, translated by Nick DeOcampo.

18 Pareja, "Roles and Image of Woman," 49.

19 *Manila Times*, September 29, 1926, 5, from Pareja's compilation, "Roles and Image of Woman," 212.

20 Quirino, *Don Jose and the Early Philippine Cinema*, 34.

21 *Manila Times*, March 13, 1927, 12. The review is in Pareja, "Roles and Image of Woman."

22 "Alleged Embezzler and Charming Incognita Left on Empress March 24," *Graphic*, April 14, 1928, 6–7.

23 "Vaudeville in the Local Theaters/Ang Mga Tala sa Bodabil," *Graphic*, July 9, 1927, 16.

24 M. San Martin, "Where Is My Wandering Girl?," *Graphic*, April 20, 1929, 4. The article mentions Anna May Wong as the only Asian actor who has made it in Hollywood. See also Lim, *Anna May Wong*.

25 I list her here as eighteen because she lists her birth year as 1909. She could have been as young as fifteen.

26 May 30, 1927, ss *Shinyo Maru* manifest. Isabel is listed among the American citizens arriving, with her father's address in Brentwood Heights, California, as her destination.

27 Elizabeth Cooper, "Meeting the Stars in Hollywood," *Graphic*, October 22, 1927, 4.

28 Cooper, "Meeting the Stars in Hollywood," 4.

29 Cooper, "Meeting the Stars in Hollywood," 5.

30 Cooper, "Meeting the Stars in Hollywood," 5.

31 "Alleged Embezzler and Charming Incognita," 6.

32 Seattle, Washington, Passenger and Crew Lists, 1882–1957. Arrival June 30, 1928 via Vancouver. An Allen Cooper is listed as arriving with Josephine Ryan along with four of her daughters with the surname Ryan.

33 Thomas Carter, in "The General's Dimples," claims that Josefina had taken up with a third American, a lawyer named Blanco. It is possible that the children born well after Thomas Ryan's death are Blanco's, and that Josefina is following him back to the United States, although I could find no archival evidence of this.

34 M. San Martin, "Stars That Shine in Philippine Filmdom," *Graphic*, October 20, 1928, 2.

35 Younger actresses such as Sofia Lotta (Ms. Cotabato) and Eva Lyn were among the ingenues named by Nepomuceno and Salumbides in late 1928 as the rising stars of Philippine film: see "Moro Girl Making Good in the Movies," *Graphic*, December 1, 1928, 7–8; M. San Martin, "Stars That Shine," 3.

36 Gleeck, *The Manila Americans*, 1929.

37 According to Carter, "The General's Dimples," those songs are "Are You Lonesome Tonight?" and "Just a Little Longer."

38 Domingo H. Soriano, "The Dancing Girls Talk of the Patrons," *Graphic*, May 7, 1930, 44–45.

39 "Who Is Who in the Philippines," *Graphic*, October 13, 1928, 9–10.

40 "Who Is Who," 9–10.

41 Petillo, *Douglas MacArthur*, 151. As noted above, a nine-year-old Allen Cooper is listed in the 1928 ship manifest, traveling with Josephine Ryan and her brood.

He would not have been in Manila to witness the story of the general meeting his sister that he relates to Petillo, and any descriptions he later shares would be secondhand.

42 Petillo, *Douglas MacArthur*, 151.

15. THE WASHINGTON HOUSEWIFE, THE HOLLYWOOD HULA GIRL, AND THE TWO HUSBANDS: REINVENTIONS

1 1940 United States Federal Census, Washington, District of Columbia, Roll T627_566, p. 17B, Enumeration District 1-387A, Official 1940 census website, National Archives, https://1940census.archives.gov/.

2 No information is recorded for her citizenship, which was required for those born in a foreign country, but perhaps the Philippines did not count as such in 1940. Franklin Kennamer, who is the informant on her death certificate in 1960, also lists her race as white. In the two decades between the 1940 census and her death, she is anything but.

3 The address listed in the 1940 U.S. Census is 900 East Fifteenth Street, Oklahoma City, OK.

4 According to Manchester, *American Caesar*, Isabel was escorted to the "Middle West," where she allegedly used the settlement from the dropped libel suit to start up a beauty shop, although no evidence is cited for this. Between the end of 1934 (after the libel suit was dropped) and February 1936, she traveled once more to Manila and, upon her return to Seattle, lists an Oklahoma address. Franklin Kennamer received his law degree from Georgetown and his undergraduate degree from a university in Oklahoma (per Franklin Burke Kennamer [his son], interview with author, March 2, 2019).

5 "General to Wed at Ceremony in New York," *Reno Gazette Journal*, April 30, 1937, 11. The MacArthurs would not return to Washington until after the war.

6 "Dimples Turns Artist, Gives Up Ambition to Greater Stage Honors." No author, publication information, or date listed, though it is likely late 1935 or early 1936. Newspaper cutting courtesy of Archivo 1985 and Juan Martin Magsanoc. The article is clearly written from a Manila perspective.

7 *President Jackson* ship manifest, February 19, 1936, Seattle, WA, port of entry, "Seattle, Washington, Passenger and Crew Lists, 1882–1957," Ancestry.com.

8 Luis F. Nolasco, "La Historia del Primer Beso de Cine en Filipinas," *Literary Song-Movie Magazine*, September 1936, 79, translated by Nick DeOcampo.

9 Franklin Burke Kennamer interview, March 4, 2019. In the undated Manila article that discusses Isabel Cooper's last visit to Manila, she is alleged to have studied at the Corcoran Arts School and the National School of Fine and Applied Arts.

10 The document cited in Ancestry.com family genealogies includes her date of death as April 4, 1938, although there are no official records that satisfy me with regard to her death. These family records seem to be based on the death of a woman named Josefina Protacia Rubin, who was living in Mexico at the time of her death, but it is unclear that she ever had any family living in Mexico. The

Josefina Rubin cited in these records is also not living with any of her progeny, which leads me to think she may not be Isabel Cooper's mother, even as she's claimed by the descendants of Isabel Cooper's half siblings. Carter states in "The General's Dimples" that Josephine Ryan, whom he knew as Asiang, died in 1937 in her early fifties, but at that point she would have been in her midforties.

11 Isabel Cooper, letter to Drew Pearson, August 7, 1942, folder 3, MacArthur, Drew Pearson Papers.

12 Alexander Korda, as quoted in Shindler, *Hollywood Goes to War*, 29.

13 U.S. Senate Resolution 152, October 1941.

14 1940 U.S. Census.

15 Isabel Cooper, letter to Drew Pearson, August 14, 1942, folder 3, Drew Pearson Papers. All letters in this chapter written by Isabel Cooper, Drew Pearson, and Sam H. Hahn are from the Drew Pearson Papers in the Lyndon B. Johnson Presidential Library.

16 Isabel Cooper, letter to Drew Pearson, August 14, 1942.

17 Drew Pearson, letter to Sam S. Hahn, August 14, 1942.

18 Sam S. Hahn, letter to Drew Pearson, September 3, 1942.

19 Drew Pearson, letter to Isabel Cooper, October 5, 1942.

20 Sam S. Hahn, letter to Drew Pearson, September 12, 1942.

21 Sam S. Hahn, letter to Drew Pearson, September 3, 1942.

22 Isabel Cooper, letter to Drew Pearson, September 2, 1942.

23 Sam S. Hahn, letter to Drew Pearson, November 5, 1942.

24 Sam S. Hahn, letter to Drew Pearson, October 16, 1942.

25 Drew Pearson, letter to Sam S. Hahn, October 7, 1942; Sam Hahn, letter to Drew Pearson, October 10, 1942.

26 Isabel Cooper, letter to Drew Pearson, October 1942 (date unclear).

27 Isabel Cooper, letter to Drew Pearson, November 26, 1942. Drew Pearson, letter to Sam S. Hahn, December 3, 1942.

28 Isabel Cooper Kannamer [*sic*], Complaint for Divorce, November 25, 1943, L.A. Superior Court.

29 Franklin Burke Kennamer interview.

30 Isabel Cooper Kennamer, Interlocutory Judgement of Divorce, March 5, 1943, L.A. Superior Court.

31 "Kennamer Film Actress Divorced from L.A. Atty," *Los Angeles Herald and Express*, undated, likely March 1943, Drew Pearson Papers.

32 Paramount Pictures, Inc., Production Notes, *So Proudly We Hail*, Special Collections, Academy of Motion Picture Arts and Sciences Margaret Herrick Library, Beverly Hills, California.

33 Paramount Pictures, Inc., Production Budget, *So Proudly We Hail*, Special Collections, Academy of Motion Picture Arts and Sciences Margaret Herrick Library.

34 Isabel Cooper Kennamer, Final Judgement of Divorce, March 8, 1944, L.A. Superior Court.

35 Photograph of Isabel "Dimples" Cooper and Rosemary Ruby "Jimmy" Ryan, a half sister, both cousins of Mercedes Sotelo-Carter, from Carter, *Then and Now*, n.p.

36 Drew Pearson, letters to Isabel Cooper, May 27, 1943, and April 21, 1943.

37 Isabel Cooper, letter to Drew Pearson, March 2, 1944.

38 Milton Moreno and Isabel Cooper, Marriage License 10282, June 22, 1944, County of Los Angeles. It is actually not clear if indeed Moreno is her relation by marriage, if not by blood, as there is little archival indication of this, but he identifies himself as white and Malay in this document. Isabel Cooper claims Caucasian and Malay identity.

39 Milton Moreno and Isabel Cooper, Marriage License 37821, November 21, 1946, County of Los Angeles.

40 "Hula Dancer Says Ex-Mate Bruised Legs," *Los Angeles Times*, September 27, 1946, A12.

41 No records of a divorce between Isabel Cooper and Milton exist in L.A. County Court records.

42 Drew Pearson, letter to Isabel Cooper, February 23, 1943.

43 Isabel Cooper, letter to Drew Pearson, February 18, 1943.

17. 1ST FILIPINA NURSE, GEISHA, ~~LITTLE SERGEANT,~~ JAVANESE NURSE, UNCREDITED

1 Allison, "Virtue through Suffering"; Koppes and Black, *Hollywood Goes to War.*

2 Hawley, "You're a Better Filipino Than I Am, John Wayne."

3 Willis, *High Contrast*; Parmar, "Hateful Contraries"; Kang, *Compositional Subjects.*

4 Hagedorn, "Asian Women in Film."

5 Cheng, *Second Skin*; Chung, *Hollywood Asian.*

6 Konzett, "War and Orientalism in Hollywood Combat Film"; Hawley, "You're a Better Filipino Than I Am, John Wayne."

7 "Filipinos Will Recall Bataan in Tableaux," *Los Angeles Times*, April 6, 1944, A1.

8 Zeiger, *Entangling Alliances*, 15.

9 Choy, *Empire of Care.*

10 Rice, *Ann Dvorak.*

11 *So Proudly We Hail* ran in the theaters with a trailer for the Army Nurse Corps and special thanks to the combat team and nurses based in Corregidor and Bataan.

12 In the film, she is not credited with her speaking part, but in the production notes for the film, she is referred to as "1st Filipino Nurse." *So Proudly We Hail*, May 5, 1945, casting document, Special Collections, Margaret Herrick Library.

13 Drew Pearson, letter to Sam S. Hahn, August 31, 1942, Drew Pearson Papers.

14 Isabel Cooper, letter to Drew Pearson, January 7, 1943.

15 Isabel Cooper, letter to Drew Pearson, January 7, 1943. She is quite specific and brutal in the way she caricatures the "author of the story" (presumably Allan Scott) as "like a poor Oklahoman who had never had anything in his life and finally oil was discovered in his back yard—newly rich. I'll bet its [*sic*] his first story."

16 Paramount Studio Pay Roll #1351, *So Proudly We Hail*, Special Collections, Margaret Herrick Library.

17 She made enough of an impression that she was converted from a daily rate to a weekly rate of $250, and likely repeated in other less-noticeable background roles. Paramount Studio Daily Production Report for *So Proudly We Hail*, December 31, 1942, Special Collections, Margaret Herrick Library.

18 Paramount Studio Production Budget, *So Proudly We Hail*, November 21, 1942, Special Collections, Margaret Herrick Library.

19 Review of *So Proudly We Hail*, *Variety*, June 23, 1943.

20 *So Proudly We Hail*. Also censorship dialogue script for *So Proudly We Hail*, May 29, 1943, New York State Archives, Albany. Censorship dialogue scripts were released for examination to state or local censorship boards in advance of the film's release.

21 Shibusawa, *America's Geisha Ally*; Kawaguchi, *Butterfly's Sisters*; Prasso, *The Asian Mystique*.

22 Manchester, *American Caesar*, 145.

23 Original print information, *The Purple Heart* (1944), Turner Classic Movies, accessed December 15, 2014, http://www.tcm.com/tcmdb/title/87382/The-Purple-Heart/original-print-info.html.

24 Its release is delayed to February 1944 by Zanuck's decision to center the demoralizing topic of torture, just when the U.S. War Department finally concedes that American prisoners of war had been tortured by the Japanese.

25 Spivak, "Can the Subaltern Speak?"

26 *Harrison's Reports*, April 29, 1944, Film Production Files, Margaret Herrick Library.

27 Cohen, "Devi Dja Goes Hollywood"; Spiller, *Javaphilia*.

28 *The Story of Dr. Wassell* cast list, 1943, Film Production Files, Margaret Herrick Library.

29 Isabel Cooper, letter to Drew Pearson, January 7, 1943. The film she is talking about in this instance is actually *So Proudly We Hail*.

30 Birchard, "*The Story of Dr. Wassell*."

19. BIT PARTS: RACIAL TYPES, ENSEMBLE

Epigraph: Isabel Cooper, letter to Drew Pearson, April 26, 1948, Drew Pearson Papers.

1 Rogin, *Blackface, White Noise*; Vera and Gordon, "The Beautiful American."

2 Courtney, *Hollywood Fantasies of Miscegenation*.

3 Brawley and Dixon, *Hollywood's South Seas and the Pacific War*; Lim, *Anna May Wong*.

4 Drew Pearson reaches out to his contacts at Warner Brothers to help out Isabel Cooper: "You may receive a call within the next week or so from a young lady of Chinese or Philippine extraction named Chabing Cooper. Confidentially, she is the former mistress of General MacArthur, and I would like to help her if possible, because she has had a tough break." He goes on to mention the card she needs, which he erroneously calls the Screen Actor's Guild (Drew Pearson, letter to William Hendricks, May 26, 1948, Drew Pearson Papers). He also reaches out

to a Robert Kenney, a former California attorney general, on her behalf (Drew Pearson, letter to Isabel Cooper, May 26, 1948, Drew Pearson Papers).

5 Isabel Cooper, letter to Drew Pearson, April 26, 1948.

6 "Hula Dancer Says Ex-Mate Bruised Legs," *Los Angeles Times*, September 27, 1946, A12; Isabel Cooper, letter to Drew Pearson, April 26, 1948.

7 The film parallels Doris Day's own meteoric rise from recording and radio artist to film star.

8 Mardo, "From UGA Booga to Hollywood Hula."

9 "Nagasaki" was a popular tune covered by big-band jazz groups in the 1930s and 1940s and was written by Harry Warren and Mort Dixon.

10 Isabel Cooper, letter to Drew Pearson, April 26, 1948.

11 Dong, *Forbidden City, USA*; Isabel Cooper, letter to Drew Person, April 26, 1948.

12 Ngô, *Imperial Blues*; Imada, "Hawaiians on Tour"; Konzett, *Hollywood's Hawaii*; Schwaller, "A Careful Embrace."

13 Isabel Cooper, letter to Drew Pearson, April 26, 1948.

14 Isabel Cooper, letter to Drew Pearson, April 26, 1948.

15 Hunt, "'Suffragettes of the Harem.'"

16 Darryl Zanuck, dir., *Anna and the King* (Twentieth Century Fox, 1946).

17 Leonowens, of course, was herself of mixed race but attained white womanhood in this filmic rendition; Heinrich, "Race and Role."

18 "Harrison's Harem," *Variety*, November 28, 1945, 6.

19 I avoid using the term "squaw" in this section's title and here even though it is in common usage during this period, and particularly in this film. See Parezo and Jones, "What's in a Name?"; Bruchac, "Reclaiming the Word 'Squaw.'"

20 Paramount Press Sheets, *Unconquered*, Margaret Herrick Library.

21 Blanke, "A New and Filmable Past."

22 "Facts about Cecil B. Demille's 'UNCONQUERED,'" Paramount Press Sheets, n.d., p. 1, Margaret Herrick Library; "Demille Presents Realistic Approach to Movie Indians," *Paramount News*, July 28, 1947, Film Production Files, Margaret Herrick Library.

23 *Unconquered*, line uttered by Chris Holden (Gary Cooper's character).

24 *Unconquered*, Shooting Report, "EXT. Guyasuta's Camp-Night-Stage 18," September 25, 1946, Production Document 11420, Film Production Files, Margaret Herrick Library.

25 Matheson, "Buckskin Fringe and Cavalier Culture"; Pavlik, Marubbio, and Holm, *Native Apparitions*; Kilpatrick, *Celluloid Indians*; Howe and Markowitz, *Seeing Red*.

26 The part is played by Katherine DeMille, the director's adopted daughter; see Downs, "The 'Enamored Indian Princess' Narrative."

27 Bird, "Introduction."

28 *Unconquered*, Daily Production Report, September 25, 1946, Paramount Studios, Margaret Herrick Library.

29 Dong, *Forbidden City, USA*, points out that a federal tax increase on cabarets in April 1944 cut the entertainment budget of many clubs, and many variety artists lost jobs or took less pay (he estimates 50 percent), 34.

30 On racial stereotypes and Charlie Chan films, see Huang, *Charlie Chan*.

31 *The Chinese Ring*, 1947, Charlie Chan's line.

32 "The Chinese Ring," *Variety*, December 7, 1947, 22. She is actually not even named in the supporting cast that is deemed average, though is listed in the supporting players.

33 Marchetti, *Romance and the "Yellow Peril"*; Lu, "Orientals in Hollywood."

34 Chabing Cooper (Belle), letter to Drew Pearson, January 24, 1951.

35 Chabing Cooper (Belle), letter to Drew Pearson, January 24, 1951.

36 Hechler and Watson, "Truman's MacArthur and MacArthur's Truman."

37 Phillips and Goldsmith, *Manila Espionage*.

38 *This Is Your Life*, NBC, March 15, 1950; Unander, "Claire Phillips"; Edwin Schallert, "Heroic Actress-Spy of Philippines Helps Screen Her Own Torture Story," *Los Angeles Times*, January 14, 1951, n.p. A copy of this article is in the Margaret Herrick Library archives; see also entry "Claire Maybelle Phillips," *The Oregon Encyclopedia*, March 17, 2018, https://oregonencyclopedia.org/articles/phillips_claire/#.XKlx-S2ZM6g.

39 Phillips files a claim with the United States Court of Claims for almost $150,000 to compensate her for her wartime services. In *Clavier v. United States* (July 12, 1957), her claim is found to be "without foundation" and it is decided that she is guilty of false testimony and fraud; see also Kaminsky, *Angels of the Underground*.

40 Feature Reviews: *I Was an American Spy*, *Boxoffice* (Archive: 1920–2000), March 31, 1951, 58, 22; Cinema, Film and Television, Entertainment Industry Magazine Archive, a15, Film Production Files, Margaret Herrick Library.

41 Rice, *Ann Dvorak*.

42 Chung, *Hollywood Asian*.

43 See Internet Movie Database site for *Anne of the Indies*, accessed May 23, 2019, https://www.imdb.com/title/tt0043288/mediaviewer/rm3282266368.

44 *I Was an American Spy* review, *Variety*, March 28, 1951, 6, Film Production Files, Margaret Herrick Library.

45 *I Was an American Spy* review, *Boxoffice*, March 31, 1951, 1246, Film Production Files, Margaret Herrick Library.

46 "Bad Direction Mars Script and Acting," no publishing information or date; "*I Was an American Spy*," review, *R.H. Picturegoer* (Archive: 1932–1960), January 5, 1952; 23, 870; William R. Weaver, *I Was an American Spy* review, *Motion Picture Herald*, n.d. All from Film Production Files, Margaret Herrick Library.

47 Sam S. Hahn, letter to Drew Pearson, July 3, 1952.

48 Sam S. Hahn, letter to Drew Pearson, September 3, 1942.

49 Maira, "Belly Dancing": Jarmakani, "Dancing the Hootchy Kootchy."

50 Quarles, *Down and Dirty*.

51 Mansbridge, "Fantasies of Exposure"; Maira, "Belly Dancing."

52 Schaefer, "*Bold! Daring! Shocking! True!*"

53 Lawrence Raimond, dir., *The Professor Misbehaves* (1954), American Film Institute catalog, https://catalog.afi.com/Catalog/moviedetails/50854.

1 The New York showing of Miljohn Ruperto's *Isabel Rosario Cooper* was held at Koenig and Clinton Gallery's Chelsea location from February 28 to April 12, 2014. The gallery has since moved to Brooklyn. The show premiered in Los Angeles. The artist has also shown the exhibit in parts at Para-Site (Hong Kong, 2016) and at ARCHIVO 1984 (Manila, 2019).

2 See also Bernabe, "Improbable Visions."

3 Sharpe, *Ghosts of Slavery*, xi.

4 Manchester, *American Caesar*.

5 Schwartz, "Passionate Letters Reveal," Morris Leopold Ernst Papers, Harry Ransom Center, University of Texas at Austin. The archive likely has this particular clip in its files because it is mentioned specifically in the article, which explains why the journalist was not allowed to reproduce the actual letters.

6 David Frum, "Top Ten Military Scandals," *Daily Beast*, November 15, 2012, https://www.thedailybeast.com/top-ten-military-sex-scandals.

7 Ernesto R. Rodriguez Jr., "Gen. MacArthur and His 'Dimples,'" *Malaya*, July 12, 1992, 12–13, in Mowelfund Library, Manila; Carter, "The General's Dimples."

8 Gordon, *Ghostly Matters*.

9 Chomet, *Asiamnesia*.

10 Lee, "Introduction," 174.

11 Chomet, *Asiamnesia*, 175.

12 Chomet, *Asiamnesia*, 180–81.

13 Chomet, *Asiamnesia*, 181.

14 Hodges, *Anna May Wong*, 63; Chomet, *Asiamnesia*, 182.

15 Chomet, *Asiamnesia*, 182–83.

16 Shimakawa, *National Abjection*.

17 Chomet, *Asiamnesia*, 183.

18 Shimakawa, *National Abjection*.

19 Dancyger and Rush, *Alternative Scriptwriting*, 85.

20 Reminiscent of Trinh T. Minh-ha's 1982 *Reassemblage*.

21 The latest, to date, is Isidra Reyes's comprehensive piece "The Colorful Life and Tragic End of the Pinay Showgirl Who Stole MacArthur's Heart!" in anticipation of Miljohn Rosario's showing in Manila (ABS-CBN, August 11, 2019, https://news.abs-cbn.com/ancx/culture/spotlight/08/11/19/the-colorful-life-and-tragic-end-of-the-pinay-showgirl-who-stole-macarthurs-heart).

23. THE SUICIDE

1 Stoler, "Introduction: 'The Rot Remains,'" 2.

2 Jaworski, "Suicide, Agency, and the Limits of Power"; Jaworski, "The Author, Agency, and Suicide." Isabel Rosario Cooper's Hollywood contemporary Lupe Vélez, the "Mexican spitfire," took her life at age thirty-six in 1944, just as Isabel Cooper's career was getting off the ground; Vogel, *Lupe Vélez*.

1925, *Miracles of Love* (Philippine Picture Plays)
Directed by Vicente Salumbides
Silent, black and white
Elizabeth "Dimples" Cooper (cover girl)
No known extant copy

1926, *Ang Tatlong Hambog* (José Nepomuceno)
Directed by José Nepomuceno
Silent, black and white
Elizabeth "Dimples" Cooper (love interest)
No known extant copy

1927, *Fate or Consequence* (Philippine Picture Plays)
Directed by Vicente Salumbides
Silent, black and white
Elizabeth "Dimples" Cooper (one of several love interests)
No known extant copy

1943, *So Proudly We Hail* (Paramount Pictures)
Directed by Mark Sandrich
Black and white
Dimples Cooper (Filipino nurse, speaking part, uncredited)

1944, *The Purple Heart* (Twentieth Century Fox)
Directed by Lewis Milestone
Black and white
Dimples Cooper (geisha, speaking part, uncredited)

1944, *The Story of Dr. Wassell* (Paramount Pictures)
Directed by Cecil B. DeMille
Technicolor
Dimples Cooper (~~Little Sergeant~~/Javanese nurse, uncredited)

1946, *Anna and the King of Siam* (Twentieth Century Fox)
Directed by John Cromwell
Black and white
Chabing (wife of king, uncredited)

1947, *Unconquered* (Paramount Pictures)
Directed by Cecil B. DeMille
Technicolor
Chabing (young Native woman, uncredited)

1947, *The Chinese Ring* (Monogram Pictures)
Directed by William Beaudine
Black and white
Chabing (Lillie Mae Wong, speaking part, credited)

1947, *Singapore* (Universal)
Directed by John Brahm
Black and white
Chabing (native woman, speaking part, uncredited)

1948, *Shanghai Crest* (Monogram Pictures)
Directed by William Beaudine
Black and white
Chabing (Miss Lee, receptionist, speaking part, uncredited)

1949, *My Dream Is Yours* (Warner Brothers)
Directed by Michael Curtiz
Technicolor
Chabing (hula dancer, uncredited)

1950, *The Great Jewel Robber* (aka *After Nightfall*) (Warner Brothers)
Directed by Peter Godfrey
Black and white
Chabing (second Chinese girl, uncredited)

1951, *I Was an American Spy* (Allied Artists)
Directed by Lesly Selander
Black and white
Chabing (Lolita, speaking part, credited)

1951, *Anne of the Indies* (Twentieth Century Fox)
Directed by Jacques Tourneur
Black and white
Chabing (slave girl, uncredited)

1953, *The Art of Burlesque* (aka *The Professor Misbehaves, Striptease College*) (Stewart-
    Raimond Productions)
Directed by Lawrence Raimond
Black and white
Chabing (Chabing, credited)

BIBLIOGRAPHY

ARCHIVES

American Historical Collection, Rizal Library, Ateneo de Manila University
Ancestry.com
Bentley Historical Library, University of Michigan at Ann Arbor
Billy Rose Theater Collection, New York Public Library
Brooke Russell Aaron Reading Room for Rare Books and Manuscripts, New York
    Public Library
Central Library, Los Angeles Public Library
Charles E. Young Library, University of California at Los Angeles
Drew Pearson Papers, Lyndon B. Johnson Presidential Library, Austin, Texas
FamilySearch.org
Harlan Hatcher Graduate Library Special Collections, University of Michigan at
    Ann Arbor
Lopez Museum and Library, Pasig, Philippines
Los Angeles County Medical Examiner
Los Angeles Superior Court Archives
Manuscripts Division, Library of Congress, Washington, DC
Margaret Herrick Library, Beverly Hills, California
Morris Leopold Ernst Papers, Harry Ransom Center, University of Texas at
    Austin
Mowelfund Library, Manila
Music Collection, British Library, London
Music Division, Library of Congress, Washington, DC
National Archives and Records Administration, Washington, DC
New York State Archives, Manuscripts and Special Collections, Albany, New York
Ortigas Library, Pasig, Manila
Performing Arts Library, University of California at Los Angeles
Periodicals Collection, Rizal Library, Ateneo de Manila University
Philippines Collection, Hamilton Library, University of Hawai'i at Mānoa
Rare Books Collection, Hamilton Library, University of Hawai'i at Mānoa

Richland County History Room, Richland Center, Wisconsin
Schomburg Center for Research in Black Culture, New York Public Library
SEA Collection, Asian Division, Library of Congress, Washington, DC
Seaver Center for Western History Research, Natural History Museum of Los
     Angeles County, Los Angeles
UCLA Moving Image Archive, University of California at Los Angeles
William Manchester Papers, Wesleyan University, Middletown, Connecticut

SECONDARY SOURCES

Allison, Tanine. "Virtue through Suffering: The American War Film at the End of
     Celluloid." *Journal of Popular Film and Television* 45, no. 1 (2017): 50–61.
Anderson, Jack, with James Boyd. *Confessions of a Muckraker: The Inside Story of
     Life in Washington during the Truman, Eisenhower, Kennedy and Johnson Years.*
     New York: Random House, 1979.
Apostol, Gina. *Insurrecto.* New York: Soho, 2018.
Arondekar, Anjali. *For the Record: On Sexuality and the Colonial Archive in India.*
     Durham, NC: Duke University Press, 2009.
Balce, Nerissa. *Body Parts of Empire: Visual Abjections, Filipino Images, and the
     American Archive.* Ann Arbor: University of Michigan Press, 2016.
Balce, Nerissa. "The Filipina's Breast: Savagery, Docility and the Erotics of the
     American Empire." *Social Text* 24, no. 2 (June 2006): 89–110.
Baldoz, Rick. *The Third Asian Invasion: Migration and Empire in Filipino America,
     1898–1946.* New York: New York University Press, 2011.
Ballantyne, Tony, and Antoinette Burton, eds. *Bodies in Contact: Rethinking Colo-
     nial Encounters in World History.* Durham, NC: Duke University Press, 2005.
Ballantyne, Tony, and Antoinette Burton. "Introduction: The Politics of Intimacy
     in an Age of Empire." In *Moving Subjects: Gender, Mobility and Intimacy in an
     Age of Global Empire,* edited by Tony Ballantyne and Antoinette Burton, 1–30.
     Urbana: University of Illinois Press, 2009.
Bautista, Julius, with Ma. Mercedes Planta. "The Sacred and the Sanitary: The
     Colonial Medicalization of the Filipino Body." In *The Body in Asia,* edited by
     Bryan S. Turner and Zheng Yangwen, 147–64. Oxford: Berghahn, 2009.
Beredo, B. Cheryl. *Import of the Archive: U.S. Colonial Rule of the Philippines and the
     Making of American Archival History.* Sacramento, CA: Litwin, 2013.
Bernabe, Jan Christian. "Improbable Visions: Filipino Bodies, U.S. Empire, and the
     Visual Archives." PhD diss., University of Michigan, 2008.
Birchard, Robert S. "*The Story of Dr. Wassell.*" In *Cecil B. DeMille's Hollywood,*
     323–28. Lexington: University Press of Kentucky, 2018.
Bird, S. Elizabeth. "Introduction: Constructing the Indian, 1830s–1990s." In *Dressing
     in Feathers: The Construction of the Indian in American Popular Culture,* 1–12.
     New York: Routledge, 1996.
Blanke, David. "A New and Filmable Past." In *Cecil B. DeMille, Classical Hollywood,
     and Modern American Mass Culture,* 129–63. New York: Palgrave Macmillan,
     2018.

Booth, Marilyn. "Fiction's Imaginative Archive and the Newspaper's Local Scandals: The Case of Nineteenth-Century Egypt." In *Archive Stories: Facts, Fictions, and the Writing of History*, edited by Antoinette Burton, 274–97. Durham, NC: Duke University Press, 2005.

Brawley, Sean, and Chris Dixon. *Hollywood's South Seas and the Pacific War: Searching for Dorothy Lamour*. New York: Palgrave Macmillan, 2012.

Bronfen, Elisabeth. *Over Her Dead Body: Death, Femininity, and the Aesthetic*. New York: Routledge, 1992.

Bruchac, Marge. "Reclaiming the Word 'Squaw' in the Name of the Ancestors." NativeWeb, November 1999. http://www.nativeweb.org/pages/legal/squaw.html.

Buhite, Russell D. *Douglas MacArthur: Statecraft and Stagecraft in America's East Asian Policy*. Lanham, MD: Rowman and Littlefield, 2008.

Burns, Lucy San Pablo. *Puro Arte: Filipinos on the Stages of Empire*. New York: New York University Press, 2013.

Camagay, Maria Luisa. *Working Women of Manila in the 19th Century*. Quezon City: University of the Philippines Press, 1995.

Campomanes, Oscar V. "Casualty Figures of the American Soldier and the Other: Post-1898 Allegories of Imperial Nation-Building as 'Love and War.'" In *Vestiges of War: The Philippine-American War and the Aftermath of an Imperial Dream*, edited by Angel Velasco Shaw and Luis H. Francia, 134–62. New York: New York University Press, 2002.

Carman, Emily. *Independent Stardom: Freelance Women in the Hollywood Studio System*. Austin: University of Texas Press, 2015.

Carter, Thomas. "The General's Dimples." *Business Journal*, August 1988, 32–39.

Carter, Thomas. *Then and Now (The Mechanics of Integration)*. Manila: Historical Conservation Society, 1983.

Castro, Alicia. *Queens of Havana: The Amazing Adventures of Anacaona, Cuba's Legendary All-Girl Dance Band*. New York: Grove, 2007.

Cheng, Anne Anlin. *Second Skin: Josephine Baker and the Modern Surface*. Oxford: Oxford University Press, 2010.

Chomet, Sun Mee. *Asiamnesia*. In *Asian American Plays for a New Generation*, edited by Josephine Lee, Don Eitel, and R. A. Shiomi, 173–203. Philadelphia: Temple University Press, 2011.

Choy, Catherine Ceniza. *Empire of Care: Nursing and Migration in Filipino American History*. Durham, NC: Duke University Press, 2003.

Chu, Richard. *The Chinese and Chinese Mestizos of Manila: Family, Identity, and Culture, 1860s to 1930s*. Amsterdam: Brill, 2010.

Chuh, Kandace. *Imagine Otherwise: On Asian Americanist Critique*. Durham, NC: Duke University Press, 2003.

Chung, Hye Seung. *Hollywood Asian: Philip Ahn and the Politics of Cross-Ethnic Performance*. Philadelphia: Temple University Press, 2006.

Cohen, Matthew Isaac. "Devi Dja Goes Hollywood." In *Performing Otherness*, edited by Matthew Isaac Cohen, 175–208. London: Palgrave Macmillan, 2010.

Courtney, Susan. *Hollywood Fantasies of Miscegenation: Spectacular Narratives of Gender and Race, 1903–1967*. Princeton, NJ: Princeton University Press, 2005.

Cruz, Denise. *Transpacific Femininities: The Making of the Modern Filipina*. Durham, NC: Duke University Press, 2012.

Dancyger, Ken, and Jeff Rush. *Alternative Scriptwriting*, 4th ed. Amsterdam: Focal Press, 2006.

DeOcampo, Nick. *Film: American Influences on Philippine Cinema*. Manila: Anvil, 2011.

Dimeglio, John R. *Vaudeville, U.S.A.* Bowling Green, KY: Bowling Green University Popular Press, 1973.

Doeppers, Daniel F. "Manila's Imperial Makeover: Security, Health, and Symbolism." In *Colonial Crucible: Empire in the Making of the Modern American State*, edited by Alfred W. McCoy and Francisco A. Scarano, 489–98. Madison: University of Wisconsin Press, 2009.

Dong, Arthur. *Forbidden City, USA: Chinese American Nightclubs, 1936–1970*. Los Angeles: DeepFocus Productions, 2015.

Downs, Kristina. "The 'Enamored Indian Princess' Narrative: Race, Sexuality, and Ancestry in the Stories of La Malinche, Pocahontas, and Sacagawea." PhD diss., Indiana University, 2017.

Fernandez, Doreen. "Philippine Theater." In *CCP Encyclopedia of Philippine Art*, vol. 7, edited by Nicanor Tiongson. Manila: Cultural Center of the Philippines, 1994.

Francia, Luis H. "A Sad Tale of Conquest and Betrayal." Inquirer.Net, March 21, 2014. http://globalnation.inquirer.net/100721/a-sad-tale-of-conquest-and-betrayal.

Fujita-Rony, Dorothy B. *American Workers, Colonial Power: Philippine Seattle and the Transpacific West, 1919–1941*. Berkeley: University of California Press, 2003.

Gleeck, Lewis E., Jr. *The Manila Americans (1901–1964)*. Manila: Carmelo and Bauermann, 1977.

Gleeck, Lewis E., Jr. *Nine Years to Make a Difference: The Tragically Short Career of James A. Leroy in the Philippines*. Manila: Loyal Printing, 1996.

Gonzalez, Vernadette Vicuña. "Illicit Labor: MacArthur's Mistress and Imperial Intimacy." *Radical History Review*, no. 123 (2015): 87–114.

Gordon, Avery. *Ghostly Matters: Haunting and the Sociological Imagination*. Minneapolis: University of Minnesota Press, 1997.

Gordon, Avery. *The Hawthorne Archive: Letters from the Utopian Margins*. New York: Fordham University Press, 2017.

Hagedorn, Jessica. "Asian Women in Film: No Joy, No Luck." *Ms. Magazine* 4, no. 4 (1994): 74–79.

Hammonds, Evelyn. "Black (W)holes and the Geometry of Black Female Sexuality." *differences: A Journal of Feminist Cultural Studies* 6, no. 2 + 3 (1994): 127–45.

Hartendorp, A. V. H. "I Have Lived: Reminisces of A.V.H. Hartendorp." Washington, DC: Manuscript Division, Library of Congress, 1970.

Hartman, Saidiya. *Wayward Lives, Beautiful Experiments: Intimate Histories of Social Upheaval*. New York: Norton, 2019.

Hau, Caroline S., Katrina Tuvera, and Isabelita O. Reyes. *Querida: An Anthology*. Mandaluyong City, Philippines: Anvil, 2013.

Hawley, Charles V. "You're a Better Filipino Than I Am, John Wayne: World War II, Hollywood, and U.S.-Philippines Relations." *Pacific Historical Review* 71, no. 3 (August 2002): 389–414.

Hechler, Ken, and Robert P. Watson. "Truman's MacArthur and MacArthur's Truman: The Roots and Ramifications of the General's Removal." In *Northeast Asia and the Legacy of Harry S. Truman: Japan, China, and the Two Koreas*, edited by James A. Matray, 203–23. Kirksville, MO: Truman State University Press, 2015.

Heinrich, Rena M. "Race and Role: The Mixed-Race Asian Experience in American Drama." PhD diss., University of California at Santa Barbara, 2018.

Hodges, Graham Russell Gao. *Anna May Wong: From Laundryman's Daughter to Hollywood Legend*. Hong Kong: Hong Kong University Press, 2002.

Hoganson, Kristin. *American Empire at the Turn of the Century*. Boston: Bedford/St. Martin's, 2016.

Hoganson, Kristin. *Fighting for American Manhood: How Gender Politics Provoked the Spanish-American and Philippine American Wars*. New Haven, CT: Yale University Press, 1998.

Howe, LeAnne, and Harvey Markowitz. *Seeing Red—Hollywood's Pixeled Skins: American Indians and Film*. East Lansing: Michigan State University Press, 2013.

Hoyt, Austin, and Sarah Holt, dirs. *The American Experience: MacArthur*. PBS Home Video, 1999.

Huang, Yunte. *Charlie Chan: The Untold Story of the Honorable Detective and His Rendezvous with American History*. New York: Norton, 2011.

Hunt, William Radler. "'Suffragettes of the Harem': The Evolution of Sympathy and the Afterlives of Sentimentality in American Feminist Orientalism, 1865–1920." PhD diss., Duke University, 2016.

Imada, Adria. "Hawaiians on Tour: Hula Circuits through the American Empire." *American Quarterly* 56, no. 1 (2004): 111–12.

James, Clayton D. *The Years of MacArthur*, vol. 1, *1880–1941*. Boston: Houghton Mifflin, 1970.

Jarmakani, Amira. "Dancing the Hootchy Kootchy: The Rhythms and Contortions of American Orientalism." In *Imagining Arab Womanhood: The Cultural Mythology of Veils, Harems, and Belly Dancers in the U.S.*, 63–101. New York: Palgrave Macmillan, 2008.

Jaworski, Katrina. "The Author, Agency, and Suicide." *Social Identities: Journal for the Study of Race, Nation, and Culture* 16, no. 5 (2010): 675–87.

Jaworski, Katrina. "Suicide, Agency, and the Limits of Power." In *Suicide and Agency: Anthropological Perspectives on Self-Destruction, Personhood, and Power*, edited by Ludek Broz and Daniel Münster, 183–204. Burlington, VT: Ashgate, 2015.

Joaquin, Nick. "Manila: Sin City?" (May 1970). In *Manila: Sin City? And Other Chronicles*, 253–71. Manila: Cacho Hermanes, 1980.

Joaquin, Nick. "A Movie Album" (1952). In *Language of the Street and Other Essays*, 167–84. Manila: Cacho Hermanos, 1980.

Joaquin, Nick. "The Way We Were." In *Writers and Their Milieu: An Oral History of First Generation Writers in English, Part 2,* edited by Edilberto Alegre and Doreen Fernandez. Manila: Anvil, 2017.

Kaminsky, Theresa. *Angels of the Underground.* Oxford: Oxford University Press, 2005.

Kang, Laura Hyun Yi. *Compositional Subjects: Enfiguring Asian/American Women.* Durham, NC: Duke University Press, 2002.

Kaplan, Amy. *The Anarchy of Empire in the Making of U.S. Culture.* Cambridge, MA: Harvard University Press, 2002.

Kawaguchi, Yoko. *Butterfly's Sisters: The Geisha in Western Culture.* New Haven, CT: Yale University Press, 2010.

Kilpatrick, Neva Jacquelyn. *Celluloid Indians: Native Americans and Film.* Lincoln, NE: Bison, 2016.

Konted. "General Douglas MacArthur and His Dimples." *Konted's Make My Day 2,* June 28, 2014 [blog]. http://kontedstories.blogspot.com/2014/06/general -douglas-macarthur-and-his.html.

Konzett, Delia. "War and Orientalism in Hollywood Combat Film." *Quarterly Review of Film and Video* 21, no. 4 (2004): 327–38.

Konzett, Delia Caparoso. *Hollywood's Hawaii: Race, Nation, and War.* Newark, NJ: Rutgers University Press, 2017.

Koppes, Clayton R., and Gregory D. Black. *Hollywood Goes to War: How Politics, Profits and Propaganda Shaped World War II Movies.* Berkeley: University of California Press, 1990.

Koshy, Susan. *Sexual Naturalization: Asian Americans and Miscegenation.* Palo Alto, CA: Stanford University Press, 2005.

Kramer, Paul. *The Blood of Government: Race, Empire, the United States, and the Philippines.* Chapel Hill: University of North Carolina Press, 2006.

Kramer, Paul. "The Darkness That Enters the Home: The Politics of Prostitution during the Philippine-American War." In *Haunted by Empire: Race and Colonial Intimacies in North American History,* edited by Ann Laura Stoler, 366–404. Durham, NC: Duke University Press, 2006.

Lacónico-Buenaventura, Cristina. *The Theater in Manila, 1846–1946.* Manila: De La Salle University Press, 1994.

Lee, Josephine. "Introduction." In *Asian American Plays for a New Generation,* edited by Josephine Lee, Don Eitel, and R. A. Shiomi, 1–10. Philadelphia: Temple University Press, 2011.

Lim, Shirley Jennifer. *Anna May Wong: Performing the Modern.* Philadelphia: Temple University Press, 2019.

Lisio, Donald. *The President and Protest: Hoover, MacArthur, and the Bonus Riot.* New York: Fordham University Press, 1994.

Lowe, Lisa. *The Intimacies of Four Continents.* Durham, NC: Duke University Press, 2015.

Lu, Megan Hermida. "Orientals in Hollywood: Asian American Representation in Early US Cinema." PhD diss., Boston University, 2017.

Lumbera, Bienvenido. "From Colonizer to Liberator: How U.S. Colonialism Succeeded in Reinventing Itself after the Pacific War." In *Vestiges of War: The Philippine-American War and the Aftermath of an Imperial Dream, 1899–1999*, edited by Angel Velasco Shaw and Luis H. Francia, 193–203. New York: New York University Press, 2002.

Mabalon, Dawn Bohulano. *Little America Is in the Heart: The Making of the Filipina/o Community in Stockton, California*. Durham, NC: Duke University Press, 2013.

MacArthur, Douglas. *Reminiscences*. New York: McGraw-Hill, 1964.

Maira, Sunaina. "Belly Dancing: Arab-Face, Orientalist Feminism, and US Empire." *American Quarterly* 60, no. 2 (2008): 317–45.

Manchester, William. *American Caesar: Douglas MacArthur, 1880–1964*. New York: Little, Brown, 1978.

Mansbridge, Joanna. "Fantasies of Exposure: Belly Dancing, the Veil, and the Drag of History." *Journal of Popular Culture* 49, no. 1 (2016): 29–56.

Marasigan, Cynthia. "'Between the Devil and the Deep Sea': Ambivalence, Violence, and African American Soldiers in the Philippine-American War and Its Aftermath." PhD diss., University of Michigan, Ann Arbor, 2010.

Marchetti, Gina. *Romance and the "Yellow Peril": Race, Sex, and Discursive Strategies in Hollywood Fiction*. Berkeley: University of California Press, 1994.

Mardo, Paola. "From UGA Booga to Hollywood Hula: A Deep Dive into America's Fascination with Tiki Bars, Tropical Drinks and the South Pacific." PhD diss., University of Southern California, 2017.

Matheson, Sue. "Buckskin Fringe and Cavalier Culture in the Hollywood Western." In *A Fistful of Icons: Essays on Frontier Fixtures of the American Western*, edited by Sue Matheson, 23–35. Jefferson, NC: McFarland, 2017.

Matsuda, Matt K. *Empire of Love: Histories of France and the Pacific*. Oxford: Oxford University Press, 2005.

May, Glenn Anthony. *Battle for Batangas: A Philippine Province at War*. New Haven, CT: Yale University Press, 1991.

McClintock, Anne. *Imperial Leather: Race, Gender and Sexuality in the Colonial Context*. New York: Routledge, 1995.

McElhinny, Bonnie. "American Mestizos in the Philippines: Ideologies of Race and Nation in a U.S. Charity for Children 'Wholly or Partly of American Blood,' 1922–1955." Paper presented at the Center for Philippine Studies Fortieth Anniversary Conference, Honolulu, April 9–10, 2015.

Mendoza, Victor Román. *Metroimperial Intimacies: Fantasy, Racial-Sexual Governance, and the Philippines in U.S. Imperialism, 1899–1913*. Durham, NC: Duke University Press, 2016.

Mendoza-Guazon, Maria Paz. *The Development and Progress of Filipino Women*. Manila: Bureau of Print, 1928.

Miller, Stuart Creighton. *Benevolent Assimilation: The American Conquest of the Philippines, 1899–1903*. New Haven, CT: Yale University Press, 1984.

Molnar, Nicholas Trajano. *American Mestizos, the Philippines, and the Malleability of Race, 1898–1961*. St. Louis: University of Missouri Press, 2017.

Moon, Katherine. *Sex among Allies: Military Prostitution in U.S.-Korea Relations*. New York: Columbia University Press, 1997.

Muñoz, José Esteban. "Ephemera as Evidence: Introductory Notes to Queer Acts." *Women and Performance: A Journal of Feminist Theory* 8, no. 2 (1996): 5–16.

Murray, Williamson, and Alan Millett. *A War to Be Won: Fighting the Second World War*. Cambridge, MA: Harvard University Press, 2001.

Ngai, Mae. *Impossible Subjects: Illegal Aliens and the Making of Modern America*. Princeton, NJ: Princeton University Press, 2005.

Ngô, Fiona. *Imperial Blues: Geographies of Race and Sex in Jazz Age New York*. Durham, NC: Duke University Press, 2014.

Nguyen, Mimi Thi. *The Gift of Freedom: War, Debt, and Other Refugee Passages*. Durham, NC: Duke University Press, 2012.

Nubla, Gladys. "The Sexualized Child and Mestizaje: Colonial Tropes of the Filipina/o." In *Gendering the Trans-Pacific World*, edited by Catherine Ceniza Choy and Judy Tzu-Chun Wu, 165–95. Amsterdam: Brill, 2017.

Ocampo, Ambeth R. "Romances in History." *Positively Filipino*, February 7, 2015. http://www.positivelyfilipino.com/magazine/romances-in-history. First published in *Looking Back*. Manila: Anvil, 1990.

Onorato, P. *Jock Netzorg: Manila Memories*. Laguna Beach, CA: Pacific Rim, 1988.

Pareja, Lena Strait. "Roles and Image of Woman in the Early Years of Philippine Cinema (1912 to 1941)." PhD diss., University of the Philippines, 1998.

Parezo, Nancy J., and Angelina R. Jones. "What's in a Name? The 1940s–1950s 'Squaw Dress.'" *American Indian Quarterly* 33, no. 3 (summer 2009): 373–404.

Parmar, Pratibha. "Hateful Contraries: Media Images of Asian Women." In *The Feminism and Visual Culture Reader*, edited by Amelia Jones, 287–93. New York: Routledge, 2003.

Pascoe, Peggy. *What Comes Naturally: Miscegenation Law and the Making of Race in America*. New York: Oxford University Press, 2010.

Pavlik, Steve, M. Elise Marubbio, and Tom Holm. *Native Apparitions: Critical Perspectives on Hollywood's Indians*, 3rd ed. Tucson: University of Arizona Press, 2017.

Pérez, Louis A. *The War of 1898: The United States and Cuba in History and Historiography*. Chapel Hill: University of North Carolina Press, 1998.

Petillo, Carol M. *Douglas MacArthur: The Philippine Years*. Bloomington: Indiana University Press, 1981.

Phillips, Claire, and Myron B. Goldsmith. *Manila Espionage*. Portland, OR: Binfords and Mont, 1947.

Pilat, Oliver. *Drew Pearson: An Unauthorized Biography*. New York: Harpers, 1973.

Prasso, Sheridan. *The Asian Mystique: Dragon Ladies, Geisha Girls, and Our Fantasies of the Exotic Orient*. New York: Public Affairs, 2009.

Quarles, Mike. *Down and Dirty: Hollywood's Exploitation Filmmakers and Their Movies*. Jefferson, NC: McFarland, 2010.

Quirino, Joe. *Don Jose and the Early Philippine Cinema*. Quezon City: Phoenix, 1983.

Rafael, Vicente. *White Love and Other Events in Filipino History*. Durham, NC: Duke University Press, 2000.

Ramos, Richard. *History of Crawford and Richland Counties. Wisconsin Illustrated,* 1881. Reprint, Springfield, IL: Unaga, 1884.

Rasor, Eugene. *General Douglas MacArthur, 1880–1964: Historiography and Annotated Bibliography.* Westport, CT: Greenwood, 1994.

Reyes, Raquel A. G. *Love Passion and Patriotism: Sexuality and the Philippine Propaganda Movement, 1882–1892.* Seattle: University of Washington Press, 2008.

Rice, Christina. *Ann Dvorak: Hollywood's Forgotten Rebel.* Lexington: University Press of Kentucky, 2013.

Roces, Mina. "Filipino Elite Women and Public Health in the American Colonial Era, 1906–1940." *Women's History Review* 25 (2016): 1–26.

Roces, Mina. "Gender, Nation and the Politics of Dress in Twentieth-Century Philippines." In *The Politics of Dress in Asia and the Americas,* edited by Mina Roces and Louise P. Edwards, 19–41. Brighton, UK: Sussex Academic Press, 2007.

Roces, Mina. "Is the Suffragist an American Colonial Construct? Defining 'the Filipino Woman' in Colonial Philippines." In *Women's Suffrage in Asia: Gender, Nationalism and Democracy,* edited by Louise P. Edwards and Mina Roces, 24–58. London: Routledge, 2004.

Roces, Mina. "Mixed Blessing: The Impact of the American Colonial Experience on Politics and Society in the Philippines." In *Women in Philippine Politics and Society,* edited by Hazel M. McFerson, 159–89. Westport, CT: Greenwood, 2002.

Roces, Mina. *Women's Movements and the Filipina, 1986–2008.* Honolulu: University of Hawaii Press, 2012.

Roces, Mina, and Louise Edwards. "Introduction." In *Women's Suffrage in Asia: Gender, Nationalism and Democracy,* edited by edited by Louise P. Edwards and Mina Roces, 1–23. London: Routledge, 2004.

Rogin, Michael. *Blackface, White Noise: Jewish Immigrants in the Hollywood Melting Pot.* Berkeley: University of California Press, 1998.

Rosca, Ninotchka. *State of War.* New York: Norton, 1988.

San Juan, Carolina de Leon. "From Vaudeville to Bodabil: Vaudeville in the Philippines." PhD diss., University of California, Los Angeles, 2010.

Schaefer, Eric. *"Bold! Daring! Shocking! True!": A History of Exploitation Films, 1919–1959.* Durham, NC: Duke University Press, 1999.

Schwaller, Shawn. "A Careful Embrace: Race, Gender, and the Consumption of Hawai'i and the South Pacific in Mid-century Los Angeles." In *Gendering the Trans-Pacific World,* edited by Catherine Ceniza Choy and Judy Tzu-Chun Wu, 366–88. Amsterdam: Brill, 2017.

Schwartz, Dan. "Passionate Letters Reveal the Sensational Love Affair of 50-Year-Old Gen. Douglas MacArthur—& a 16-Year-Old Filipino Girl." *National Enquirer,* September 21, 1976.

Sharpe, Jenny. *Ghosts of Slavery: A Literary Archaeology of Black Women's Lives.* Minneapolis: University of Minnesota Press, 2003.

Shibusawa, Naoko. *America's Geisha Ally.* Cambridge, MA: Harvard University Press, 2006.

Shimakawa, Karen. *National Abjection: The Asian American Body Onstage*. Durham, NC: Duke University Press, 2002.

Shindler, Colin. *Hollywood Goes to War: Films and American Society, 1939–1952*. New York: Routledge, 2015.

Sobritchea, Carolyn Israel. *Women's Role in Philippine History: Selected Essays*, 2nd ed. Diliman, Quezon City: University Center for Women's Studies and the University of the Philippines, 1996.

Spiller, Henry. *Javaphilia: American Love Affairs with Javanese Music and Dance*. Honolulu: University of Hawai'i Press, 2015.

Spivak, Gayatri Chakravorty. "Can the Subaltern Speak?" In *Marxism and the Interpretation of Culture*, edited by Cary Nelson and Lawrence Grossberg, 271–313. Urbana: University of Illinois Press, 1988.

Spivak, Gayatri Chakravorty. "The Rani of Sirmur: An Essay in Reading the Archives." *History and Theory* 24 (1985): 247–73.

Stein, Charles W. *American Vaudeville as Seen by Its Contemporaries*. New York: Alfred A. Knopf, 1984.

Stoler, Ann Laura. *Along the Archival Grain: Epistemic Anxieties and Colonial Common Sense*. Princeton, NJ: Princeton University Press, 2009.

Stoler, Ann Laura. *Carnal Knowledge and Imperial Power: Race and the Intimate in Colonial Rule*. Berkeley: University of California Press, 2012.

Stoler, Ann Laura, ed. *Haunted by Empire: Geographies of Intimacy in North American History*. Durham, NC: Duke University Press, 2006.

Stoler, Ann Laura, ed. *Imperial Debris: On Ruins and Ruination*. Durham, NC: Duke University Press, 2013.

Stoler, Ann Laura. "Introduction: 'The Rot Remains': From Ruins to Ruination." In *Imperial Debris: On Ruins and Ruination*, ed. Ann Laura Stoler, 1–36. Durham, NC: Duke University Press, 2013.

Tadiar, Neferti Xina M. *Fantasy-Production: Sexual Economies and Other Philippine Consequences for the New World Order*. Hong Kong: Hong Kong University Press, 2004.

Tan, Antonio S. *The Chinese Mestizos and the Formation of Filipino Nationality*. Quezon City: Asian Center, University of the Philippines, 1984.

Teng, Emma Jinhua. *Eurasian: Mixed Identities in the United States, China, and Hong Kong, 1842–1943*. Berkeley: University of California Press, 2013.

Torres, Cristina Evangelista. *The Americanization of Manila, 1898–1921*. Quezon City: University of the Philippines Press, 2010.

Trouillot, Michel-Rolph. *Silencing the Past: Power and the Production of History*. Boston: Beacon, 1995.

Unander, Sig. "Claire Phillips: Forgotten Hero." *1859: Oregon's Magazine*, January 1, 2016. https://1859oregonmagazine.com/think-oregon/art-culture/claire-phillips/.

Vera, Hernán, and Andrew M. Gordon. "The Beautiful American: Sincere Fictions of the White Messiah in Hollywood Movies." In *White Out: The Continuing Significance of Racism*, edited by Ashley W. Doane and Eduardo Bonilla-Silva, 113–28. New York: Psychology Press, 2003.

Vogel, Michelle. *Lupe Vélez: The Life and Career of Hollywood's "Mexican Spitfire."* Jefferson, NC: McFarland, 2012.

Weinbaum, Alyse Eve, Lynn M. Thomas, Priti Ramamurthy, Uta G. Poiger, Madeleine Yue Dong, and Tani E. Barlow. *The Modern Girl around the World: Consumption, Modernity, and Globalization.* Durham, NC: Duke University Press, 2008.

Welch, Richard E., Jr. "American Atrocities in the Philippines: The Indictment and the Response." *Pacific Historical Review* 43, no. 2 (May 1974): 233–53.

Wexler, Laura. *Tender Violence: Domestic Visions in an Age of U.S. Imperialism.* Chapel Hill: University of North Carolina Press, 2000.

Willis, Sharon. *High Contrast: Race and Gender in Contemporary Hollywood Film.* Durham, NC: Duke University Press, 1997.

Winkelmann, Tessa Marie. "Dangerous Intercourse: Race, Gender and Interracial Relations in the American Colonial Philippines, 1898–1946." PhD diss., University of Illinois at Urbana-Champaign, 2014.

yamomo, meLê. *Theatre and Music in Manila and the Asia Pacific, 1869–1946: Sounding Modernities.* New York: Palgrave Macmillan, 2018.

Zeiger, Susan. *Entangling Alliances: Foreign War Brides and American Soldiers in the Twentieth Century.* New York: New York University Press, 2010.

INDEX

affair, 1, 5, 16, 19–20, 22, 78, 100–101, 106, 112,
    121, 150–51, 153, 188n42
Ahn, Philip, 124, 142, 144
Alien Exclusion Act, 25, 43
Allied Artists, 140–41, 143
American Caesar (Manchester), 2–3, 13
American Mestizo Association, 55
Ang Tatlong Hambog, 77–78, 83
Anna and the King of Siam, 110, 132–34
Anne of the Indies, 144
antimiscegenation laws, 33, 39, 44–45, 89, 95,
    185n52
Appearance of Isabel Cooper, The (Ruperto),
    158
archive, 5, 9, 12, 20, 26–27, 32, 51, 149,
    156
Arden Cho as Isabel Rosario Cooper (Ruperto),
    156–57
"Are You Lonesome Tonight?," 67–68,
    190n37
Art of Burlesque, The, 145–47
Asiamnesia, 152–55, 159

Baby Girl (Isabel Cooper), 19–20, 23, 71
bailerina, 55, 60
Bataan, 99, 116, 118, 143
Beaudine, William, 137
Benevolent Assimilation Proclamation, 35
Boaz, Wisconsin, 35, 39, 182n10
bodabil, 59, 60, 64, 68, 73, 88, 187n30
Bonus Army, 22–23
brownface, 124, 128

cabaret, 40, 57, 60, 63, 195n29
Calle Herrán, 19, 57, 83, 85, 93n1, 187n17
Canson, John, 40, 55
Carter, Thomas, 67, 93, 107, 181n5, 184n42,
    186n66, 187n26, 188n39, 189n8, 190n33,
    191n10
casting couch, 52, 82–84, 129
Cavite, 38, 127, 144
Chabing (Isabel Cooper), 49–55, 63, 66, 108,
    110, 128–47, 158
Chan, Charlie (character in *The Chinese
    Ring* and *Shanghai Crest*), 129, 136–38
Chaplin, Charlie, 59, 64, 98
Chastleton Hotel, 15–16, 21–23, 95–98, 156–57
Chinese Ring, The, 136–37
Chomet, Sun Mee, 152–53, 159
Colbert, Claudette, 117, 119–21
comedy, 64, 68, 79, 155–56, 170, 187n30
Cooper, Allen, 85, 89, 179n28, 184n43, 185n60,
    190n32, 190n41
Cooper, Bruce (brother of IC), 41, 69–70,
    182nn9–10
Cooper, Bruce (son of IC and PR), 23, 42, 46,
    70, 99, 184nn43–44, 185n60, 187n17
Cooper, Bruce (son of IC and RR), 41, 69,
    184n38
Cooper, Elizabeth (Isabel Cooper), 73–74,
    77–84
Cooper, Gary, 124, 128
Cooper, Isaac (IC), 23, 33–47, 57, 69–70, 81, 89,
    99, 181n7, 182nn9–10, 183n13, 184n38, 185n47,
    185n52, 185n55, 185n57, 185n60, 186n65

Corregidor, 99, 118, 121–22, 143
Cowper, John C., 67–68, 188n31
Cromwell, Louise, 62, 63, 115
Culver City, 3–5, 152

Dalagang Bukid, 58
Davis, T. J., 71, 92
Day, Doris, 129–31, 195n7
death certificate, 4, 13–14, 44–45, 108, 148,
    165–66, 169, 181n7, 191n2
de la Cruz, Katy, 64, 68
de la Rama, Atang, 58–59, 76, 187n22
Delongpre Ave, 13, 165–66
DeMille, Cecil B., 105, 116–17, 124, 134–35
desire, 2, 7, 15, 19, 22, 27, 34, 42, 47, 100, 102, 112,
    123, 134, 142, 151, 153, 157; archival, 7, 9, 11,
    155; imperial, 6, 12, 17, 20, 26, 32, 49, 54–56,
    62, 66, 81, 85, 113, 115, 122, 125; racial, 128, 133
Detzer, Dorothy, 3, 21, 171n21
Diamond, David, 51–53
Dimples (Isabel Cooper), 49, 56, 60–68,
    73–75, 79–80, 86–92, 96, 151, 154, 170–71
Dimples (Ruperto), 155–57
Dunne, Irene, 132
Dvorak, Ann, 51, 116, 140

Ernst, Morris, 18, 23–24, 26, 28, 29, 180n36,
    180n40
Escolta, Manila, 39–40
Eurasian, 2–3, 8, 100–101, 152

Faircloth, Jean, 95–96
Fate or Consequence, 79
Filipina: as colonial gendered/sexualized
    labor, 6, 17–18, 33–34, 38–39, 40–42, 55, 57,
    62–63, 85; representations of, 30–31, 73–74;
    social and political debates about, 31, 58–59,
    64, 76–77, 81. *See also* New Filipina
Filipinization, 43
Filipino cinema, 7, 20, 58–59, 73, 77, 187n26
Fuentes, Dorothy (character in *I Was an
    American Spy*), 141, 143–44

Gardner, Ava, 128, 139
geisha, 112, 116, 121–23, 128, 152, 158
genre, 1–3, 5, 8, 11–12, 150, 156–57, 169

Georgetown University, 95–96, 191n4
Gibson, Martha (character in *My Dream Is
    Yours*), 129–31
Gleeck, Lewis, 60, 67
Goddard, Paulette, 117, 121, 134
Goldstone, Nat, 100, 102
gossip, 2–3, 11–12, 21, 38–39, 51, 68, 73, 81, 83–87
Graphic, 58–59, 65, 67, 81–84, 87–88, 188n39
Great Depression, 21–22, 97
Great Jewel Robber, The, 139

Hahn, Sam, 100–102, 105–6, 131, 145
harem, 132–33, 146–47, 158
Harrison, Francis Burton, 57
Harrison, Rex, 110, 132–33
Hartendorp, A. V. N., 38, 60
"Has Anyone Seen My Kitty?," 60, 62, 146,
    188nn40–41
haunting, 133, 149–52, 154, 159
Havana, 21–22
Holy Cross Cemetery, 3–4, 8
Hoover, Herbert, President, 15, 22
hula dancer, 94, 103, 108, 110, 129–31, 136, 155,
    166, 170

Indians, 35, 37, 134–35
innocence, 19, 177n1; as colonial posture, 17,
    22, 49, 54–56, 66; as a stage act, 56, 60–66,
    73, 76, 79, 146
intimacy: and empire, 5–8, 27, 32, 34, 40–41,
    53–57, 66, 112–15, 121, 126, 154; as labor,
    17–20, 26, 116, 144; policing of, 6, 39, 185n53;
    as public spectacle, 72, 81
Isabel Rosario Cooper (Ruperto), 116, 149–50,
    155–59, 197n1
I Was an American Spy, 51, 53, 116, 127, 139–45

Joaquin, Nick, 60
Jones Act, 43
Jose Reyes Studios, 103–4, 155
"Just a Little Longer," 91, 190n37

Kennamer, Franklin Burke (son of FK),
    167–68
Kennamer, Franklin E. (FK), 4, 13–14, 24,
    94–99, 105–6, 108, 165–68

Kennamer, Isabel (Isabel Cooper), 94–101, 105, 110
kiss, 19, 72, 76–79, 82–83, 89, 91, 142–43, 146, 152, 159
kundiman, 58, 64

Lake, Veronica, 117, 121
Leonowens, Anna (character in *Anna and the King*), 132–33, 195n17
libel, 17–18, 23–24, 49, 100, 107, 151, 191n4
"little brown brothers," 66, 181n1
Little Sergeant (excised character in *The Story of Dr. Wassell*), 124–26
Lolita (character in *I Was an American Spy*), 127, 139–44
Loo, Richard, 122–23, 144
Los Angeles County Court, 108–9
Los Angeles County Department of Public Health, 165–66
Los Angeles County Medical Examiner's Office, 169
Los Angeles Herald and Express, 106
Los Angeles Times, 108, 114–15, 140
love, 5, 17, 19–23, 26, 74, 79, 86, 124, 142–43, 150; colonial, 2, 8, 11–12, 32, 97, 126, 155, 186n5; unrequited, 1, 2, 14, 125, 154, 168

MacArthur, Arthur, 35, 37, 183n18
MacArthur, Douglas, 37, 41, 48–49, 101, 106–7, 110, 139–40, 150–51, 167; affair with Isabel Cooper, 1–8, 13, 15–29, 51–54, 66–67, 71, 85, 89, 91–95, 100, 120, 145, 152–56; as chief military advisor to Philippine commonwealth, 95–96; as chief of staff of United States Army, 15, 18, 94, 121; as commanding general of Philippine Department, 84, 89–92; marriage to Jean Faircloth, 95–96; marriage to Louise Cromwell, 62–63, 84, 115; as World War II general, 72, 98–99, 112–16, 121–23
MacArthur, Pinky, 15–16, 26, 95
Madame Butterfly, 135, 144
Majestic Theater, 89
Manchester, William, 2, 3, 13, 14, 150, 153, 179n21

Maricopa, Arizona, 44, 56, 185n53
Mariveles, 118
McKinley, William, 35, 181n1, 182n13
mestiza/mestizo, 8, 25, 30, 39, 55, 57, 74, 90, 141, 181n5, 187n10. *See also* mixed-race category
Miracles of Love, 73–74, 76, 89–90
Miss Columbia, 114–15, 123
Miss Lee (character in *Shanghai Crest*), 137–38
mistress, 1–2, 5–8, 14, 38, 51, 94, 96, 99, 110, 112, 115–16, 122, 152–53, 168; as master of, 8, 27, 31, 136, 141–43
mixed-race category, 6–8, 26, 32–33, 42–43, 51–52, 55–57, 60, 81, 96, 99, 102, 106, 113, 128, 152, 181n5, 185n52, 187n8. *See also* mestiza/mestizo
Mongkut (character in *Anna and the King*), 132–33
Moreno, Milton, 108–10, 181n7, 186n1, 193n38
My Dream Is Yours, 129–31

"Nabasag ang Banga," 58, 76
Nagcarlan, Laguna, 33, 41
National Enquirer, 13, 150–51, 179n18, 179n21
Nepomuceno, José, 58, 73, 76–79, 83–84, 187n21, 190n35
New Filipina, 64, 72, 76–79, 81–83, 96, 129
nurse, 106, 112, 116–21, 124–25, 128, 158

Oklahoma, 24, 95, 180n41, 191n4
Olympic Stadium, 59, 85, 91
Oyuki (character in *Asiamnesia*), 152, 154

pacification, 6, 32, 37, 54, 72, 112, 183n15
Pacific theater, 100, 105, 113
Paco, Manila, 19, 38, 57, 74–75, 86
Paramount Studios, 102, 119, 124, 135
paramour, 19, 101, 120, 153, 170
Pearson, Drew: correspondence with Isabel Cooper, 20, 49, 51–53, 66, 97–108, 110, 113, 124, 129, 139, 142, 145, 155; MacArthur libel suit against, 17, 18, 23–26, 29, 151, 179n15, 180n33, 180n36, 191n4

performance, 11, 41, 58–59, 64, 67–68, 79, 84, 86, 91, 95, 102, 119, 121, 131, 139, 145, 147, 157, 170
Pershing, John, 62, 115, 188n42
Pershing Square, 114–15
Philippine-American War, 6, 32–33, 37–38, 54, 72, 182n8, 183n17
Philippines Free Press, 21, 58–59
Phillips, Claire (character in *I Was an American Spy*), 51, 140–44, 196n39
prostitution, 39–40
Purple Heart, The, 121–23, 194n24

querida, 6, 38. *See also* mistress
Quezon, Manuel, 46, 57, 63, 95–96

Reappearance of Isabel Rosario Cooper, The (Ruperto), 149–50, 155, 158
redface, 128, 134–36
repertoire, 59, 73, 77, 84, 121, 148
Rivoli Theater, 60–61, 64, 68, 70, 73, 83–84, 90–91
RKO, 52, 102
romance, 1–3, 17, 26, 41, 63, 82, 96, 118, 156, 168; as film genre, 73–74, 139
Rubin, Protacia, 33–34, 41–47, 56, 70, 73, 89, 110, 181n7, 184n40, 184n42, 185n55, 185n57, 186n66, 191n10. *See also* Ryan, Josefina
rumor, 3, 11–12, 20, 68, 78, 83, 85–86, 115, 151, 188n42
Ruperto, Miljohn, 116, 149–50, 155–59, 167
Ryan, Josefina, 46–48, 57, 63, 70, 74–75, 83–85, 97, 184n40, 187n17, 189n8, 190n33, 191n10. *See also* Rubin, Protacia
Ryan, Josephine Margaret, 46, 63
Ryan, Rosemarie Ruby, 63, 106–7
Ryan, Rubia, 41, 69, 184nn38–39
Ryan, Thomas Bernard, 46, 57, 63–64, 74–75, 84, 189n8, 190n33

Salumbides, Vicente, 73–74, 76, 79, 84
Sandrich, Mark, 117
Santa Ana Cabaret, 40, 55, 57, 60
sarswela, 58–59, 187n22, 187n30
Sato, Betty Yoshiko, 167

Savoy Nifties, 67, 188n31
Savoy Theater, 60, 64, 67–68, 84, 86
scandal, 3, 5–8, 14, 32–33, 42, 46–47, 66, 72–84, 89, 96–97, 115, 146, 151, 155–56
Schwartz, Dan, 13–14, 179n18, 179n21, 197n5
Seven Seas, 130–31, 166
sex, 17–18, 26, 32, 38, 55–57, 72, 133, 181n3, 183n20, 183n29
sexuality, 3, 6, 17, 25, 32, 58–62, 128, 133, 154, 181n46
Shanghai Crest, 137–38
Singapore, 139
Sirena Theater, 60, 64
So Proudly We Hail, 106, 117–22, 193n11
Sotelo, Mercedes, 89, 93, 107, 188n39, 192n35
Spanish-American War, 32, 35
Story of Dr. Wassell, The, 116–17, 123–25
suicide, 2–3, 8, 13–14, 151–52, 154, 165–69

Teatro Libertad, 59
That Hamilton Woman, 98
Thurston, Carol, 124
Tillotson, L. S., 24
Tin Pan Alley, 62, 67–68, 73, 130, 170
Tremartini (character in *The Story of Dr. Wassell*), 124–25
Tuason, Luis, 78–79
Tydings-McDuffie Act, 25

Unconquered, 134–35

Variety, 116, 123, 137, 144, 170
variety act/show, 67–68, 80, 188n30, 195n29
vaudeville, 1, 7, 10, 20–21, 41, 59–60, 63, 65, 67–68, 73, 82, 90, 94, 118, 144, 146, 151, 170, 187n30. *See also* bodabil
violence, 150–51; colonial 5, 8, 17, 72; military, 37, 112, 125; as personal assault, 83–84; racial, 25, 35

ward, 41–42, 52; as colonial status, 7, 15, 17–18, 24–25, 43, 54–55, 63, 177n12
West Point, 37, 41, 62
Winters, Roland, 136–38
Wong, Anna May, 190n24
Wong, Anna May (character in *Asiamnesia*), 152, 154–55

Wong, Lilly Mae (character in *The Chinese Ring*), 136–37
World War I, 44, 46, 56
World War II, 1, 72, 98, 105, 112–21; films about, 112–27, 139–45. *See also* Pacific theater

yellowface, 128, 132–33, 136–38

Zanuck, Darryl F., 122, 132, 194n24
Ziegfeld Follies, 68, 131
Zorilla Theater, 59

Printed in the USA
CPSIA information can be obtained
at www.ICGtesting.com
CBHW071912300424
7702CB00004B/13